COLORA
MOUNTAIN CLUB
GUIDEBOOK

GUIDE TO WESTERN NATIONAL MONUMENTS

MIKE ENDRES

Live A Great Story Art!

The Colorado Mountain Club Press
Golden, Colorado

Guide to Western National Monuments
© Mike Endres 2021

PUBLISHED BY

The Colorado Mountain Club Press
710 10th Street, Suite 200, Golden, CO 80401
303-996-2743 email: cmcpress@cmc.org
website: www.cmc.org

Founded in 1912, The Colorado Mountain Club is the largest outdoor recreation, education, and conservation organization in the Rocky Mountains. Look for our books at your local bookstore or outdoor retailer or online at www.cmc.org

CORRECTIONS: We greatly appreciate when readers alert us to errors or outdated information by emailing cmcpress@cmc.org.

Mike Endres: author and photographer
Takeshi Takahashi: designer
Jodi Jennings: copyeditor
Elle Klock: production assistant

Cover photo: The unique Navajo Sandstone of The Wave was formed millions of years ago. Consider yourself extremely fortunate if you get a permit to visit this restricted area. Photo by Mike Endres.

DISTRIBUTED TO THE BOOK TRADE BY:

Mountaineers Books
1001 SW Klickitat Way, Suite 201, Seattle, WA 98134, 800-553-4453
www.mountaineersbooks.org

We gratefully acknowledge the financial support of the people of Colorado through the Scientific and Cultural Facilities District of greater metropolitan Denver for our publishing activities.

TOPOGRAPHIC MAPS created with Gaia GPS software.

Printed in the United States of America

21 / 10 9 8 7 6 5 4 3 2 1

ISBN 978-1-937052-55-3

Contents

An autumn mist rises from a river valley near Mount St. Helens. Much of the land surrounding the monument is open to the public for outdoor recreation.

Introduction

The Antiquities Act of 1906 gave US presidents the authority to establish national monuments as an expedient method to protect natural and historically significant areas in the United States. The first monument, Devils Tower, was designated by President Theodore Roosevelt on September 24, 1906. This established a long-standing tradition followed by all but two presidents (Richard Nixon and Donald Trump), resulting in the current list of 129 national monuments at the time of this writing.

Many previously designated monuments have transitioned to national parks (such as White Sands National Park in 2019) or another status, while others have been turned over to state control or simply disbanded.

The true value of monuments can be experienced firsthand by visiting any of those listed in this guide. Perhaps the most striking and familiar example is the Grand Canyon. First designated as a national monument in 1908, it is now a world-famous national park, attracting nearly six million visitors annually from around the world, according to National Park Service data from 2019. Nearly half of our current national parks began life as a national monument.

The 129 current monuments are managed by eight different agencies within five separate departments of the federal government. The vast majority fall under the management of the Department of the Interior, and of those, the National Park Service oversees most of them. You can purchase an Interagency Annual Pass to these lands for only $80 from nps.gov. It will allow you access to areas managed by the US Forest Service, National Park Service, US Fish and Wildlife Service, Bureau of Land Management, Bureau of Reclamation, and the Army Corps of Engineers.

This guide, while not all-encompassing, is intended to showcase those national monuments that have a more natural, outdoor recreation-focused appeal. For that reason, some monuments are excluded. The omissions include those that are more of a historical site or those that represent a notable time period in our nation's history. Other monuments in the West are not covered here because they are inaccessible to most people or are not located in the contiguous United States.

Leave No Trace

Leave the areas you visit better than you found them. For more information on Leave No Trace ethics, visit lnt.org.

Camp on durable surfaces and never cut switchbacks: If you decide to go off-trail, groups should spread out instead of walking single file to avoid trampling resources and creating new trails.

Respect wildlife: If an animal appears agitated by your presence, you're probably too close.

Dispose of waste in a responsible manner: Pack it in, pack it out.

Fires: Be careful with your campfires, research and obey burn warnings and fire bans, and consider foregoing a fire altogether in the backcountry when camping. Drown your fires completely before leaving them.

The Ten Essentials

Navigation (map and compass): Carry an up-to-date map and an accurate compass. Know how to use them. GPS units and modern smartphone apps are a nice backup.

Sun protection (sunglasses and sunscreen): The sun can sap your energy and motivation surprisingly quickly. Lather up and protect yourself every day.

Bend in the Green River near Echo Park, Dinosaur National Monument.

Sunset on the rock formations at Cedar Breaks National Monument.

Insulation (extra clothing): Carry enough insulation to keep you warm in any condition you might reasonably experience, no matter how close to the car you plan on being. Carry reliable rain gear and protect your supplies from water. Avoid cotton clothing, which absorbs water and resists drying.

Illumination (headlamp/flashlight): A quality headlamp (with extra batteries) should have a place in every daypack or overnight kit. Don't get caught in an emergency situation made worse by a lack of visibility.

First-aid supplies: Carry and stock a first-aid kit suitable for your group. Know how and when to use the supplies and how to make informed decisions about medical situations in the backcountry. A Wilderness First Aid (WFA) course is a highly recommended first-step investment in yourself.

Fire (waterproof matches/lighter/tinder): If you need a fire to stay warm, know how to start and maintain one.

Repair kit and tools: Carrying gear patches, extra buckles, a knife, and cord is always a wise choice.

Nutrition (extra food): Prepare for the worst-case scenario.

Hydration (extra water): Consume plenty of water and consider a water filter or purifying tablets on longer hikes.

Emergency shelter: For the day hiker, a bivy sack or other emergency shelter is a good idea. They're light and packable and may very well make the difference for you if you end up stranded overnight.

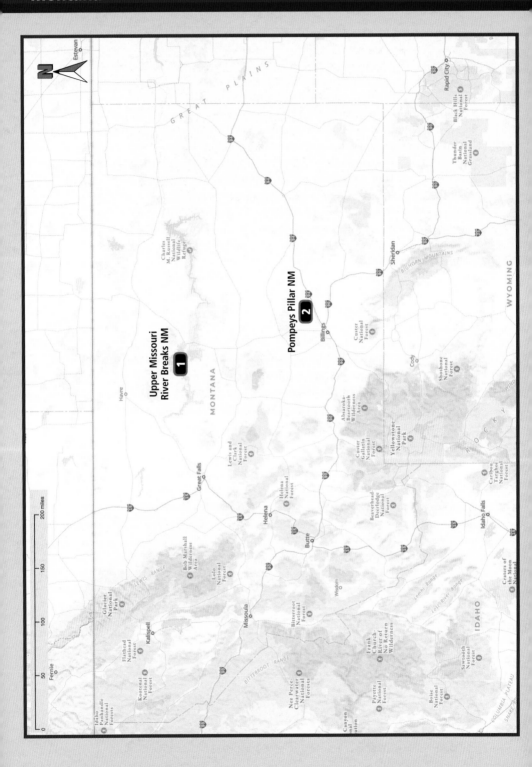

1. Upper Missouri River Breaks National Monument

NEAREST TOWN:	Fort Benton, MT
SIZE:	495,502 acres
BEST SEASON(S):	Spring through fall
NOTABLE ACTIVITIES:	Wildlife viewing, boating/rafting, historic Lewis and Clark Trail, photography, hiking

THE MONUMENT:
Located in north-central Montana, "The Breaks" were proclaimed a national monument by President Bill Clinton on January 17, 2001. Encompassing 495,502 acres, these public lands were previously managed by the Bureau of Land Management and currently contain multiple tracts of private inholdings as well as state properties. Present-day management of these mixed lands includes the recognition of historical uses, such as the grazing of as many as 10,000 head of cattle. Efforts to protect the natural resources of these lands continue alongside grazing, hunting, and fishing.

Sunrise from our first campsite on the river.

Some of the Chalk Cliffs the monument is so well known for in the warmth of the early morning sun.

The portion of the Missouri River within the Breaks was designated as a Wild and Scenic River in 1976, adding to the overall appeal of the national monument. The river itself forms the western boundary, while the Charles M. Russell National Wildlife Refuge abuts the eastern margin.

The Lewis and Clark Expedition passed through here in 1805, and several of their campsites are marked on the Bureau of Land Management (BLM) Boater's Guide for each of the two river sections within the national monument. An excellent account of their travels can be found in Stephen E. Ambrose's book, *Undaunted Courage*. This book would make an outstanding read on any float of the river, allowing you to relive the journey of Lewis and Clark with all of today's comforts and none of their suffering.

Another good pack-along reference book is *Montana's Wild and Scenic Upper Missouri River* by Glenn Monahan and Chan Biggs, which provides an excellent historic narrative. Both men are intimately familiar with the river and its history; one runs a river outfitting business, and the other is a retired BLM river ranger.

Typical of the American Plains, the weather is generally mild in the summer with highs in the low 80s and nighttime lows in the upper 40s to 50s. Winter is cold with highs in the 30s and lows into the low teens. Precipitation is just under 17 inches with most falling in the spring and summer months. Snowfall can be an impressive 5 feet in the winter.

Steamboat Rock, named for its resemblance to the chimneys on the old paddlewheel boats that used to ply these waters, transporting goods and passengers.

Jake, in his default position. The waters in August were perfect for a relaxed and lazy float between campsites.

THINGS TO DO:

The best way to see and experience the Breaks is to take a float trip down all or part of the 149-mile river corridor. Spring floats can include high water at a rather fast flow, making it more challenging for the inexperienced. Late summer, while warmer, sees a flow of around 2.5 miles per hour—which is much more manageable. One can easily traverse the distance between campsites in four to five hours with minimal effort. In addition to being more relaxing, a slower pace also allows considerable time for viewing the sights and exploring the surrounding public lands on foot. This area has remained essentially unchanged since the time of the Lewis and Clark Expedition in 1805.

There are two river sections for floating. The first, and shortest, typically begins at Coal Banks Landing northeast of Fort Benton and ends at Judith Landing, traveling approximately 47 miles and requiring roughly two or three days. Mile zero for the entire float, however, is at Chouteau County Fairgrounds in Fort Benton, which also has camping, showers, and electrical hookups. From here, it is 41 miles to Coal Banks Landing, a comfortable two-day effort. Another good put-in is at Wood Bottom, which is easily accessed from Fort Benton and adds only another 21 miles to the total trip length to Judith Landing. I found this stretch to have a preponderance of wildlife when I did the first section in late August, including several bald eagles and numerous ospreys.

The second section picks up at Judith Landing and goes through the eastern portion of the national monument for roughly 61 miles to Kipp Recreation Area, ending at the Fred Robinson Bridge on MT Highway 191. Most

A For the longest time I had always thought of pelicans as coastal birds, never knowing how widespread the American white pelican is throughout the West. This is a non-breeding adult due to the lack of a prominent knob of tissue on its bill. **B** A mule deer doe with her spotted fawns comes to the riverbank for water after feeding all night. **C** A variety of prairie wildflowers decorate the landscape here. **D** The American badger, widespread throughout the open grasslands of the American prairie, also inhabits the desert scrub.

people float only the first portion, leaving the second half relatively untraveled. This is unfortunate, as considerable wildlife, including mule deer, elk, bighorn sheep, and hundreds of species of birds, are found in this region.

This section is also where the true "Missouri Breaks" topography can be found, along the Judith River Formation. The layers of rock and sediment were deposited here in a horizontal fashion as part of a great inland sea that covered most of the Great Plains. Over time, these different deposits were folded, uplifted, sculpted by glacial activity, eroded, and otherwise altered to create the Breaks as we know them today. Sturgeon, northern pike, walleye, paddlefish, and channel catfish are among the forty-nine species of fish found throughout the river.

THINGS TO SEE:
A visit to the Missouri Breaks Interpretive Center in Fort Benton is a great place to start your exploration of the monument. Here you'll be able to study

the natural and cultural history of the region. You can also obtain boating information to help you plan your float trip, including a Boater's Guide to whichever section of the river you're floating.

The first half of the river within the monument contains the well-known Chalk Cliffs, which can be quite impressive in the reflected light of early morning or evening. Composed of white-colored Eagle sandstone, these formations can reach heights of 300 feet. In some areas within the sandstone cliffs there are dark-colored injections of hot magma that have proven to be highly resistant to erosion, creating what Meriwether Lewis called "scenes of visionary enchantment." Other interesting geological features

One can pull out anywhere on public property along the river to go hiking or simply to take a rest and relax.

include the aptly named Pedestal Rocks, which are small pinnacles of softer sandstone capped by the harder magma inflows, much like hoodoos in other parts of the country.

GETTING THERE:

While you can access several portions of the river system for viewing and floating, most people choose Fort Benton as their first stop. It is located on US Highway 87 approximately 40 miles northeast of Great Falls and 70 miles southwest from Havre. Supplies and outfitters can be found in all three towns.

FACILITIES:

For those camping, the seven RV and twenty primitive tent sites at the Chouteau County Fairgrounds on the western side of Fort Benton are quiet, have electrical hookups, and offer showers. You are just a few steps from the river if this is where you plan to put in. The fairgrounds also provide long-term secure parking for floaters.

A solitary canoer idly drifting by some of the Chalk Cliffs of the monument nearing sunset.

A few additional RV parks and hotels are available in Fort Benton. There are several excellent restaurants in town, including some that specialize in serving up some very good Montana-style cooking.

On the river itself there are several established camping areas within reach of a half-day's paddling. Most have some form of exclusion fencing to keep cattle out. These sites are often on private land and represent a partnership between the landowner and the BLM, so be respectful and clean up after yourself to avoid souring this relationship. Campsites that lack the exclusion fencing are less desirable, as cows are allowed to walk and defecate freely throughout the area, which tends to draw an abundance of flying insects. There is also an ongoing effort to increase the number of cottonwood trees at several of these campgrounds, and floaters are encouraged to water the saplings as the campgrounds are typically above the river's high-water mark. Dispersed camping is allowed on BLM lands along the river corridor; however, absolutely no camping is permitted on any of the private lands within the monument.

USEFUL CONTACTS:

**Upper Missouri River Breaks
National Monument**
920 NE Main Street
Lewistown, MT 59457
406-538-1900

blm.gov/programs/national
 -conservation-lands/montana-dakotas
 /upper-missouri-river-breaks

visitmt.com/listings/general
 /national-monument/upper-missouri
 -river-breaks-national-monument

fortbenton.com/river

missouribreaks.org

2. Pompeys Pillar
National Monument

NEAREST TOWN:	Billings, MT
SIZE:	51 acres
BEST SEASON(S):	Spring through fall
NOTABLE ACTIVITIES:	History, birding, short walks

THE MONUMENT:

Previously designated a National Historic Landmark in 1965, President Bill Clinton changed the status of Pompeys Pillar to a national monument on January 17, 2001. This move enhanced the site's significance and afforded increased protection and improved management.

At only 51 acres, it is one of the smallest national monuments in the country. Located along the banks of the Yellowstone River and 32 miles northeast of Billings, the monument contains the only physical evidence of the famed Lewis and Clark Expedition. Captain William Clark etched his signature in the rock on July 25, 1806, as his party was returning from the Pacific coast. The name of the pillar comes from Sacagawea's son, Jean Baptiste Charbonneau, whose Anglican nickname was Pompey.

One can easily imagine the Lewis and Clark Expedition of 1803 floating downstream along the Yellowstone River.

At Pompeys Pillar, a short hike will take you to the top with sweeping views of the Yellowstone River and surrounding lands.

The original sandstone inscription of William Clark during the Lewis and Clark Expedition of 1803.

The site has long been a landmark for nomadic Indigenous peoples, as well as a place for ritual and religious activities. The Crow people named the pillar Mountain Lion's Lodge, and humans have occupied the area for more than 11,000 years. Hundreds of petroglyphs and other archaeological artifacts can be found in the area, along with evidence of trappers and early settlers.

The weather is mild, with summer highs in the mid-80s and winter lows in the teens. Annual precipitation is less than 14 inches, mostly in the form of rain during the spring and summer months. Winds are ever-present, however, particularly during the winter. Average wind speeds are around 15 mph in the winter and 10 mph in the summer, the latter making for a comfortable day lounging alongside the Yellowstone River.

THINGS TO DO:

Before or while visiting this monument, I strongly encourage you to read the accounts of the Lewis and Clark Expedition, an intrepid group of men and women. *Undaunted Courage* by Stephen E. Ambrose is a great account of this spectacular adventure. The effort the participants took to make the journey—documenting flora and fauna along the way, living off the land, and dealing with political pressures—makes for one of history's exciting adventure narratives.

A walk through the monument's interpretive center is worthwhile. The monument is open daily from 8 a.m. to 4 p.m., May through September. If you visit outside these months, you may still walk in from the front gate (about 1.0 mile) from dawn to dusk.

There is a concrete walkway, with a likeness to the nearby Yellowstone River, which has signs along the way with quotes from Clark's journals, telling the story of the expedition's passage.

Birding is popular here, given the nearby water source and numerous cottonwood and willow trees. Warblers, vireos, tanagers, kingbirds, osprey, and bald eagles may be seen.

Each year, at the end of July, you can attend Clark Days, with traditional Native American dancers, cowboy poetry and music, and a pancake breakfast. This is the only time you can camp on the grounds, on both Friday and Saturday nights of the festival. The cost is free.

The quiet setting, right off I-94, is also a great place to have a leisurely picnic, perhaps with a walk around the grounds.

THINGS TO SEE:

Taking the short walk to the top of Pompeys Pillar is a popular activity. The views from the top are all-encompassing, allowing visitors to see for miles in every direction. You'll also notice the protected signature of William Clark on the sandstone wall by the walkway. With a little imagination one can easily see the same landscape Clark encountered stretched out before you. Imagine yourself preparing to set off on the Yellowstone River, heading home after more than two years of exploring the great American West.

GETTING THERE:

Conveniently located about 32 miles northeast of Billings and right off I-94, this is one of the most accessible monuments in this guide.

FACILITIES:

There is no camping within the monument, in part due to its small size and seasonal operating hours. Free camping is allowed on the grounds during Clark Days in late July. Additional camping is available in both Billings and Hardin. Billings has all the usual amenities associated with a large city.

USEFUL CONTACTS:

Pompeys Pillar
National Monument
Bureau of Land Management
3039 US Highway 312
Pompeys Pillar, MT 59064
406-896-5013

blm.gov/visit/pompeys-pillar
  -national-monument

pompeyspillar.org

visitbillings.com

billingschamber.com

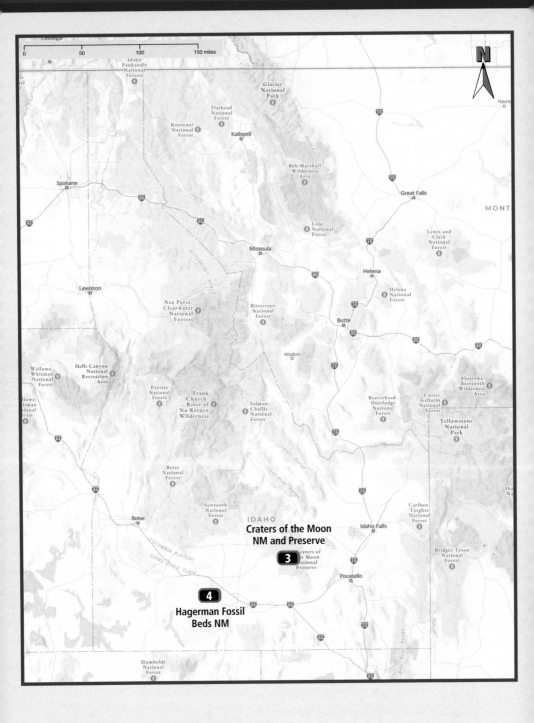

3. Craters of the Moon
National Monument and Preserve

NEAREST TOWNS:	Arco or Carey, ID
SIZE:	750,000 acres
BEST SEASON(S):	Year-round
NOTABLE ACTIVITIES:	Solitude, hiking, birding, geological features, cross-country skiing, wilderness camping, lava tube exploration, astronomy, NASA history

THE MONUMENT:

Through the efforts of local citizens, this area of unique geological importance was set aside and protected as a national monument. The determination of two men in particular, Robert Limbert and Harold Stearns, led President Calvin Coolidge to create this 750,000-acre monument on May 2, 1924.

Limbert was a local taxidermist, and Stearns was a geologist visiting Idaho with a government expedition in 1923. Both men clearly saw the exceptional landscape represented here as unique within the continental United States. The region includes remnants of volcanic eruptions as old as 15,000 years and as recent as 2,000 years ago. A deep fissure, the Great Rift, runs 62 miles in length across the monument, and the peculiar landscape is

Sunrise is scenic from the top of the Inferno Cone, a short but stiff 0.2-mile hike.

A tree mold, created when the lava formed around the tree, which later died, leaving this circular hole.

dotted with cinder cones, lava tubes, and kipukas, which protect islands of natural sagebrush steppe. What sets this landscape apart is that it was formed by the flow of lava from the fissures and spatter cones—basically miniature volcanoes—rather than large singular volcanoes such as Mount St. Helens. The monument itself is managed jointly by both the Bureau of Land Management and the National Park Service.

The weather here, being a high-desert arid climate, sees little in the way of precipitation except during the winter months. There's plenty of hot sunshine in the summer. The black lava rock absorbs and then radiates much of this sunlight back at the hiker, resulting in air temperatures as high as 170 degrees! The winds blow regularly throughout the year and contribute to the dryness. It can get quite cold in the winter, as low as minus 30 degrees.

The air here can be some of the clearest in the nation, allowing you to see the Grand Tetons 140 miles distant. But it can also be some of the haziest, due to the pollution that often comes from faraway coal-fired power plants and other industrial activities.

THINGS TO DO:

Stop first at the visitor center to get oriented, pick up a brochure, watch the video, talk with a ranger, and peruse the exhibits. If you want to explore one of several caves that are open to the public, you will need a permit. You also must ensure that you have no clothing or equipment that was previously taken into another cave and not yet disinfected. This is to reduce the spread of white-nose syndrome, a fungus that can be fatal to cave-dwelling bats.

The very popular 7.0-mile Loop Road will take you past many of the monument's most interesting features. Trailheads are located along the road itself or off one of three spur roads. The drive also brings you to the Big Sink Overlook, which offers tremendous views in all directions of lava flows and lava fields. This drive is closed from November to April due to snow and ice, when it becomes a great cross-country ski outing.

Spatter cones, miniature volcanoes, so named because of how they spit and sputtered, spewing rocks, ash, and lava.

Rabbitbrush and a true lunar landscape. Astronauts from the Apollo 14 mission trained here in 1969 due to its similar geology with the moon.

There are at least six trails available for hiking, depending on the weather. Take into consideration the heat, your energy level, and your abilities. One of the easiest and most accessible trails starts at the visitor center, the 0.3-mile North Crater Flow Trail, which provides views of one of the youngest flows within the monument.

The Devils Orchard Trail is a 0.5-mile walk that brings you to a landscape dotted with lava fragments protruding from a sea of cinders. Hiking a stiff 0.2 mile up the Inferno Cone rewards you with views of cinder cones lined up along the Great Rift. The Spatter Cones are accessible via a short trail where you can see these miniature volcanoes firsthand. A steeper 0.25-mile hike takes you to commanding views of the Big Craters to the southeast. Devils Orchard and Spatter Cones trails are both wheelchair accessible.

Longer hikes include the Tree Molds Trail, which features imprints of lava-charred trees along its 1.0-mile length. Broken Top Trail circumnavigates its namesake 6,058-foot cinder cone for a total of 1.8 miles. The Wilderness Trail takes you to molds of upright trees, known as lava trees, about 2.0 miles from the trailhead. It also continues out into the wilderness area within the monument for those wishing to explore further or partake in an overnight backpacking trip. If you are camping, let the staff at the visitor center know of your plans and obtain the necessary permits. You must be fully self-sufficient. There are no water sources; carry all you'll need. Appropriate clothing and shelter, a map and compass with the skills to use them, and plenty of water are essential for backcountry travel at Craters of the Moon.

A 0.8-mile trail toward the end of the Loop Road will bring you to four different lava tubes: Dewdrop, Boy Scout, Beauty, and Indian Tunnel. Explore these caves at your leisure, once you've obtained the required permit, and be mindful of those sections that are marked or deemed hazardous by the monument staff.

With an average snow depth of 26 inches, the park offers cross-country skiing and snowshoeing as popular winter activities when the Loop Road is closed, and a ski track is maintained along its course. There are also ranger-led winter ecology walks offered in January and February.

THINGS TO SEE:

Despite its apparently barren landscape, there are actually a good number of wildlife and plant species to be found. The key to sightings is both the time of year and the time of day. Most wildlife species are more active in the evening, overnight, and in the early morning, when the temperatures are more manageable. Springtime also brings a rush of reproductive efforts among birds, including sage grouse, with their unique mating display on historic leks—the name for areas where sage grouse congregate in the spring.

While the more fragile annuals bloom in late May after the snow melts, wildflowers reach their peak typically in mid-June. The hardier, drought-resistant species blossom throughout the summer and into mid-September.

Craters of the Moon is a designated International Dark Sky Park, which recognize skies that are predominantly free of light pollution from outside sources. Visitors can spend the evening stargazing for individual constellations or taking in the entirety of the Milky Way. Star parties are held each spring and fall, sponsored by the Idaho Falls Astronomical Society. This group provides telescopes, as well as the expertise necessary to fully appreciate the heavens. There are also ranger-led full moon walks during the summer months.

An interesting side note: Craters of the Moon served in 1969 as a training labora-

USEFUL CONTACTS:

Craters of the Moon
National Monument and Preserve
1266 Craters Loop Road
Arco, ID 83213
208-527-1300
nps.gov/crmo

Shoshone Field Office
Bureau of Land Management
400 West F Street
Shoshone, ID 83352
208-732-7200
blm.gov/office/shoshone-field-office

tory for astronauts on the 1971 Apollo 14 mission. Since they were all trained primarily as pilots, the astronauts had limited knowledge of geology and what types of rock samples would be best to bring back from the moon, which shares a similar landscape to the monument. This training allowed them to make the most of their limited time and payload capacity.

GETTING THERE:

The monument is roughly equidistant from the towns of Arco and Carey, both of which are about 20 miles from the entrance. Carey is 65 miles from Twin Falls on US Highway 26/93, and Arco is 61 miles from Blackfoot on US Highway 26. Both are larger cities and are located on I-84 and I-15, respectively.

The rock wren, a common resident of scrublands and arid talus slopes, hence the name.

FACILITIES:

There is a forty-seven-site campground just beyond the entrance to the monument that can accommodate RVs and tents. There are no hookups, and generators cannot be used after 10 p.m. There is potable water at several spigots located throughout the campground, as well as vault toilets. Wood fires are prohibited. The campground is first-come, first-served, and payment is by credit or debit card only. There is also a kiosk at the monument entrance where you can register and pay for your campsite 24/7, again using plastic. Group sites can be reserved ahead of time using recreation.gov.

The nearest towns are Arco to the northeast and Carey to the southwest. Both are relatively small communities, with only Carey offering limited lodging and restaurants. Arco's historical claim to fame is that it was, in 1955, the first city to be powered by nuclear energy. There is a KOA campground in Arco with full services.

The bigger towns of Ketchum or Sun Valley are your best bet for lodging, dining, and supplies near the monument. Traveling farther in either direction will get you to the larger metropolitan areas of Idaho Falls, Pocatello, and Twin Falls, all located off I-84.

4. Hagerman Fossil Beds
National Monument

NEAREST TOWN:	Hagerman, ID
SIZE:	4,351 acres
BEST SEASON(S):	Year-round
NOTABLE ACTIVITIES:	Museum, hiking, birding

THE MONUMENT:

About 44 miles west of Twin Falls along the Snake River, Hagerman Fossil Beds National Monument is best known for its rich collection of fossils from the Pliocene era, 3.5 million years ago. Fossils of the Hagerman Horse (*Equus simplicidens*), a species unique to this area, only exist in the Hagerman Horse Quarry in the northern reaches of the monument. The remains of an extinct genus of camel, *Camelops hesternus*, is also found here. More widespread than the Hagerman Horse, fossilized remains of Camelops can also be seen at the George C. Page Museum in Los Angeles and at Waco Mammoth National Monument in Waco, Texas.

Designated a national landmark in 1975, the Hagerman Fossil Beds were further protected as a national monument on November 18, 1988. A 3.0-mile segment of the famous Oregon Trail runs through the monument,

Snake River. Many of the fossils found here came from the unstable bluffs along the river.

once used by early pioneers to cross the vastness of the West seeking better lives on the frontier. Comprising 4,351 acres, including an eastern boundary that parallels the Snake River for 6 miles, this monument remains largely undeveloped with limited access points. Most of the focus is on paleontology and the work of students and professionals to recover valuable fossils.

Temperatures reach the low 90s in July and August, while in the winter they drop to the 30s and 40s. Spring and fall are the most comfortable times to visit, with highs in the 60s and nighttime lows in the 30- to 40-degree range. Annual precipitation is just over 10 inches, with little to no snowfall.

THINGS TO DO:

The visitor center is in the nearby town of Hagerman, on the eastern side of the Snake River. The small museum features fossils from the area and a very knowledgeable staff. You can also browse information on the history of the monument, including details about some of the more notable paleontological discoveries from this region.

There are two designated overlooks within the monument. The first is the Snake River Overlook on Bell Rapids Road, off Highway 30 south of Hagerman. It offers beautiful views across the prairie to the Snake River and the monument's eastern boundary. You'll also be able to clearly see the sedimentary soil that lends itself very well to the preservation and excavation of fossilized remains. The other viewpoint, the Oregon Trail Overlook, is named for the view it affords of the Oregon Trail below. There is a designated hiking trail between the two overlooks, about 3.0 miles one-way, as well as a short interpretive walk. Continuing along Bell Rapids Road, you can take 400 East for about 3.5 miles to 5700 North, then take the first right-hand turn off 5700 North, which leads to the Snake River. The last section of road may be blocked, necessitating a short walk to the river's edge.

Despite the open nature of the monument, cross-country travel is prohibited, ostensibly to protect visitors from snakes and other hazards but more likely to discourage fossil-hunters who might plunder the excavation sites or ruin ongoing research. Additionally, the sedimentary banks of the Snake River, where most of the fossils are found, can be extremely unstable and subject to sliding.

THINGS TO SEE:

Nearby is the Minidoka National Historic Site, a former Japanese internment camp from World War II and a reminder of a darker period in our nation's history.

Southeast of Twin Falls is City of Rocks, an exceptional rock-climbing destination featuring excellent granite. There are over 500 established routes for climbers of all abilities. In addition, visitors can see signatures that early explorers wrote on the rock faces with axle grease.

Craters of the Moon National Monument is about 90 miles to the northeast of Twin Falls and offers camping and a look into the area's volcanic past. It was also a training ground for astronauts in the 1960s as they prepared for the first lunar landings.

If you're visiting in the winter, Sun Valley Resort offers excellent skiing about 92 miles north on Highway 75. Sun Valley receives about 120 inches of snow annually.

The Morley Nelson Snake River Birds of Prey National Conservation Area, to the west of Hagerman Fossil Beds, has the greatest concentration of nesting raptors in North America and perhaps the world. Here you can see bald and golden eagles, osprey, northern harriers, peregrine falcons, and even migrating gyrfalcons, along with many more raptor species. Just south of Boise, it's a good place to spend a few days searching for some of these magnificent birds and their offspring.

USEFUL CONTACTS:

Hagerman Fossil Beds Visitor Center
221 North State Street
Hagerman, ID 83332
208-933-4100
nps.gov/hafo

visitidaho.org/places-to-stay
    /Hagerman

visitsouthidaho.com/visitor-info
    /twin-falls-visitor-center

GETTING THERE:

The monument is adjacent to Hagerman, which sits 8 miles south of I-84 along US Highway 30. Hagerman is 38 miles northwest of Twin Falls on US Highway 30.

FACILITIES:

There are no facilities within the monument. Food, fuel, and lodging can be found in nearby Hagerman. More amenities are available in Twin Falls, about 38 miles to the southeast on I-86. Lacking nearby public lands, there isn't much in the way of dispersed camping in the immediate area. Camping is available at both Three Island Crossing State Park and Bruneau Dunes State Park, roughly 25 or 30 miles to the west, respectively. Camping is also available to the east at Lake Walcott State Park near Minidoka, about an 83-mile drive.

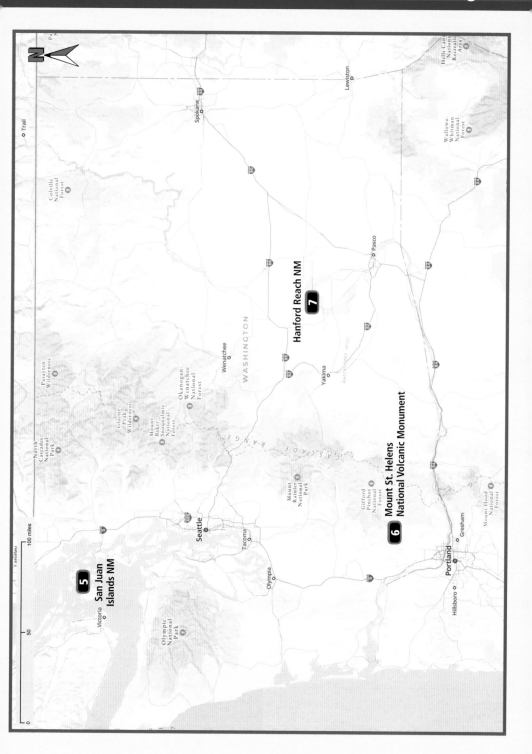

San Juan Islands NM **5**

Mount St. Helens National Volcanic Monument **6**

Hanford Reach NM **7**

5. San Juan Islands
National Monument

NEAREST TOWN:	Anacortes, WA, and small communities on each of the islands
SIZE:	1,000 acres (all of the archipelago)
BEST SEASON(S):	Year-round
NOTABLE ACTIVITIES:	Hiking, birding, wildlife and plant viewing, photography, geology, astronomy, mountain biking (limited), marine life, whale watching, kayaking

THE MONUMENT:

Officially proclaimed San Juan Islands National Monument on March 25, 2013, by President Barack Obama, the monument comprises approximately 1,000 acres spread over seventy-five different sites on six primary islands within the San Juan archipelago, the entirety of which is managed by the Bureau of Land Management (BLM). While the BLM continues to oversee these sites, they are now permanently protected from common uses on other BLM lands, including grazing, mining, energy production, off-road vehicle use, and sale.

A trio of orcas, circling and feeding collectively on a sea lion.

The excellent Washington State Ferries can take you and your vehicle to the various islands of the monument. Be sure to make reservations in advance.

The ferry coming into the port of Orcas Island. Your initial ticket gives you access to all the islands of the monument.

The monument is in Washington's northern Puget Sound, just west of Seattle. It encompasses over 450 separate islands, rocks, and pinnacles, and is home to numerous species of mammals, birds, and insects. The marbled butterfly, previously thought to be extinct, can be found here. Archaeological sites and historic lighthouses are scattered throughout the islands. Surprisingly, researchers have uncovered the skeletons of ancient bison, approximately 10,000 to 12,000 years old, at some of these sites. Habitats within the monument include wetlands, grasslands, open woodlands, and large stands of forest. This diversity of habitat supports an equally wide range of wildlife. Here you'll encounter orcas, seals, black-tailed deer, bald eagles, peregrine falcons, and marbled murrelets.

Given its position in the ocean waters where the Strait of Juan de Fuca and the Strait of Georgia meet, the weather here is classic Pacific Northwest. Expect lots of rain, with serious storms possible year-round. Summers are mild with highs in the 70s and lows in the 50s, while winters cool down to the upper 40s and mid-30s. Precipitation is an impressive 28 inches of rainfall, with barely 3 inches of snow annually.

THINGS TO DO:

Accessing the monument isn't particularly difficult, although it takes some planning, especially during the peak months of summer. The only practical way to get to any of the main islands with your vehicle is by boat. Fortunately, the state of Washington has an excellent ferry system. Once you're on the islands, going from one to another is as easy as getting in line for the next ferry. There are no additional charges for island hopping. Being on the

The diminutive black-tailed deer, a subspecies of mule deer, is a fairly common resident of the lush forests on these islands.

Looking across the archipelago from Mount Constitution on Orcas Island.

ferries themselves is an interesting and enjoyable experience. Various waterfowl can be seen, and the views of Mount Baker are stunning. Anacortes on Lopez Island, the typical jumping-off point for trips to the San Juan Islands, is accessible via highway from the mainland.

THINGS TO SEE:
The scenery is what most people come for, but the host of other activities in the area is why they stay. One of the more popular outings is watching for gray whales during their biannual migration every spring and fall. It's likely you'll also see other wildlife along the way, including orcas, stellar sea lions, bald eagles, or even Dall's porpoise. There are numerous outfitters and sightseeing tour operators on the San Juan Islands, as well as in Anacortes or Bellingham. Most have comfortable boats and ample viewing opportunities, with morning and afternoon departures. Tours tend to last from three to four hours.

Island hopping is a great way to experience the monument. Ferries connect you to different ports within the archipelago, allowing you to follow your inclinations with relative ease. Island hopping takes a bit of planning and coordination, but it also allows you to explore each of the major islands with your own vehicle.

GETTING THERE:
Anacortes, on WA Highway 20 just 15 miles west of I-5, is the most popular gateway for a visit to this archipelago. From here you'll need to board a ferry to access and travel among the islands.

Mount Baker, 10,781 feet, is part of the North Cascade Range, seen from the ferry to Orcas Island.

FACILITIES:

Vehicle camping at commercial sites is available and easily accessible on the larger islands. There are also several state parks with campgrounds. Again, given the monument's proximity to the Seattle metropolitan area and the popularity of the islands, planning ahead is the best way to avoid disappointment.

If you choose to travel by private boat to or among the islands, the BLM offers additional information on marine camping parks on several of the islands. These are typically restricted to boat-only access, and often to only kayaks or wind-powered vessels. The beauty and appeal of these sites is that you have reduced crowds and stunning scenery. They're great for wildlife viewing and photography as well. Local tour operators offer a wide range of kayak trips.

USEFUL CONTACTS:

At the time of this writing there is no official visitor center.

blm.gov/programs/national-conservation
  -lands/national-monuments
  /oregon-washington/san-juan-islands

go-washington.com/San-Juan-Islands

visitsanjuans.com
  (general information)

wsdot.wa.gov/ferries

wta.org/signpost/hike-the-new-san-juan
  -islands-national-monument

6. Mount St. Helens
National Volcanic Monument

NEAREST TOWN:	Castle Rock, WA
SIZE:	110,000 acres
BEST SEASON(S):	Year-round
NOTABLE ACTIVITIES:	Hiking, mountaineering, birding, wildlife and plant viewing, photography, volcanic geology, astronomy, solitude, mountain biking, climbing, skiing, lava tube exploration

THE MONUMENT:

Recognizing the significance of the eruption of Mount St. Helens in 1980, President Ronald Reagan established this monument only two years later on August 27, 1982. This unique landmark was the first national monument managed by the US Forest Service, and it covers 110,000 acres.

Within the boundaries of the monument, the environment was left untouched after the 1980 eruption to allow scientists and educators the opportunity to witness firsthand the natural recovery of this distinctive

Mount St. Helens from Windy Ridge, a good place to view the northeastern aspect of the mountain.

A composite of Mount St. Helens, 8,364 feet, at sunset, showing much of the north side that was blown out in 1980.

landscape. Indigenous peoples in the Pacific Northwest called the mountain "Louwala-Clough," or "Smoking Mountain." The current name is attributed to Captain George Vancouver, an early explorer of the Northwest, who named the mountain in honor of Alleyne Fitzerbert. Fitzerbert held the title of Baron St. Helen.

Mount St. Helens is a composite volcano, also known as a stratovolcano. These are typically steep-sided symmetrical cones that tend to erupt quite explosively. Shortly after 8:32 a.m. local time on May 18, 1980, Mount St. Helens did exactly that. The eruption was in response to a magnitude 5.1 earthquake that struck about a mile beneath the volcano. The resulting devastation created a cloud of volcanic ash that spread as far as Minnesota on the prevailing winds, rising to an altitude of about 16 miles in less than 15 minutes. The speed of the lateral blast was calculated to be nearly 670 mph. Mudflows in the Toutle River drainage ultimately deposited more than 65 million cubic yards of debris downstream, causing the Columbia River navigational channel to drop from 39 feet to less than 13 feet. Mount St. Helens presently reaches an altitude of 8,364 feet, about 1,313 feet lower than it was before the eruption. The total area impacted by the blast was over 230 square miles of forestland.

There is a visitor center at Silver Lake, close to I-5 and about 30 miles west of the mountain itself. It is run by Washington State Parks, and there's

It will take many generations for this landscape—decimated by the 1980 eruption—to return to the days of lush conifers and flowing streams so typical of the Pacific Northwest.

a small entrance fee. Mount St. Helens is not visible from this location. While there are no roads that travel through the entirety of the monument, there are several that provide views of Mount St. Helens from the north, south, and east.

The Johnston Ridge Observatory offers excellent views of the north side of the mountain, including the vast crater and dome, as well as an informative visitor center. You can get there by driving Highway 504 to its end at the observatory. Windy Ridge is another excellent viewpoint, weather allowing, that shows the northeast side of the volcano and the crater. Roads 81 and 83 grant access to the south side. Both head north from Highway 503, which parallels the Swift Reservoir.

The weather in nearby Randle is a typical mountain climate, with summer highs in the 70s and lows in the upper 40s. Winters only reach the 40s during the day, while nights can see sub-freezing temperatures. Add to that a few thousand feet of elevation gain to get to the Johnston Ridge Observatory, and you can easily see a drop of 10 degrees or more in temperature. Annual precipitation, given that the monument is in the Pacific Northwest, totals an impressive 60 inches or more with at least 5 feet of snowfall.

THINGS TO DO:

There are a variety of activities centered on the mountain itself. Driving to one of the many viewpoints is a popular way to experience the monument and witness the devastation, provided the weather allows. Highway 504, on the north side of the monument, will take you to the Johnston Ridge Observatory with several scenic pullouts along the way. This location offers stunning views of the crater and the ever-growing lava dome within it. You

Some of the blast devastation on the southern aspect of a slope above Spirit Lake.

Logs felled by the explosion and blown into Spirit Lake clearly be seen, floating on the far shore.

can also clearly see where the mudflow poured over the North Fork of the Toutle River Valley.

A more unique way to experience the mountain is to climb it. Most hikers start from the south side. Permits are required and can be obtained from mshinstitute.org. While not a technical climb, it can be exhausting. The ascent involves an elevation gain of approximately 4,500 feet over a 5.0-mile one-way route on boulders and very loose volcanic ash. Sturdy hiking boots, gaiters, food, lots of water, and an early start are all recommended. Due to the removal of glacial accumulation zones after the eruption, there is no risk from crevasses, unlike many other Cascade volcanoes. The climbing season generally runs from May through November, barring activity from the volcano itself, which may necessitate closures. Permits are limited to 500 people per day between April 1 and May 14, and 100 people per day from May 15 to October 31. Plan accordingly.

Many climbers opt to ski or snowboard down the mountain after reaching the summit. Not as outlandish as it might seem, this is a common outing for ski mountaineers in spring and early summer. Crampons and an ice ax are recommended when climbing on snow. Please note that, even though the slope angles are similar to what might be found at a ski resort, the setting is much wilder. Climbing Mount St. Helens requires a certain level of mountaineering competence, trip planning experience, knowledge of local weather patterns, physical fitness, appropriate gear and clothing, and comfort moving safely over varied terrain. Guides are available for hire for less experienced climbers.

Mountain biking is also a popular activity, with several trails within the monument dedicated to the sport. One of the more popular is the Ape

My daughter, Sara, making her way up the last bit of the climb on the south side of the mountain. As you can see, without snow cover it's a long slog up volcanic debris.

Canyon Trail, which takes you on a 24-mile out-and-back ride through vibrant green forests. As you ascend, you'll encounter remnants of the destruction from 1980, including still-standing trees and fields of pumice rock. You'll also witness nature's ongoing efforts to restore the area, such as flowing streams with vegetation, herds of elk, wildflowers, and a slow but steady regrowth of the great forests that once blanketed this region.

THINGS TO SEE:

Wildlife, while perhaps not as abundant as before the eruption, is still present in good numbers. It's not unusual to spot herds of elk in the open areas below the Johnston Ridge Observatory. Wildflowers are prevalent within the monument, with over 300 documented species. This diversity of plants is likely due to the wide range of distinct ecosystems within the monument's varied elevations.

The lava tubes known as the Ape Caves are probably the most intriguing and popular attraction, other than the mountain itself. Formed by the movement of hot lava flowing away from the mountain nearly 2,000 years ago, some of these tubes are quite high and as long as 2.4 miles. A local logger, Larry Johnson, first discovered the lava tubes in 1951.

Caves are isolated ecosystems and must be treated with care. The temperature is a constant 42 degrees, and the cave interiors are, of course, very wet. The walls have cave "slime," a fungus that serves as a critical food source for cave-dwelling organisms. It should not be touched or damaged. White-nose syndrome, a condition that affects bats and triggers them to awaken when they should be hibernating, is primarily transmitted by people. Please follow the guidelines posted at the ranger kiosks. Wear sturdy hiking shoes along with warm clothes and a water-resistant outer layer. The most critical piece of equipment is a good light source with extra batteries, as there is

The Lava Tubes at Ape Cave are intriguing to explore. Just make sure you have at least two sources of light and extra batteries.

absolutely no natural light within the cave. The main entrance offers access to both the upper and lower portions of the cave, with the former being the more difficult route.

GETTING THERE:

From the north, take Exit 63 off I-5 onto WA Highway 505 in Toledo. Join WA Highway 504 east and follow this for 30 miles to the monument. From the south, take Exit 49 at Castle Rock to WA Highway 504E and join WA Highway 504 east as described above. To visit Ape Caves Lava Tubes on the south side of the monument, take Exit 21 off I-5 at Woodland and follow WA Highway 503 for 21 miles to Cougar to pick up your permit. From there it's about 5 miles to the site.

FACILITIES:

While there are no campgrounds in the monument itself, there are numerous campgrounds, both private and government run, in the surrounding Gifford Pinchot National Forest. Camping is permitted in the monument where overnight backpacking is allowed. There are several private camping resorts along Highway 503 on the south side of the monument. Lodging can also be found in the nearby towns of Castle Rock, Kelso, Kalama, and Woodland off of I-5. These all put you within easy driving distance for a day trip to the monument.

USEFUL CONTACTS:

Mount St. Helens National Volcanic Monument
Gifford Pinchot National Forest
fs.usda.gov/giffordpinchot
360-449-7800

mshinstitute.org

mountsthelens.com

7. Hanford Reach National Monument

NEAREST TOWN:	Richland, WA
SIZE:	195,000 acres
BEST SEASON(S):	Year-round
NOTABLE ACTIVITIES:	Hiking, birding, wildlife and plant viewing, photography, geology, astronomy, solitude, mountain biking, hunting, fishing, history

THE MONUMENT:

Hanford Reach National Monument started out as part of the security buffer surrounding Hanford Nuclear Reservation. Since 1943, it has become a largely untouched area of public land protected by monument status as of June 9, 2000, by President Bill Clinton. Named after the Hanford Reach, the last non-tidal and free-flowing portion of the mighty 1,212-mile long Columbia River, it is also one of only eight national monuments overseen by the US Forest Service. Part of the monument is contained within the Hanford site, and is thus managed by the Department of Energy (DOE). The monument's horseshoe shape covers 195,000 acres, surrounding the Hanford site on three sides.

The Hanford Reach of the mighty Columbia River offers up world-class fishing as well as lazy float trips downstream to Richland.

A pleasant place to while away the day, the White Bluffs Boat Launch area.

Human history here dates back 10,000 years to the ancestors of the Wanapum peoples, Yakima Nation, Confederated Tribes of the Colville and Umatilla, and the Nez Perce. These inhabitants call this land home, where they historically were able to freely fish, hunt, and harvest other natural resources from this area. Evidence of winter "house pits" has been found here, suggesting year-round living. Fur trappers in the 1800s were among the first non-natives to arrive, with the Lewis and Clark Expedition of 1804 leading the way. White Bluffs, with its ferry crossing of the Columbia, was a major supply depot for the region. Steamboats plied the river ferrying goods and taking gold from the Rocky Mountains to the Pacific Coast. All this human activity led to increased agricultural production and cattle grazing as well. The construction of the Hanford Ditch in 1907 allowed water to be pumped from the river and to the nearby farms, while the Milwaukee Road became a major thoroughfare for colonial settlers.

This area has nine nuclear reactors, including the famous "B Reactor," which provided the plutonium for the world's first nuclear explosion and the atomic bomb, "Fat Man," which was dropped on Nagasaki, Japan, in 1945.

There are two areas in the monument that are closed to the public for research purposes: the Saddle Mountain National Wildlife Refuge and the Fitzner-Eberhardt Arid Lands Ecology Reserve. Any lands that are managed by the DOE or that lie within the Hanford Nuclear Reservation are off-limits to the general public. Limited access notwithstanding, there is plenty of land to explore, including both river and desert habitat, each with its own wildlife and plant species.

The striking purple of these flowers in mid-winter suggests that wildflowers can be found year-round here, given the fairly mild climate.

Weather is mild, except for summers when temperatures reach the upper 80s and sometimes as high as 100 degrees. The air is especially dry with high fire danger. Summertime lows are a comfortable upper 50s. Winter is mild and temperatures rarely drop below freezing, even at night. Highs are in the low- to mid-40s, so it never gets "warm" in the winter months. Spring and fall are the best seasons to visit, as the wildlife tends to be more active and visible and the temperatures are in the 60s and 70s. Here in the rain shadow of the Cascades, precipitation is low, with less than 8 inches annually. Very little falls during the summer. Snowfall can amount to as much as 6 inches per year.

THINGS TO DO:

Information on the monument can be found at the Reach Museum in Richland.

A popular activity involves finding an abandoned military or service road and seeing where it takes you. There are over 57,000 acres available to the public for exploration. The White Bluffs North and South Slope Trails offer easy walking along the bluffs of the river. They are both out-and-back loops that, at their longest, are about 8 miles. To reach the trails from the north, take WA 24 to just past mile marker 64 and turn onto a gated gravel road. Follow the road for about 4 miles to the turn for the North Slope Trailhead and continue toward the trailhead for 1.5 miles. Going another 4 miles on the gravel road past the North Slope Trailhead turnoff leads to the South Slope Trailhead.

The short and easy 2.6-mile Crab Creek Trail Loop passes through riparian habitat on the Columbia National Wildlife Refuge. Expect to see a variety of birds here such as sparrows, buntings, wrens, orioles, and sandhill cranes during spring. To reach this trail from Othello, WA, follow West McManaman Road northwest out of town to the trailhead. A brochure is available through the US Fish and Wildlife Service (USFWS). These same roads also serve as mountain bike routes. Many are paved and offer a smooth surface.

The river is a big draw for anglers and boaters, and the White Bluffs Boat Launch is a common put-in site. Floating the Hanford Reach from Priest Rapids Dam to Richland, a 51-mile outing, is a popular two-day getaway. This world-class fishery offers the chance to catch steelhead, white sturgeon, chinook salmon, and bass along the Reach. Hunters can search out likely habitat for chukar and California quail, a variety of waterfowl, as well as mule deer and elk. The USFWS has additional information on boating, fishing, and hunting.

THINGS TO SEE:

Elk, native to this area for 10,000 years, were reintroduced in the 1930s from Rocky Mountain stock. Protected from hunting and human interference in the Arid Lands Reserve, they have thrived here, where there are few natural predators. It is believed that they arrived in the Reach by natural migration from stock introduced near Mount Rainier National Park. They were first seen within the monument in 1972 and are best viewed in the winter along the east side of WA 240.

The marsh wren, a resident of marshes in this area, can be hard to spot and rarely sits still.

The draw of this monument is the preservation of sagebrush steppe habitat, which had been largely intact for more than sixty years. The sagebrush is critical both for food and as a source of shelter for numerous species of birds, mammals, and reptiles. While adjacent lands have been overgrazed and are contaminated with pesticides and herbicides, Hanford Reach remains undisturbed and thus allows researchers and visitors to experience what Eastern Washington was like before massive agricultural development occurred.

Mule deer, coyotes, darkling beetles, and Upper Columbia River steelhead trout can all be found here. Roughly 238 species of birds have been documented in the monument, including white pelicans, bald eagles, horned larks, loggerhead shrikes, burrowing owls, Say's phoebe, migrating sandhill cranes, and chukars, all of which are habitat dependent.

The Reach Museum in Richland has galleries that discuss the Ice Age floods, the Manhattan Project, the Columbia River and surrounding lands, as well as an outdoor gallery that includes a Cold War bus, metal cutouts of the twenty-two animals that are native to this region, and a garden of local plants. While it is not an official monument visitor center, it has information on exploring the monument on your own.

GETTING THERE:

Accessing this horseshoe-shaped monument depends on the direction you're coming from.

From Yakima to the west, follow WA Highway 24 for 25 miles to its junction with WA Highway 240. Turn south here and follow along the monument's eastern border.

From Richland to the south, take WA Highway 240 for about 20 miles along the monument's eastern border.

From the northeast, leave Othello going south on WA Highway 24 for 35 miles to its junction with WA Highway 240 as described above.

From Vantage off I-90, take WA Highway 243 for 23 miles to its junction with WA Highway 240 and drive south as described above.

> **USEFUL CONTACTS:**
>
> **The Reach Museum**
> **1943 Columbia Park Trail**
> **Richland, WA 99352**
> **509-943-4100**
> **visitthereach.org**
>
> **fws.gov/refuge/Hanford_Reach**
>
> **visittri-cities.com**

FACILITIES:

There are no facilities within the monument. Although cell coverage is good, bring what you may need and start out with a full tank of gas. The Vernita Bridge Rest Stop on WA Highway 24 has flush toilets, picnic sites, shade, water, and general information. It's open twenty-four hours year-round. Camping can be found at Benton County Horn Rapids Park and Kennewick's Columbia Park. Richland, Kennewick, Othello, and Yakima all offer numerous food, fuel, lodging, and entertainment options.

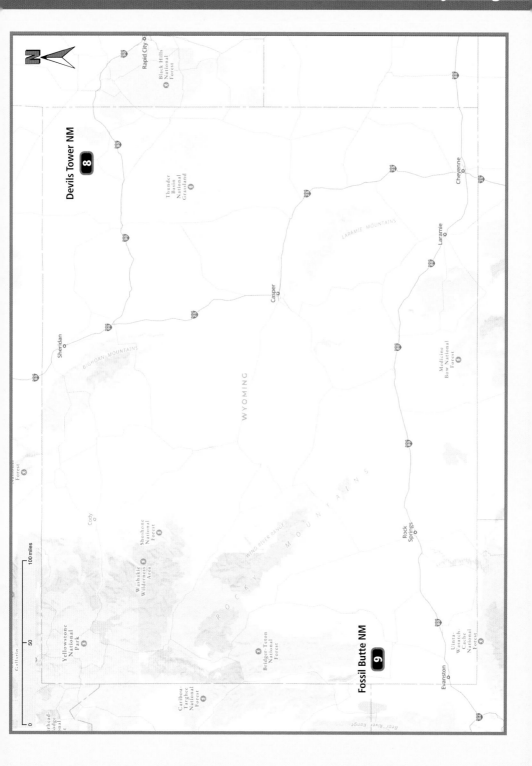

N

Devils Tower NM

8

Rapid City

Black Hills National Forest

Thunder Basin National Grassland

Cheyenne

LARAMIE MOUNTAINS

Laramie

Casper

Sheridan

BIGHORN MOUNTAINS

WYOMING

Medicine Bow National Forest

Forest

Cody

Shoshone National Forest

Washakie Wilderness Area

WIND RIVER RANGE

R O C K Y   M O U N T A I N S

Rock Springs

100 miles

50

0

Gallatin

Yellowstone National Park

Bridger-Teton National Forest

Fossil Butte NM

9

Caribou-Targhee National Forest

Uinta-Wasatch-Cache National Forest

Evanston

Bear River Range

8. Devils Tower National Monument

NEAREST TOWN:	Sundance, WY
SIZE:	1,347 acres
BEST SEASON(S):	Spring through fall
NOTABLE ACTIVITIES:	Hiking, birding, wildlife and plant viewing, photography, unique geology, astronomy, solitude, mountain biking, rock climbing

Devils Tower with a trio of Texas longhorns lounging in the grasslands.

THE MONUMENT:

Devils Tower was the first national monument established under the Antiquities Act, by President Theodore Roosevelt on September 24, 1906. It was designated to protect the unique geology and cultural significance of the tower. Managed by the National Park Service, the monument encompasses 1,347 acres, of which about 1.25 acres, the size of a football field, is located on top of the tower. Devils Tower is known as "Mato Tipila Paha" in the Lakota language, or "Mato Tipila," which means "Bear Lodge."

There are several scientific explanations for the formation of the tower, which began as an intrusion of magma that solidified before reaching the surface and was then exposed through erosion. But the Kiowa oral history of the tower is far more intriguing. According to the legend, seven girls were being chased by bears and jumped on a low rock to escape. One girl prayed to the rock for help, and the rock began to grow upward. As the bears tried to reach the girls high on the rock, they scratched and clawed at its sides, forming the characteristic columns. The rock went ever higher into the sky until the seven girls became seven little stars in a group known as The Pleiades. On winter nights these seven stars are visible directly over the tower.

The Red Beds Trail alongside a stream flowing along red clay banks in the early morning, showing the Spearfish Formation.

The monument's current name came from Col. Richard Dodge, who claimed that a Native American tribe had called it Bad God's Tower during his 1875 scientific expedition. Hence the name Devils Tower.

In October 1941, parachutist George Hopkins attempted to make history by parachuting onto the tower's summit. While the jump itself was successful, the rope by which he planned to descend missed its mark, and Hopkins could not retrieve it. He had to wait six days for a team of professional climbers, led by Jack Durrance and Paul Petzoldt, to ascend the tower and rescue him.

The climate in this region is mild in the summer with highs in the 80s and lows in the 50s. Winter is not exceptionally cold, with temperatures averaging in the mid-30s, but it can be windy, and over 6 feet of snow falls here annually. Most precipitation occurs from spring through fall, totaling less than 20 inches.

Viewing sunrise on the tower is a fine way to start your day. Taking in the night sky under the tower is another option that many overlook.

White-tailed deer are one of many species of wildlife that can be found in the monument.

THINGS TO DO:

For many, climbing Devils Tower is a lifelong goal. There are over 220 established climbing routes. The first ascent, via a 350-foot wooden ladder, was made by William Rogers and Willard Ripley on July 4, 1893. During the climb, their wives ran a refreshment stand below. It was quite a spectacle, and the gathering turned into an annual get-together for the ranchers who inhabited the surrounding area. Two years later, Mrs. Rogers made the first female ascent using the same ladder. Today, upwards of 6,000 climbers visit each year from around the world to ascend the unique rock of Devils Tower. Climbers are required to register with a ranger before beginning their attempt. Out of respect for Indigenous ceremony, there is a voluntary climbing closure of the tower during the entire month of June.

Three hiking trails lead around the tower. The Tower Trail is a 1.3-mile loop around the base that has close-up views of the rock and climbers on its flanks. This trail is primarily within a pine forest and features benches for rest breaks. The longer, more strenuous 2.8-mile Red Beds Trail takes you past the namesake bluffs of red rock. The Joyner Trail is another loop trail of 1.5 miles, north of the tower; it follows a ridge and drops down a sandstone cliff into a meadow below. If you see a prayer cloth or bundle, be respectful and leave it alone.

None of these trails is wheelchair accessible. Despite being paved, the Tower Trail is neither smooth nor level.

THINGS TO SEE:

The tower, of course! At 867 feet, it is easily the tallest object around for hundreds of miles. You're bound to be impressed by this solitary formation and intrigued by its creation.

A population of black-tailed prairie dogs is visible from three pullouts along the road at approximately 0.5 mile into the monument. Be aware that these are wild animals and have been known to bite and carry diseases.

With over 150 species of birds documented, this area is rich in wildlife. Whitetail deer are abundant and are easily identified by their characteristic white tail.

The world-renowned Sturgis Motorcycle Rally takes place during the first full week of August each year. The "Ride to Devils Tower" typically occurs on Wednesday of that week, with thousands of motorcyclists in attendance. While the monument steps up its efforts to accommodate the crowds to include a 45-minute round-trip shuttle bus, it is a popular time to visit. The paved parking lot at the visitor center is set aside for motorcycles, and monument staff suggests arriving before 8 a.m. or after 5 p.m. to minimize the congestion. The entire area surrounding the monument is impacted by the rally, which make patience and caution essential.

The 12-foot-high Wind Circle or Circle of Sacred Smoke sculpture is located across from the picnic area along the road to the campground, about 1 mile into the monument. Designed and

A team of climbers ascending the phonolite porphyry of the tower.

A closer view of the same climbers on one of the many excellent parallel cracks of varying difficulty.

created by Japanese sculptor Junkyu Muto, it represents a gesture of international good will. The sculpture was donated to the National Park Service in 2008; the park only had to pay transportation costs. This is the third of seven proposed Muto sculptures to be created for sites around the world. The other two are at the Vatican and Buddha Gaya in India.

GETTING THERE:

Traveling east on I-90, take Exit 153 and travel north on US Highway 14 for 28 miles to the junction with WY Highway 24. From here, it's another 4 miles to the entrance.

Traveling west on I-90, take the Sundance Exit onto US Highway 14 and continue for 24 miles to the junction with WY Highway 24. Then drive north for 4 miles to the entrance.

FACILITIES:

There is a fifty-site seasonal campground along the Belle Fourche River about 2 miles into the monument. It can accommodate RVs up to 35 feet. It is first-come, first-served, and there are no hookups, although potable water and restrooms are available. There is no access to the river from here, as it is on private land and fenced off. Immediately before the entrance to the monument, there is a KOA campground with full-service hookups, showers, laundry, and a nearby post office. They even have nightly showings of *Close Encounters of the Third Kind*, which featured Devils Tower, in an open-air setting.

Keyhole State Park, approximately 20 miles south of Devils Tower on WY Highway 14, offers numerous outdoor activities along with ten different year-round campgrounds for a total of 286 RV and tent sites, although only the Tatanka Campground has hookups for water and electric. Reservations are required from May 1 through September 30. Keyhole State Park features a large reservoir, so fishing, boating, and other water sports are quite common.

The nearest town of any size is the small community of Hulett, with fewer than 400 people, about 9 miles from Devils Tower. Hulett has small-town amenities, including a few nice bed and breakfasts.

USEFUL CONTACTS:

Devils Tower National Monument
WY-110
Devils Tower, WY 82714
307-467-5283 (x635)

nps.gov/deto

wyoparks.state.wy.us/index
.php/places-to-go/keyhole

9. Fossil Butte
National Monument

NEAREST TOWN:	Kemmerer, WY
SIZE:	8,198 acres
BEST SEASON(S):	Fall through spring
NOTABLE ACTIVITIES:	Hiking, birding, wildlife and plant viewing, photography, geology, astronomy, solitude, mountain biking

THE MONUMENT:

Located in the southwestern corner of Wyoming about 10 miles west of the town of Kemmerer, this monument contains 8,198 acres and is home to a 50-million-year-old lakebed, Fossil Lake. Fossil Lake was originally 40 by 60 miles in size but dried up long ago. Created on October 23, 1972, by Congress and managed by the National Park Service, the Fossil Butte National Monument attracts nearly 20,000 annual visitors, despite its relatively remote location.

The very colorful buttes of Fossil Buttes National Monument.

Moose are somewhat common in this area, having found habitat that is to their liking.

This monument represents another collaborative effort by local communities to preserve a significant part of geological history. This area lies within the transition zone between the relatively flat deserts of central Wyoming and the massive Rocky Mountains. Elevations range from 6,600 feet at the entrance to over 8,000 feet along the summit of the Bull Pen. The climate reflects this high desert setting, and it is often quite cold in the winter months, occasionally reaching minus 30 degrees. While the area receives 9 to 12 inches of precipitation annually, most of it arrives in the form of snow. Summer highs can reach the upper 70s, with nighttime lows in the 40s. The region has shifted from a sub-tropical lake ecosystem to a very dry, high-altitude desert setting over the course of 50 million years.

Shrublands are the most prominent plants in this area, with larger trees uncommon and riparian zones practically nonexistent. One stream, Chicken Creek, drains nearly two-thirds of the monument's lands, but it's both interrupted and intermittent. Twelve invasive exotic plant species have been identified in the monument and represent a threat to the continuation of native species. There is a continuous effort by monument staff to control these invasive species through mowing, spraying, and hand pulling.

THINGS TO DO:

First, things not to do: collecting any artifacts from the monument is strictly prohibited. All fossils here are protected by federal law.

The visitor center should be your first stop, not only to gain a sense of your surroundings but also to appreciate the 300 fossil exhibits on display. The fossils are primarily fish and fish-related species but also include plants and insects that would have thrived in the wetlands surrounding Fossil Lake. The detail in some of the fossils is extraordinary, with teeth, scales, and even skin preserved. Literally a look into the prehistoric past, the visitor

Sunsets can be very vibrant here, with open skies and a bit of dust to add warmth to the sky.

center is a great educational resource for children and adults alike. Other good resources are *The Geological History of Fossil Butte National Monument* by Paul Orman McGrew (1975) and *Fossil Butte National Monument Geological Resources Inventory* by the National Park Service (2013).

Hiking, as always, is a popular and informative way to experience the monument. Remember to dress for the conditions and bring plenty of water, as this is a very dry climate at higher altitude.

The 1.5-mile Nature Loop Trail, with nearby picnic tables, is a trail of moderate difficulty winding through sagebrush and an aspen grove. The longer, 2.5-mile loop Historic Quarry Trail provides an opportunity to view a quarry that was active in the 1960s. Exhibits along both trails describe the area's natural history as well as the geology.

Bicycles are allowed in the monument but are restricted to designated roadways and are not allowed on the trails.

Driving the 7.5-mile Scenic Drive, when open, is a great way to see much of the monument from above. RVs and trailers are not recommended beyond the picnic area, as the 4-mile gravel road beyond can be narrow and steep.

THINGS TO SEE:

There are 109 species of birds within the monument, distributed throughout the three zones within the area: low-elevation riparian, pinyon-juniper, and sage shrubland. You can expect to see warblers, hummingbirds, vireos, pinyon jays, grosbeaks, and mourning doves, among many others.

For visitors from places that have considerable light pollution, the Fossil Butte area is a remarkable experience once the sun goes down. With little to no man-made light, the night skies above are filled with stars and the Milky Way. Although the monument is closed after sunset, the entire area boasts excellent night sky viewing. If you happen to be there in July or August, the

Perseids meteor shower may be visible overhead from mid-July thru August 24, with peak viewing occurring from around August 9 to 14. Midnight to dawn is typically the best time for viewing the meteor shower.

Mule deer and antelope are fairly common and easy to view. Elk sightings have been reported, especially in late fall or winter. Interestingly, people have even seen beaver and moose in the monument, despite the lack of wetlands or other habitat seemingly more suitable to these species.

If you are traveling in the vicinity of Green River, take some time and drive the well-maintained (May through October) gravel road between I-80 and US Highway 191. This area, Pilot Butte, is home to about 250 wild horses that can easily be seen from the road. Additionally, the nearby Killpecker Sand Dunes, the largest active dunes in North America, along with the White Mountain Petroglyphs, are easily accessed during a day trip. Boar's Tusk, an ancient 400-foot volcanic plug, is readily visible from the gravel road.

GETTING THERE:
From I-80, take US Highway 189 or WY Highway 30 north, depending on your direction of travel, for 45 miles to Kemmerer. Then go west on US Highway 30 for an additional 9 miles.

FACILITIES:
The visitor center is open year-round, but the front gate closes during severe winter storms. The upper road, accessing the Chicken Creek Nature Trail, closes on November 1 and typically reopens in late May.

There is no camping within the monument, although the nearby Bridger-Teton National Forest offers several campgrounds to the north. This is convenient, especially if you are on the way to Grand Teton National Park or Yellowstone National Park. The nearby towns of Kemmerer, Evanston, and Green River offer the typical range of amenities common to small cities.

USEFUL CONTACTS:

Fossil Butte
National Monument
864 Chicken Creek Road
Kemmerer, WY 83101
307-877-4455

nps.gov/fobu

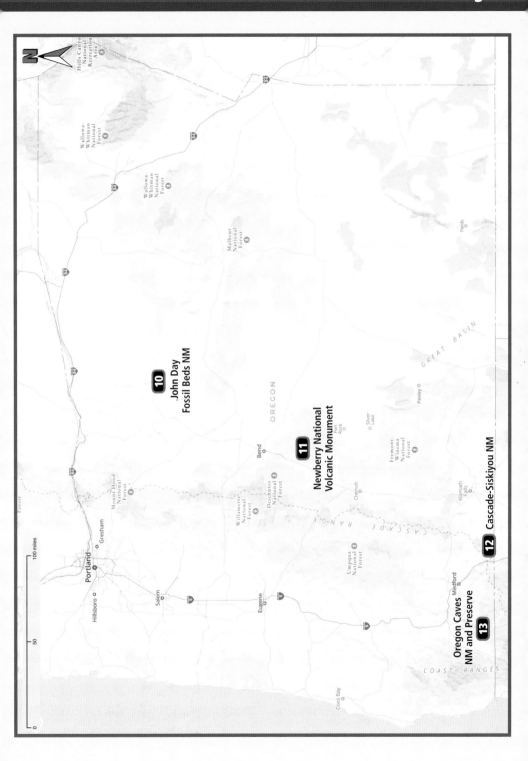

N

Hells Canyon National Recreation Area

Wallowa Whitman National Forest

Wallowa Whitman National Forest

Malheur National Forest

GREAT BASIN

Fields

10 John Day Fossil Beds NM

OREGON

Paisley

Silver Lake

Fremont Winema National Forest

11 Newberry National Volcanic Monument

Fort Rock

Bend

Chemult

Klamath Falls

Deschutes National Forest

Willamette National Forest

Mount Hood National Forest

Forest

100 miles

50

0

Portland

Gresham

Hillsboro

Salem

Eugene

Umpqua National Forest

Medford

12 Cascade-Siskiyou NM

CASCADE RANGE

13 Oregon Caves NM and Preserve

Coos Bay

COAST RANGES

55

10. John Day Fossil Beds
National Monument

NEAREST TOWNS:	Dayville, Mitchell, and Antelope, OR
SIZE:	14,402 acres
BEST SEASON(S):	Year-round
NOTABLE ACTIVITIES:	Hiking, birding, wildlife and plant viewing, photography, geology, astronomy, solitude, mountain biking, fossil viewing

The John Day River flows beneath the multi-layered Cathedral Rocks.

THE MONUMENT:

The John Day Fossil Beds National Monument in central Oregon consists of three separate units: Sheep Rock, Clarno, and Painted Hills. While sharing a common geological history, each unit has its own unique appeal. The three noncontiguous units total 14,402 acres, the result of a convoluted political history preceding national monument status. President Gerald Ford designated the area John Day Fossil Beds National Monument on October 26, 1974. But it wasn't until July 1, 1975, that the proceedings were actually completed and the state lands were transferred to the National Park Service. After a further delay waiting for the Department of the Interior to publish the required Federal

The multicolored rocks of the Painted Hills Unit can be viewed after a short hike to a high point. The different-colored layers represent a history of past climate change. Iron red indicates a warm and moist environment while the yellow-tan layers are reflective of a drier climate. The black spots are concentrations of manganese, likely fixed by a plant.

Register notice, the monument was finally, officially established on October 8, 1975.

In the rain shadow of the Cascade Mountains, the area receives a maximum of about 16 inches of precipitation annually. Snow is not uncommon in the winter. Though the temperature averages 42 degrees during the day, it can drop below freezing at night. The nearby town of Mitchell recorded a record high of 107 degrees in 1972, while average July and August temperatures are around the mid-80s during the day, dropping to low 50s at night. The elevation of the monument is roughly 2,200 feet.

Native Americans, namely the Sahaptin, frequented the area before European colonizers arrived in the mid-1800s. Eventually, many of the Indigenous peoples were forcibly removed to reservations as more and more European settlers arrived.

THINGS TO DO:

First, go to the Thomas Condon Paleontology Center. It is named for the renowned 19th-century pastor from Oregon who was influential in recognizing the scientific importance of the fossil beds. Although he was an amateur geologist, his enthusiasm for the area and promotion of its importance earned him Oregon's first appointment as state geologist in 1872. Located in the Sheep Rock unit, the 11,000-square-foot paleontology center is home to over 500 fossil specimens representative of the area.

The visitor center also serves as a research facility for the National Park Service, which conducts ongoing exploration and cataloging of monument fossils. If the staff is working inside, you can watch their meticulous and painstaking work through the laboratory's viewing window. The center also has eight different exhibits representative of distinctive periods of the fossil history of the area, going back as far as fifty-five million years.

Hiking in the Clarno Unit is easily accessible but somewhat limited. Three interconnected trails are open to the public: the Geological Time Trail, Trail of Fossils, and the Clarno Arch Trail. Each has interpretive plaques that explain the geological history. The Trail of Fossils has in situ fossils along the trail. The 0.5-mile Clarno Arch Trail leads to a natural arch.

The Sheep Rock Unit offers eight separate trails, from short and easy to longer and more strenuous. There are also two roadside stops at Cathedral Rock and Goose Rock with views of the area's distinctive geology. Sheep Rock itself is the dominant feature across the road to the east of the visitor center. Blue Basin has an easy 1.3-mile trail that wanders among the colorful badlands. The 3.25-mile Overlook Trail ascends to the basin's rim, where you'll be rewarded with outstanding vistas of the valley below. This trail has a high point of 2,920 feet after gaining 760 feet of elevation. The John Day River, which passes through the monument, is the longest undammed tributary of the mighty Columbia River. Rafting is available from commercial outfitters, although most runs do not traverse the monument.

The Painted Hills Unit is likely the most striking and memorable for visitors, and it is highly photogenic. The stunning, multicolored hues of the volcanic deposits beg to be photographed. The layering of different colored soils tells

USEFUL CONTACTS:

John Day Fossil Beds National Monument
32651 OR Highway 19
Kimberly, OR 97848
541-987-2333

nps.gov/joda

A slight contrast in colors at the base of Sheep Rock.

the story of climate change over millions of years. The reddish colors are consistent with a warm and moist climate, which produced damp soil and numerous ponds and lakes. Yellow and tan layers indicate the presence of a much drier climate. The concentrated black layers are thought to be caused by concentrations of the compound manganese, which was "fixed" by plant life. Manganese is one of nine essential nutrients for plant life, required for photosynthesis. The best time for photos is late afternoon, looking eastward, as the sun sets at your back. Scout out a suitable location earlier in the day and return at the appropriate time.

Hiking off-trail is illegal, as is mountain biking, although numerous biking trails can be found in the nearby Malheur National Forest. Tracks made here last for years in the fragile soil. Collecting artifacts within the monument boundaries is also strictly prohibited. Water is seasonally available, so prepare accordingly.

Visiting the James Cant Ranch House is an interesting look at one family's struggles to survive while homesteading the area. James Cant Sr., an immigrant from Scotland via South America, arrived in Dayville in 1905 and started out herding sheep for a local family. He eventually acquired a

Mule deer can be found here, although they don't often stick around, especially a large buck such as this.

ranch and 680 acres, on which he began his own ranching operation. The ranch house itself, built in 1917, was often open to travelers and fossil hunters, including the distinguished Dr. John C. Merriam. The ranch house and surrounding buildings were listed on the National Register of Historic Places in 1984, and it served as the first headquarters for the newly formed monument.

THINGS TO SEE:
Fossils of course, hundreds of them! Most of the fossils are preserved as a result of the volcanic activity that occurred thirty-five million years ago in the Cascade Range. The relatively rapid deposition of volcanic ash allowed for the remarkable preservation of a variety of plants and animals.

There are over fifty species of birds within the monument, although some are seasonal or migratory. Birds that are easily seen here include red-tailed hawks, American kestrels, great blue herons, Canada geese, hummingbirds, warblers, canyon wrens (with their distinctive calls), and mountain bluebirds. At the right time of year, primarily in the spring, flocks of sandhill cranes fly overhead as they migrate northward.

Elk, mule deer, pronghorn, and the elusive cougar represent mammals within the monument. Bighorn sheep, extirpated in the early 20th century, were reintroduced in 2010 and may be found in the Foree Area of the Sheep Rock Unit.

Numerous snakes, including rattlesnakes, live here, as well as a variety of lizards, toads, and salamanders. Butterflies are abundant; fifty-five different species were documented during a 2003–2004 survey.

GETTING THERE:
The roads are slow, and the distance between units is deceptively far. It is not recommended to drive to all three units in a single day. Fuel is scarce, so top off when you can.

Sheep Rock Unit: The Sheep Rock Unit, site of the visitor center, is approximately 80 miles on US Highway 26 from Baker City, which sits alongside I-84 east of the monument. From the west, take OR Highway 126 out of Redmond for 18 miles to Prineville. Then take US Highway 26 an additional 75 miles to the site.

Painted Hills Unit: From the Sheep Rock Unit it is 30 miles to the Painted Hills Unit, again on US Highway 26 going west. From Redmond, take OR Highway 126 for 18 miles to Prineville. Then take US Highway 26 an additional 40 miles to the site.

Clarno Unit: From Mitchell on US Highway 26, take OR Highway 19 for 41 miles north to Fossil. Go west on OR Highway 218 approximately 15 miles to the Clarno Unit. Alternatively, from Willowdale on OR Highway 191, go 3 miles to the junction with OR Highway 293 and follow this for 12 miles to Antelope. Then take OR Highway 218 for 15 miles to the site.

FACILITIES:
No camping is allowed in the monument's three units, but the link in the "Useful Contacts" section provides an excellent map of the area with towns, services, campgrounds, RV parks, and state parks. There are many state and private campgrounds throughout the area, and the nearby small towns offer services such as gas, lodging, groceries, and restaurants.

11. Newberry
National Volcanic Monument

NEAREST TOWN:	Bend, OR
SIZE:	54,000 acres
BEST SEASON(S):	Year-round
NOTABLE ACTIVITIES:	Hiking, birding, wildlife and plant viewing, photography, geology, astronomy, solitude, mountain biking, lava tube exploration, skiing, fishing, snowmobiling

THE MONUMENT:

The Newberry Caldera is as distinctive as the world-famous Crater Lake Caldera, 70 miles south of this monument. The Newberry Caldera is protected for the same reasons; it is a rare expression of geological forces at work. Designated on November 5, 1990, by an act of the 101st Congress and signed into law by President George H. W. Bush, the monument encompasses roughly 1,200 square miles, an area about the size of Rhode Island. While often referred to as a crater, it's actually a 17-square-mile caldera, formed when the rocks lying over the magma chamber collapsed into the failing chamber below. As such, it has no natural outlets for the water that collects here throughout the year.

Rime-encrusted cliffs along the flanks of Paulina Peak, 7,985 feet, during the depths of winter.

The caldera lies within the boundaries of the Deschutes National Forest, and the monument is managed by the US Forest Service. It has typical Pacific Northwest weather. About 20 inches of annual snowfall falls primarily between November and March, with nearly 5 inches of rain in the other months. Temperatures in July and August can reach the 80s, while winter temperatures can drop to the low 20s. Highs in winter are 40-plus degrees. Mid-summer is the best time for cloud-free skies, while the winter is often overcast with reduced visibility.

THINGS TO DO:

A stop at the nearby Lava Lands Visitor Center is an excellent starting point. Here you can explore exhibits, ask questions, and plan your stay. There is a short paved walkway, the Trail of Molten Lands, which shows where NASA astronauts underwent training for their mission to the moon in the 1960s.

There are numerous trails of varying difficulty within the monument. The 5.5-mile Crater Rim Trail #3957 takes you to the top of 7,985-foot Paulina Peak while enjoying the quiet and solitude of the forest. It's a difficult trail that gains about 1,700 feet from near the Paulina Lodge junction to the summit. Depending on your skills, you can ascend this trail year-round. For those not interested in climbing, the Newberry Crater Road leads to the same summit area, when it is open. This

A popular 5.7/C0 route goes up this side of the pillar known as Monkey Face at nearby Smith Rock. Once on top, there's a 200-foot free-hanging rappel back down to the ground, just to make sure you get your money's worth.

Skiing is an ideal way to experience the monument during the winter months. There are numerous trails separate from those used by snow machines and a few warming huts to help keep you comfortable in the freezing temperatures.

A pair of male northern pintail ducks square off with each other during the spring mating season.

A very large mountain lion, common in this region, who lost no time putting distance between us.

Obsidian, highly prized for its near surgical sharpness, was a valuable trading commodity for the Indigenous peoples of this region.

is not a road for long vehicles or trailers, as it is both steep and rough, with tight turns as you near the top. In the winter one can ski, snowshoe, or take a snowmobile to the summit. For mountain bikers, the 20-mile loop along the Crater Rim Trail offers superb views and a good day trip with easy access. To access this trail, take US Highway 97 to the Paulina-East Lake Road. Turn on Paulina-East Lake Road and follow it to its intersection with US Forest Service Road 21.

The 3.9-mile National Forest Trail is an easy year-round outing just south of Bend. This trail is essentially level as it winds its way through the forest, offering scenic views along the way.

You can also enjoy the monument in winter. The main road typically closes at mile 10, where you can find ample parking, vault toilets, and a warming hut. The trails are marked for snowmobiles or human-powered recreation, such as cross-country skiing or snowshoeing. Some have avalanche hazards, so be prepared with a beacon, shovel, probe, and a partner. Maps are available at the warming hut.

Nearby Smith Rock State Park outside of Bend, long considered the birthplace of American sport climbing, offers world-class rock climbing with routes ranging from 5.5 to 5.14. America's first 5.14, "To Bolt or Not to Be," was put up here. At 5.14c, "Just Do It" remains one of the most difficult routes in the world. The 350-foot rock formation Monkey Face is worth the hike,

Some plants just don't take no for an answer, as evidenced by this sapling in the midst of the Big Obsidian Flow.

The terminus of the Big Obsidian Flow, a 700-acre flow that formed just 1,300 years ago.

even if you don't intend to climb it. The standard route up the southeast side of the tower goes at 5.7 and C0. There are also several hikes within the state park that allow you to leisurely explore this unique setting.

THINGS TO SEE:
Attractions within the area include Lava Butte and Lava River Cave to the north, and the Lava Lands Visitor Center, about halfway between Bend and La Pine. Driving to the top of Lava Butte is restricted during the busy summer season; there is a shuttle system in place and private vehicles are allowed by lottery only. Either way, you'll have tremendous views of the central Oregon landscape. You can also hike along the road to the top, which is about 1.5 miles from the visitor center. Once on top you can hike the 0.25-mile Rim Trail for truly grand views of the Cascades, the monument's southern portion, and the extensive lava fields below.

A trip to the Lava River Cave, a 1.0-mile hike over varying terrain, provides a look into the life of a lava tube. These are underground flows of lava that melted through the underlying rock and dirt, cooled, and left a tube in their wake. Today these tubes maintain a constant temperature of 42 degrees year-round and are home to bats and other underground life. There is a self-guided tour, but be sure to take at least one source of light for each person. If you have been in other caves, do not wear the same shoes or clothing to avoid spreading a fungus that can be fatal to the bats.

You can also hire a helicopter for an aerial view of the monument through a local operator (see the "Useful Contacts" section).

Seeing the Big Obsidian Flow requires a moderate 2.0-mile round-trip hike. The obsidian rock here was highly prized by Native Americans as a cutting tool for its extreme natural sharpness.

With peaks reaching to 10,000 feet, the southern Cascades offers mountaineers, skiers, and hikers endless opportunities for recreation.

GETTING THERE:

The entrance to the monument is 13 miles south of Bend on US Highway 97 and about 20 miles north of La Pine, which is also on US Highway 97.

FACILITIES:

There is seasonal camping within the monument at Prairie, Pine Mountain, Cinder Hill, East Lake, Little Crater, and Paulina campgrounds. Some sites have access to the lake and boat ramps. There is also lodging at the Paulina Lake Lodge. The nearby La Pine State Park offers 82 full-hookup sites, 47 sites with electric and water, and 10 log cabins. Sites 1 through 44 are open year-round, although water is typically shut off in the winter. The park has hot showers and flush toilets. The area around Twin Lakes/Crane Prairie Reservoir Recreation Area has numerous campgrounds and dispersed camping.

Nearby La Pine offers food, fuel, and lodging, while the larger city of Bend has just about everything you need for your visit.

USEFUL CONTACTS:

Lava Lands Visitor Center
58201 S. Highway 97
Bend, OR 97707
541-383-5300

fs.usda.gov/visit/destination
  /newberry-national-volcanic
  -monument-0

visitbend.com

flycascades.com

12. Cascade-Siskiyou National Monument

NEAREST TOWNS:	Ashland and Keno, OR
SIZE:	86,000 acres
BEST SEASON(S):	Year-round
NOTABLE ACTIVITIES:	Hiking, birding, wildlife and plant viewing, photography, geology, astronomy, solitude, mountain biking, boating

THE MONUMENT:

President Bill Clinton proclaimed Cascade-Siskiyou a national monument on June 9, 2000, in order to preserve the area's unique biological diversity. To provide further protection, President Barack Obama expanded the monument on January 12, 2017, to a total of over 86,000 acres to include both southern Oregon and northern California.

Cascade-Siskiyou is often referred to as the "Galapagos of North America" due to its abundance of plant and animal life. Located at the junction of the Siskiyou, Klamath, and Cascade mountain ranges, each with its own rich ecosystems, the monument harbors an incredible array of species, many of which are rare and endemic only to this area. The Bureau of Land Management (BLM) has identified five distinctive ecoregions within the monument: grassland and shrubland, Garry and California oak woodlands, juniper scablands, mixed conifer and white fir forests, and wet meadows and riparian forests.

Hyatt Reservoir with a typical symmetrically shaped volcano in the distance.

Given an elevation range of 1,500 to 6,000 feet, temperatures vary from summer highs in the 80s to lows in the upper 40s. With average lows in the 30s, snow is common in the winter months, especially at higher altitudes, which limits access to some areas. Winter highs rarely exceed 50 degrees. Precipitation is abundant, particularly in the winter, with an average of 2 inches per month in rain and snow.

THINGS TO DO:

There is no visitor center within the monument, but there is an information station along OR Highway 66 in the small community of Green Springs, where you can obtain maps of the monument, a bird checklist, a colorful brochure of the native flowers, and information on local activities.

A 19-mile segment of the Pacific Crest National Scenic Trail (PCT) traverses the monument. Hiking all or a portion of the PCT is one of the better ways to experience much of what this monument has to offer. The easiest way to access the PCT is where it crosses OR Highway 66 at Green Springs. Here you can begin out-and-back day hikes to Hobart Bluff and Soda Mountain or coordinate a vehicle shuttle as you hike 12 miles to Pilot Rock. This prominent volcanic plug was referred to as Tan-ts'at-seniptha by the Indigenous Takelma peoples. Translated, it means "Stone Standing Up," an apt description. Reaching a height of 5,910 feet, Pilot Rock is easily visible to travelers on the I-5 corridor several miles away.

If you have limited time, there are a few shorter hikes in the Green Springs area. The Green Springs Mountain Loop Trail is an easy, fairly level 2.2-mile hike. To get there, drive about 0.75 mile north from the information station on Little Hyatt Road until you reach BLM 39-3E-32, which you'll follow to the road's end and a small parking turnaround.

The monument provides a variety of relaxing activities from hiking to birding to paddling a canoe in the crisp autumn air.

Lounging around Hyatt Reservoir is a fine way to spend a relaxed day taking in the views of nearby Mount McLoughlin and watching wildlife on the lake. Depending on the season, you may spot bald eagles. If you're fortunate, you'll see a rare and endangered great grey owl in the neighboring forest.

For something a little different but enjoyable, the Oregon Shakespeare Festival, started in 1935, runs from mid-February through early November and presents 11 different plays on three stages in nearby Ashland.

Several additional attractions exist near the monument that are worth the time and effort to explore. Crater Lake National Park, a few hours to the north, offers stunning views of the deepest lake

A great grey owl scratching an itch and showing the talons that make them such efficient predators.

in the western hemisphere. Both the Upper and Lower Klamath National Wildlife Refuges boast dozens of bird species and serve as gathering places for hundreds of bald eagles during the winter months. Putnam's Point, in Klamath Falls, is the best and most reliable location for viewing Clark's and western grebes in the spring as they perform their ritual mating dance on the water. Oregon Caves and Lava Beds National Monuments are relatively close by. Both monuments are covered in more detail within this guide.

THINGS TO SEE:

Both paved and unpaved roads provide access to the monument, although some of the unpaved roads may not be suitable for passenger cars. Historic Route 66, also known locally as the Green Springs Highway, traverses the northern portion of the monument. It's a scenic way to view parts of Cascade-Siskiyou if you're pressed for time.

Over 200 species of flowering plants have been identified within the monument. Given the region's ample rainfall, this is not surprising, as many species thrive in the cool moist environment. Depending on the season and elevation, one may find the striking scarlet fritillary, fawn lilies, or the diminutive yet colorful draba verna, also known as shadflower. Junipers thrive in the higher elevations, as do populations of white fir. Pacific madrone can be found in the northern and western reaches, while oak woodlands are more prevalent in the Emigrant Creek region and to the south of Pilot Rock.

On clear days, and from a high vantage point, you can see the nearby volcanoes of Mount Shasta and Mount McLoughlin and the rim of Crater Lake to the north.

GETTING THERE:

From the north on I-5, take Exit 14 south of Ashland onto OR Highway 66. Follow this for approximately 20 miles along a rising and winding roadway.

From the south, take Exit 6 onto OR Highway 273 for about 20 slow and winding miles, which will bring you to the junction with OR Highway 66. Follow OR Highway 66 as described above.

From the east, leave Klamath Falls on OR Highway 66 and follow this for about 33 miles.

FACILITIES:

Dispersed camping is allowed throughout most of the monument, but you must stay within 50 feet of the roadway and visitors are strongly encouraged to use existing sites. No cross-country travel by vehicle or bike is allowed. Hyatt Lake Recreation Area, north of Route 66, offers the only developed camping within the monument boundaries, along with boating and fishing. There is also a horse camp if you are an equestrian. Reservations are made through recreation.gov. Asperkaha County Park sits on Howard Prairie Lake to the north and offers camping and boating. There is also camping at Emigrant Lake on the western side of the monument, just north of the junction of Route 66 and OR Highway 273.

Nearby Ashland to the west offers a range of accommodations and dining to suit just about every taste and budget. To the east, Klamath Falls provides similar options.

USEFUL CONTACTS:

Cascade-Siskiyou
National Monument
Medford District BLM
3040 Biddle Road
Medford, OR 97504
541-618-2200

blm.gov/programs/national
  -conservation-lands
  /national-monuments/oregon
  -washington/cascade-siskiyou

cascadesiskiyou.org

pcta.org

traveloregon.com/things-to-do
  /outdoor-recreation/camping
  /cascade-siskiyou-national-monument

klamathbirdingtrails.com

13. Oregon Caves
National Monument and Preserve

NEAREST TOWN:	Cave Junction, OR
SIZE:	480 acres
BEST SEASON(S):	Year-round, with weather closures in winter
NOTABLE ACTIVITIES:	Hiking, birding, wildlife and plant viewing, photography, geology, astronomy, solitude, mountain biking, cave exploration, history

THE MONUMENT:

You won't likely visit Oregon Caves National Monument and Preserve by accident; it's at the end of a 20-mile road leading from the small community of Cave Junction. Declared a monument on July 12, 1909, by President Howard Taft, it comprises 480 acres above ground, but its principal attraction is the network of underground passages and caverns that make up the cave itself. In 2014 Congress enlarged the protected area to a total of 4,070 acres and added the designation of Preserve to the monument's name.

The monument was first discovered by Elijah Davidson, who was searching for his lost dog while out hunting bear. The extent of the cave's 15,000

Stalagmites grow upwards while stalactites form from the top down.

Fall colors and the visitor center, your first stop for information and reservations for cave tours.

The elusive varied thrush, occasionally heard but rarely seen, is a fairly common resident of the Pacific Northwest.

The Townsend's bat is highly vulnerable to white-nose syndrome, which is deadly to bats and easily transmissible.

feet was not fully mapped until the late 1970s. The River Styx (Cave Creek), which flows through the cave system, is the first and so far only underground river in the National Wild and Scenic Rivers inventory. The cave itself is composed primarily of marble formed from limestone that was exposed to intense heat. The cave is formed by the process of carbon dioxide in the above-ground soils mixing with water and creating a weak acid, which ends up dissolving the marble and forming the cavities.

The road into the monument is not suitable for trailers or large RVs; these can be parked at the Illinois Valley Visitor Center in Cave Junction. Weather in nearby Cave Junction is typical for the Pacific Northwest. Winters can be cold and damp with temperatures in the low 30s and highs averaging 50 degrees. Summers can be surprisingly warm, often reaching into the 90s during the day and down to the 50s at night. The highest recorded temperature was a remarkable 114 degrees in 2008! The monument may be closed at times during winter due to the weather, because the majority of the precipitation occurs during those months.

THINGS TO DO:

If you plan to explore the cave, don't bring or wear anything from trips to other caves. This is part of an effort to limit the spread of white nose syndrome among the bats. This fungal infection has been associated with the deaths of 5.7 million bats in the United States alone and has been found in 29 states.

Guided cave tours are offered from March 25 through November 5 from 10:00 a.m. until 4:00 p.m. There are 500 steps along the course of the tour, many of them steep and uneven. The lowest height is a mere 45 inches, so a bit of stooping is necessary. As with most caves, the temperature is a cool and damp 44 degrees on average. Warm clothing and sturdy hiking shoes are essential. Children must be at least 42 inches tall and are not allowed to be carried through the cave for safety reasons. There is also a candle-light tour, which offers a sense of some of the difficulties early cave explorers encountered. While you can just show

Some of the formations within the cave system are lit, lending an interesting color to the scene.

up and sign on for a tour, reservations through recreation.gov are strongly encouraged, as you may have to wait up to two hours during the busier summer months. The trip through the cave lasts about ninety minutes.

In addition to touring the cave, you can enjoy several trails around the visitor center. Both the Cliff Nature Trail and the Old Growth Trail are fairly short and should take no more than an hour or so. Each offers a chance to see some of the surrounding forest and gain a sense of the place. Longer trails such as the Big Tree Trail bring you to the widest-girthed Douglas fir in Oregon. Be prepared to spend up to three hours walking the entire loop. If you're looking for a full day of hiking, the Bigelow Lakes–Mount Elijah Loop is just over 9 miles and leads through mountain meadows and by lakes. The trail ends at the summit of 6390-foot Mount Elijah, and on clear days you can see Mount Shasta in northern California.

The visitor center has an informative exhibit on the geology of caves and the hardy creatures that inhabit them.

THINGS TO SEE:
The historic Chalet Visitor Center itself is worth a walk around to appreciate the effort that went into creating this structure that blends with the sur-

roundings. Park staff lives on the upper floor, allowing them to be on-site and avoid the lengthy drive to and from the monument.

The Chateau at the Oregon Caves is another interesting structure on the monument grounds. It was designed and built by locals in 1934 and is made of natural materials. Located across from the visitor center, it too blends in with the environment, and even has a stream running through the main dining area. The restaurant offers locally procured meat, vegetables, cheeses, and wines, continuing a long-standing connection to the surrounding communities. The coffee shop and deli offer sandwiches, salads, and of course, coffee.

The Civilian Conservation Corps was busy here and constructed trout pools, retaining walls, waterfalls, and a campfire circle. All these structures blend in with the surrounding elements, creating an ambience of relaxation and immersion with the nearby old growth forests.

The Smokejumper Museum on US 199 is an interesting side trip. The structure was built in the 1940s as protection against Japanese balloon firebombs. It recognizes the skill and daring of firefighters in the most remote areas of our National Forests.

GETTING THERE:

Drive to Cave Junction, OR. From Grants Pass, OR, go about 30 miles south on US Highway 199. From Crescent City, CA, drive north 53 miles on US Highway 199. From Cave Junction, it's about 20 miles on US Highway 46 to the monument.

USEFUL CONTACTS:

Oregon Caves
National Monument and Preserve
19000 Caves Highway
Cave Junction, OR 97523
541-592-2100

nps.gov/orca

facebook.com/OregonCavesNPS

FACILITIES:

A great way to relax and experience the whole setting of Oregon Caves is to spend the night in the Chateau at the Oregon Caves. It offers a variety of room accommodations, excellent dining, and a charming setting, all conducive to unwinding among the old growth Douglas fir forest.

There is no camping within the small monument, but sites can be found at Cave Creek Campground (not suitable for RVs), Grayback Campground (RVs allowed), and Lake Selmac County Park (91 sites with 39 full RV hookups). There are numerous private campgrounds in the surrounding area that can accommodate everything from tents to RVs.

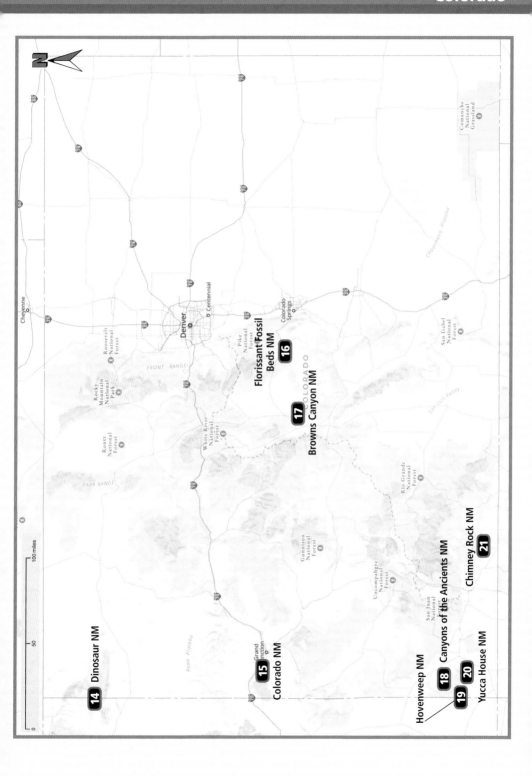

N

100 miles
50
0

Cheyenne

Comanche National Grasland

Roosevelt National Forest

Denver
Centennial

Colorado Springs

Pike National Forest

COLORADO

Florissant Fossil Beds NM **16**

FRONT RANGE

Rocky Mountain National Park

Browns Canyon NM **17**

Routt National Forest

White River National Forest

San Isabel National Forest

San Luis Valley

PARK RANGE

Rio Grande National Forest

Gunnison National Forest

Roan Plateau

Uncompahgre National Forest

Chimney Rock NM **21**

Grand Junction

San Juan National Forest

Colorado NM **15**

Canyons of the Ancients NM **18**

Hovenweep NM

Dinosaur NM **14**

Yucca House NM **20**

19

75

14. Dinosaur
National Monument

NEAREST TOWNS:	Dinosaur, CO, and Vernal, UT
SIZE:	211,000 acres
BEST SEASON(S):	Year-round
NOTABLE ACTIVITIES:	Hiking, birding, wildlife and plant viewing, photography, geology, astronomy, solitude, mountain biking, fossil viewing, boating, fishing, rafting, kayaking

THE MONUMENT:

On October 4, 1915, President Woodrow Wilson declared the initial 80 acres surrounding the Dinosaur Quarry a National Monument. On July 14, 1938, President Franklin D. Roosevelt expanded the monument to its present size of nearly 211,000 acres. A significant portion of the monument (91 percent) is also designated a part of the National Wilderness Preservation System.

The topography here consists of open sagebrush, deep canyons, and the river bottoms of the Green and Yampa Rivers. Temperatures in the summer months can exceed 90 degrees during the day with nighttime lows in the lower 50s. Winter can be quite cold with highs in the 30s and lows dip-

A panorama overlooking the vastness of the monument.

ping to single digits. Precipitation is sparse, barely reaching one inch during the wettest months of May, September, and October. Snowfall can be significant and averages seven inches in both December and January, totaling 35 inches for the year.

THINGS TO DO:

There are several roads into the monument, some better than others. Check with the monument headquarters near Dinosaur for road conditions as some roads become impassable when wet, even for 4WD vehicles.

For many people, driving through may be the best way to experience the monument. It is a rugged landscape that is far from assistance; towing charges from here can exceed $1,000! Off-road driving is prohibited for all vehicles, including ATVs and UTVs, which are not permitted on any monument roads.

Looking down from an overlook at the Green River on the north side of the monument.

A compass, a partial moon, and a 75-minute exposure create an interesting composition for Steamboat Rock along the Green River.

The Harpers Corner Scenic Drive is a 31-mile (one-way) paved road with several stunning overlooks, ending with broad views of the monument and three deep canyons. The Harpers Corner Trailhead is here. This is a 2.0-mile out-and-back trail reaching an elevation of 7,500 feet.

The Yampa Bench Road, for high-clearance and 4WD vehicles only, leads into the southern part of the monument, an area few people ever see. This unpaved road has a few narrow, steep sections and stream crossings that may include mud as well as several areas of soft sand. If in doubt, turn around; it's much easier, and less expensive, than getting stuck or needing a tow.

Floating the Green or the Yampa Rivers is a great way to see parts of the monument that are not accessible any other way. There are several outfitters in the area that provide complete trips or can assist you with your own canoe or raft.

THINGS TO SEE:

A visit to the Quarry Exhibit Hall, in the Utah portion of the monument, should be the first stop if you are driving to the west side of the monument. This remarkable structure allows you to see, firsthand and up close, a 150-foot wall with more than 1,500 actual fossils still embedded in the rock. An early paleontologist, Earl Douglass, had the idea in 1923 that leaving the bones and skeletons in a protected and viewable form would create "one of the most outstanding and instructive sights imaginable." The Hall was

Looking across the Green River near Split Mountain Campground.

originally built in 1957 on top of an unstable rock formation that pushed the Hall upward, eventually making it unsafe. It was closed to the public in 2006 for extensive repairs and reopened in 2011.

Of the many species of wildflowers found here, the Dinosaur milkvetch can only be seen within the monument and its immediate surroundings.

GETTING THERE:

To access the Quarry Visitor Center on the western side of the monument, take US Highway 40 east from Vernal, UT, for 13.0 miles to Jensen, UT. Drive north from here on UT Highway 149 for 7 miles.

From the seasonal Canyon Visitor Center, located a few miles east of Dinosaur, CO, take the Harpers Corner Road for 31 miles to Harpers Corner.

To access other roads into and around the monument, it's advisable to first check with the visitor center to determine its current status and suitability for your vehicle.

Dramatic curving strata along the Green River.

Cottontail rabbits are a common sight within the monument.

Petroglyphs at the McKee Spring petroglyph site, along the Island Park Road on the north side of the monument.

FACILITIES:

There are six campgrounds located throughout the monument, three in Utah and three in Colorado. Only Green River Campground is seasonal, open from early April to mid-October. The others are open year-round, but water is either not present or available only during the warmer months. All are located at or above 4,900 feet, which can make it more comfortable during the hotter months. Green River Campground has eighty sites for both RVs and tents but no electricity or showers. Split Mountain Group Campground has four sites suitable for RVs and tents. No hookups are available and there are no showers. These two campgrounds can be reserved at recreation.gov, while the others are first-come, first-served. Gates of Lodore is also suitable for RVs. Rainbow Park and Deerlodge Park are tent camping only. Echo Park is open to high-clearance vehicles and is impassable during wet weather, snow, or rain. Backcountry camping is allowed, but sites along the Green and Yampa Rivers are reserved for boaters during the high-use season.

The nearby towns Hulett, Moorcroft, Sundance, and Gillette all offer lodging, meals, and fuel.

USEFUL CONTACTS:

Dinosaur National Monument
11625 E. 1500 S
Jensen, UT 84035
435-781-7700

nps.gov/dino/planyourvisit
  /commercialguidedrivertrips.htm
  (approved outfitters for floating
  the Yampa River)

colorado.com/colorado-official
  -state-welcome-center
  /colorado-welcome-center-dinosaur

visitutah.com/places-to-go
  /parks-outdoors
  /dinosaur-national-monument

15. Colorado
National Monument

NEAREST TOWNS:	Grand Junction and Fruita, CO
SIZE:	20,533 acres
BEST SEASON(S):	Year-round, depending on activity
NOTABLE ACTIVITIES:	Hiking, birding, wildlife and plant viewing, photography, geology, astronomy, solitude, mountain biking, American history, rock climbing

THE MONUMENT:

Colorado National Monument was established on May 24, 1911, by President William Taft. It is a brilliantly colored, 32-mile landscape of twisting canyons and towering sandstone formations. Over a billion years of geological history can be witnessed from its canyon rims.

The monument rises from 4,000 feet to nearly 7,000 feet in a semi-desert climatic region in western Colorado. Pine and Utah juniper are the most common trees while sagebrush, rabbitbrush, cacti, and yucca can be found

View from the second pitch of Otto's Route, 5.8+, on Independence Tower, 5,739 feet.

Scenes like this, with a rising fog, often occur after a heavy, wet snowfall followed by a warmer, sunny day.

in abundance. About 110 flowering plant species have been identified within the monument, most blooming in the wetter spring and fall seasons. Birds here include ravens, chukar, Gambel's quail, canyon wrens, and over 60 other species. The National Audubon Society identified the monument as an Important Bird Area in 2000. Mammals range from the antelope ground squirrel to desert bighorns and mountain lions. Numerous reptiles and amphibians also inhabit the monument.

Temperatures range from the 30s in winter to the 90s during the summer. Nights are generally cool and comfortable, except in winter when temperatures can drop into the teens. Rain amounts to a scant 9 inches annually, falling mostly during the spring and fall seasons. Surprisingly, there is an average of 20 inches of snowfall annually.

USEFUL CONTACTS:

Colorado National Monument
1750 Rim Rock Drive
Fruita, CO 81521
970-858-3617 ext. 360

nps.gov/colm

THINGS TO DO:

The 23-mile Rim Rock Drive traverses the monument from a high vantage with numerous pullouts that offer stunning vistas of the landscape below. A number of trails, ranging from 0.25 mile to 8.5 miles, offer a more intimate and adventurous way to experience the monument. A popular trail is the Monument Canyon Trail, which travels into the depths of the main canyon with views of soaring towers and possibly desert bighorn sheep. This is an 11-mile out-and-back trail of moderate difficulty, gaining 1,500 feet if you follow it to the end. This trail starts at a parking area 0.25 mile off Broadway on the east side of the monument. Even though it looks as if you're driving into someone's backyard, just keep going and you'll reach the obvious trailhead sign. Otto's Trail, 0.7-mile, is an easy out-and-back hike from the canyon rim to an overlook with grand views of the canyon and several large towers, including Independence Monument. It starts about 1.0 mile east of the visitor center on Rim Rock Drive.

Rock climbing is permitted in the monument, but climbers should check-in at the visitor center first. There is an annual ascent of Independence Tower every Fourth of July to commemorate both our nation's day of independence and the first ascent by John Otto in 1911. Otto's Route, the classic route up the west side of Independence Tower, goes at 5.9 with two cruxes. One is on the second pitch, an awkward off-width, and the second is the final, airy pitch that struggles up the exposed caprock to the summit. Bike riding is popular, particularly along Rim Rock Drive, but is not permitted on trails or off-road. With adequate snow, cross-country skiing is

A juniper titmouse contemplating where to go to enjoy its morning snack.

A chukar partridge, first introduced in North America as a game species in the 1930s, has readily adapted to the arid mountains of the American West.

Desert bighorn sheep rams during rut, sizing one another up for the inevitable head-butting.

Independence Tower at sunrise. The standard climbing route, Otto's Route, goes up the right side of the spire in four pitches, out of sight in this photo.

also a common and enjoyable activity within the monument.

THINGS TO SEE:
The Monument has a considerable variety of wildlife and plant life, given its austere setting. Pinyon pine and Utah juniper are easily found along the higher elevations, while the Rio Grande cottonwood and single-leaf ash are more common in the lower, wetter areas. Here you'll also find many of the sixty-three breeding bird species that call the monument home. Several of the raptor species can be seen along the high sandstone walls. The visitor center has a checklist for birds and a log of recent sightings.

GETTING THERE:
From Fruita, take Exit 19 off I-70 and drive 4.0 miles to the West Entrance.
From the center of Grand Junction, take Broadway, which becomes Monument Road, approximately 4 miles to the East Entrance.

FACILITIES:
Camping is available year-round within the monument, which has fifty-one sites at the Saddlehorn Campground near the visitor center. While suitable for both tents and RVs up to 40 feet, there are no electric hookups or showers. A-Loop sites are available on a first-come, first-served basis while B-Loop sites can be reserved up to six months in advance at recreation.gov. All sites offer a table, charcoal grill, restrooms, and drinking water. Backcountry camping is allowed anywhere within the monument at least 0.25 mile away from the road and 150 feet from trails. Water is not readily available in the backcountry; you must carry your own. At least one gallon per person per day in the summer months is recommended. Wood fires are not permitted anywhere within the monument. The towns of Fruita and Grand Junction are nearby.

16. Florissant Fossil Beds
National Monument

NEAREST TOWN:	Florissant, CO
SIZE:	6,278 acres
BEST SEASON(S):	Year-round
NOTABLE ACTIVITIES:	Hiking, birding, wildlife and plant viewing, photography, geology, astronomy, mountain biking, fossil viewing, history

THE MONUMENT:

Florissant, a French word for flowering, is an apt description of this area in the summer. Although the valley itself was originally named after Florissant, Missouri, it describes these 6,000 acres of Colorado quite nicely during the flowering season. A local collaborative effort secured the monument's designation, and President Nixon conferred national monument status on the 5,998-acre site on August 20, 1969.

Thirty-four million years ago this area was home to a large lake, Lake Florissant. There was volcanic activity in the nearby Guffey volcanic complex, and the climate was temperate. These factors combined to create an

The homestead of Adeline Hornbek, built in the late 1800s, is a popular site for visitors.

The red fox, a wide-ranging species, can be found in the woodlands of the Rocky Mountains.

environment suitable for the preservation of many of the fossilized species discovered here. Life forms ranged from large spiders and insects to various fish, birds, and a few mammals. No amphibians have been unearthed among the nearly 40,000 fossilized specimens collected from this area.

There is evidence that the Utes occupied land or traveled through this area. Over ninety culturally modified trees have been identified within the monument. These include trees from which a portion of the tree's inner bark was peeled, trees which were bent when young to permanently grow horizontal to the ground, trees (typically juniper or cedar) that may have been planted when a tribal leader died, and trees (usually aspens) that were carved to indicate a significant event.

As with any monument or other protected place, collecting artifacts, plants, or other "souvenirs" is strictly prohibited.

The climate here is high-altitude Rocky Mountains with summer highs in the low 80s and lows of 40 to 45. Winter brings lows in the teens and highs in the mid-30s. Nearly two feet of rain falls here annually along with about nine inches of snow during the winter.

THINGS TO DO:
Hike one or all of the nine trails to experience the site and view some of the petrified redwoods. There are over 14 miles of trails for all levels, but the monument sits at 8,500 feet, so be aware to not overexert yourself. The 1.0-mile self-guided Petrified Forest Loop travels alongside the interpretive

excavation site (only open in summer) as well as the Big Stump, a massive redwood 38 feet in circumference!

Don't miss the visitor center. While the center offers numerous fossils to view, the majority of those excavated have long since been moved to museums and private collections. In response, monument staff photographed over 5,000 notable fossils from seventeen different museums and placed them on a virtual online museum at nps.gov/flfo. You can also check this site for the schedule of activities hosted by monument staff.

A visit to the adjacent Hornbek Homestead is a unique look at the homesteading challenges of life in the late 1800s. Adeline Hornbek came to Florissant Valley in 1878 and soon became engaged in many local activities, including serving as secretary of the school board and running the local mercantile. As a single parent (her husband disappeared three years earlier), she worked hard to make a living from the land and raise her children. Hers was the first home in the valley to have a second story and also boasted a dozen glass-paned windows, a rarity when many homes were little more than sod shanties.

If you enjoy rock climbing, nearby Eleven Mile Canyon has some of the best traditional and sport routes in the region. The rock is solid granite with routes from 5.5 to 5.13c. Mueller State Park also has a few domes that offer mostly sport routes at higher grades.

High Park Road is a pleasant drive in the area. To reach it, take the paved two-lane road from the monument, Teller County Road 1, south to CR 11 and follow this to its junction with CO 9. This leads to US 50 and the nearby Royal Gorge. From Cañon City, take Shelf Road, which follows the Gold Belt Byway but is generally limited to vehicles less than 25 feet. This road is narrow and winding and may require a 4WD vehicle, especially when wet.

Nearby Spinney Mountain State Park has world-class trout fishing in a quiet mountain setting on its 2,500-acre reservoir. It opens only after the ice has melted from the lake surface. Boat rentals are available at the 11 Mile Marina. Given the lake waters and the surrounding riparian zones, there are ample birding opportunities year-round. There is no camping here, although picnicking is allowed.

THINGS TO SEE:
The night sky here is relatively free of light pollution despite its proximity to Colorado Springs. The staff holds regular Night Sky Programs throughout the year and is supported by the Colorado Springs Astronomical Society. The viewing goes on regardless of the weather. No reservations are required,

but you should call ahead in the event of severe thunderstorms or snow. Dress warmly as the nights can be cold due to the altitude. The program schedule is at nps.gov/flfo/night-sky-programs.htm.

Wildlife is plentiful in the area, and visitors may see elk, mule deer, and black bears. Roughly 110 species of birds have been observed in the monument. While many are common and year-round residents, a good number only pass through during a particular season. Occasionally, mountain lions are observed in the area.

Wildflowers are seasonally abundant in the surrounding meadows and forests. As of 2013, about 448 species of flora reside within the monument, as documented by the on-site herbarium in the visitor center.

GETTING THERE:
Drive 30 miles from Manitou Springs on US Highway 24 to Florissant. Then take County Road 1 for approximately 4 miles to the visitor center.

FACILITIES:
There is no camping within the monument, but nearby Mueller State Park and Pike National Forest offer numerous sites. The State Park has 132 sites; 22 are walk-in, and one is a group RV site. There are seasonal showers, laundry, and restrooms along with 20- and 30-amp hookups. Three cabins are available for four to eight people. Nearby Florissant has limited services that include restaurants, gas, and convenience stores.

Woodland Park, about 20 minutes east of the monument, offers the usual range of amenities of a moderately sized town. Colorado Springs, about an hour east, has plenty of lodging and dining options as well as commercial campsites and notable attractions such as the Air Force Academy, Garden of the Gods, and Pikes Peak.

USEFUL CONTACTS:

Florissant Fossil Beds National Monument
P.O. Box 185
Florissant, CO 80816
719-748-3253
nps.gov/flfo

colorado.com/national-monument
 /florissant-fossil-beds-national-monument

17. Browns Canyon
National Monument

NEAREST TOWNS:	Buena Vista and Salida, CO
SIZE:	21,586 acres
BEST SEASON(S):	Year-round
NOTABLE ACTIVITIES:	Hiking, birding, wildlife and plant viewing, photography, geology, astronomy, solitude, mountain biking, rafting/kayaking, hunting, fishing

THE MONUMENT:

President Barack Obama declared this area a national monument on February 19, 2015, to protect its unique ecological resources. It comprises former Bureau of Land Management (BLM), US Forest Service, and some state lands. The monument also includes the Browns Canyon Wilderness Study Area. Its 21,586 acres include deep granite canyons, pristine high-altitude backcountry, and the renowned Arkansas River.

The Arkansas River and Mount Princeton, 14,196 feet, at dawn.

Situated halfway between the mountain towns of Salida and Buena Vista, elevations range from 7,300 to 10,000 feet with indigenous plant and wildlife reflecting this difference. Much of the monument is subalpine grasslands, offering rich food sources for wildlife including mule deer, elk, and Rocky Mountain bighorn sheep, as well as black bears and the occasional mountain lion. Plant life is represented by a wide assortment of wildflowers along with aspen, limber pine, and Douglas firs, depending on the elevation.

Summer temperatures here can reach highs in the mid-80s, coupled with a scorching sun, given the altitude. Choose your outing based on your abilities and adjust for heat and elevation. Winters are relatively mild, with high temperatures in the 40s and lows in the teens. While it snows in the Arkansas Valley, the snow tends to melt quickly, meaning access to most of the monument is year-round.

THINGS TO DO:

There are several hikes in the area. The River Bench Trail #6045A starts in the Ruby Mountain Campground area. To get to the trailhead, take Highway 285 to County Road 301 and head east on CR 301 for about 1.0 mile. Then turn onto CR 300 south and follow it to the campground and the Turret Trail Trailhead #6045. This trail leads through the northern portion of the monument along the Arkansas River, treating you to stunning views of the nearby Collegiate Peaks, a few of Colorado's fifty-four peaks over 14,000 feet. The best time for this hike is early morning when the sunrise bathes these high mountains in warm alpenglow. It also allows you to avoid the heat during the spring through summer when it can approach 100 degrees. The trail is not well marked, but it heads south, splitting from #6045 and finishing along the river.

Another longer hike is the Turret Trail #6045 from either its starting point in the Ruby Mountain Campground or at the end of CR 84. The easiest way to do this hike is to set up a car shuttle at each end, one car at Ruby Mountain Campground and another near the small off-grid community of Turret. Or hike the entire trail as an out-and-back. To reach the Turret Trailhead, take CO 291 north from Salida to CR 175, a good gravel road, about 9 miles to its junction with CR 184 atop a plateau with outstanding views. Take CR 184 to the town of Turret and connect with FR 184, which leads to the end of the road and the trailhead. This is a wonderful multiday backpack trip and allows you to see a good portion of the monument, likely without running into many others along the way. Certainly, doing a portion of this hike from either direction is pleasant and offers numerous

A A prairie falcon in flight—it weighs only about 1.6 pounds (720 grams) but can attain speeds of up to 100 mph. **B** The prairie rose, also known as the climbing rose, is widespread throughout eastern and central North America. **C** A family of common mergansers negotiating the high flow of the Arkansas River in early summer. **D** A western swallowtail butterfly gathering nectar from a thistle top during its fairly short lifespan from June to July.

viewpoints and scenery. Be advised that water is sparse in the monument, aside from the river, so you'll need to carry enough for your needs.

The famed Arkansas River runs along the western boundary of the monument. Known for its world-class trout fishing and recognized as a Gold Medal fishery, the Arkansas is also the country's most popular whitewater destination. Commercial raft operators and professional fishing guides are based in nearby Buena Vista and Salida. The river's headwaters originate 40 miles away near Fremont Pass, and the river gains strength and volume along the way. Snowmelt and rain are the primary water sources for the river, which can run as high as a formidable 3,600 cubic feet per second.

A nice short day hike, roughly 1.0 mile one-way, starts from the Hecla Campground, CR 194, heading south to a site along the river called "Seidel's Suckhole," Class IV–V, named for the suckhole here that can become like a washing machine to those river runners caught in its powerful churning

Rafting the Arkansas River is a very popular activity; being caught in an upswell at Siedels Suckhole is an added bonus.

waters. Hang out for an hour or two and you're sure to witness some thrilling action as river runners negotiate this difficult river section. Even though there's a well-traveled trail to this site, be prepared to get your feet wet if the water level is up. You can also go upstream for one to three miles to view several other challenging Class III–IV sections of the river: Pinball (IV), Widowmaker (IV), and Raft Ripper (III–IV). The names themselves give you an idea of the seriousness of running this section of the river, even with a commercial outfitter.

There are a half dozen 14ers within sight, including 14,443-foot Mount Elbert, the highest peak in Colorado. All are considered day hikes except during winter months when the approaches are considerably longer. Most high peaks in the region require an early start to avoid afternoon thunderstorms and allow sufficient time to achieve the typical 3,000 feet or more of elevation gain. The only exception is Mount Antero, where you can drive a high-clearance 4WD vehicle up a rough trail to about 12,000 feet, thus cutting your ascent on foot by about a thousand feet. Check out *The Colorado 14ers: The Best Routes* guidebook from CMC Press for more information.

The nearby Mount Princeton Hot Springs has on-site lodging. It's a nice retreat after a day of hiking in the monument or rafting on the Arkansas. Salida also has indoor hot springs open to the public.

There are also five ghost towns in the area, St. Elmo being the most accessible and popular. It has over thirty original structures still standing and offers a unique look into Colorado's extensive mining history.

If you're an off-road enthusiast, or like to see some hard-core four-wheeling, the aptly named Carnage Canyon (FR 6042) and Chinaman's Gulch (FR 6044) will appeal to you. Both are accessible from CR 301, east of Johnson

Village, and are located within the Four-Mile Recreation Area north of the monument. These are two of the most difficult 4WD trails in the state and are often the site of epic catastrophes! So go there only if you know your stuff. Check out funtreks.com for updates and additional information. The gravel road leading to these sites is limited to vehicles 50 feet or shorter and has few opportunities for turning around easily. The 4WD trails are to be traveled counterclockwise only.

If you're visiting during the winter ski season, both Monarch Mountain and Ski Cooper are within an hour's drive. Both lift areas have exceptional and challenging skiing on natural snow no matter your ability level.

THINGS TO SEE:

Looking for wildlife is always an enjoyable outing, even if you don't see anything more than a common ground squirrel or two. Many animals are wary of humans and in areas where hunting is allowed, as it is here, they are especially cautious. Early mornings and late evenings are your best bet for seeing the larger mammals such as deer and elk, which typically feed in the open meadows at those times. Seeing an elusive bear, or even a mountain lion, is a matter of being in the right place at the right time and being observant.

As mentioned earlier, a view of the Collegiate Peaks can be as easy as sitting alongside the river at the Ruby Campground. A short walk from your campsite to the river's edge provides gorgeous views of Mount Princeton, Mount Harvard, and Mount Columbia as the rising sun warms their eastern slopes.

GETTING THERE:

There are several access points scattered along US Highway 285 between Buena Vista and Salida. Most are associated with the type of activity you wish to engage in.

USEFUL CONTACTS:

BLM, Rocky Mountain District
3028 E. Main Street
Canon City, CO 81212
719-269-8500

USFS, Salida Ranger District
5575 Cleora Road
Salida, CO 81201
719-539-3591

Arkansas Headwaters Recreation Area
307 West Sackett Avenue
Salida, CO 81201
719-539-7289

cpw.state.co.us/placestogo/Parks
   /ArkansasHeadwatersRecreationArea

Four-wheeling in Carnage Canyon in the National Forest adjacent to the monument's northern boundary.
Photo by Dustin Kemp

The Hecla Campground can be reached via County Road 194, approximately 18 miles south of Buena Vista and about 5 miles north of Salida.

The Ruby Mountain Campground can be reached by turning onto County Road 301, which is roughly 14 miles south of Buena Vista and 9 miles north of Salida.

To reach the Turret Trailhead, take CO Highway 291 north from Salida to County Road 175, a gravel road, about 9 miles to its junction with County Road 184, which is atop a plateau with outstanding views. Take County Road 184 to Turret and connect with Forest Road 184, which will take you to the end of the road and the trailhead for #6045.

FACILITIES:

There are nineteen campsites beside the Arkansas River at the Ruby Mountain Campground. Tent sites 14 through 19 are situated along the river's edge and have some shade, while the remainder of the sites are in the open but offer great views of the Collegiate Peaks. There are vault toilets but no hookups, potable water, or RV dumps here.

Another campground on the western side of the monument is at Hecla Junction, about 6 miles south of Nathrop and a few miles east on CR 194, a well-maintained gravel road. This is a popular put-in/take-out for rafters on the Arkansas as well, so expect some traffic, especially during the peak season. There are twenty-two sites here and no services are available aside from vault toilets.

18. Canyons of the Ancients
National Monument

NEAREST TOWNS:	Cortez and Pleasant View, CO
SIZE:	176,000 acres
BEST SEASON(S):	Year-round, weather permitting
NOTABLE ACTIVITIES:	Archaeological site viewing, hiking, birding, wildlife and plant viewing, photography, geology, astronomy, solitude, mountain biking, Ancestral Puebloan culture

THE MONUMENT:

Canyons of the Ancients National Monument was established on June 9, 2000, by President Bill Clinton. This 176,000-acre tract of protected land is administered by the Bureau of Land Management as part of its 32-million-acre National Conservation Lands. With over 6,000 distinct archaeological sites, Canyons of the Ancients has one of the largest concentrations of protected ruins in the United States and includes Lowry Pueblo Ruins Archaeological Site, just west of Pleasant View, which was incorporated into the monument in 2000. Built and occupied around mid-1,000

View across the monument looking at Sleeping Ute Mountain, 9,984 feet.

CE, it once held up to 100 people, mostly farmers of Ancestral Puebloan heritage. To reach it, take Montezuma County Road CC west from Pleasant View for about 9 miles to the ruins. Much like Casa Grande, it now sports a roof to protect it from the elements.

Because of its remote location and inadequate funds for staffing, it faces ongoing threats. Roads created for oil and gas exploration or off-road travel render many of these sites particularly vulnerable to vandalism and looting. The BLM designated this as an Area of Critical Environmental Concern in 1986. The intent of this designation is to prohibit additional leases for oil or natural gas.

The weather here is characteristic of a high-desert environment in the west, with moderately hot summers and precipitation measured in mere inches. Summer temperatures can reach the upper 80s with lows in the mid- to upper 40s, while winters are in the 40s during the day and dip into the teens at night. Rainfall occurs throughout the year at an average rate of one inch per month, except for June, which barely reaches half an inch. Snow-fall occurs, but it neither accumulates significantly nor tends to last long. Note that precipitation in any form can make the back roads of this region impassable. Elevations range from 5,300 feet to as high as 6,600 feet.

More than 150 species of mammals, birds, reptiles, and amphibians inhabit the monument. Large mammals such as mule deer, mountain lions, and coyotes are dispersed throughout the monument, while most bird species are found along streams and year-round water sources. There are no fish here.

THINGS TO DO:

First, visit the Canyons of the Ancients Visitor Center and Museum in Dolores, which has helpful staff to assist with making the most of your time here.

A popular hike within the monument is the 6.5-mile Sand Canyon Trail, which can be reached from either the north or, more easily, from the south. The south trailhead is accessed off CR G, about 12 miles west of Cortez. If you want to hike the length of the canyon, a shuttle is recommended, otherwise you can hike as much or as little as you wish from either trailhead. Make an early start while it's still cool, and hike from a lower elevation to a higher one early in the morning so your hike back is more leisurely and comfortable. If you're hiking the length of the canyon, start from the Sand Canyon Pueblo so most of the hike is downhill. There are several ruins along the canyon, notably the Castle Rock Pueblo near the southern trailhead, and Saddlehorn Pueblo located about 1 mile upcanyon from the south.

Almost all the canyons and mesas within the monument on BLM lands are available for hiking, but you must have a good topographic map and know how to use it.

THINGS TO SEE:

Given the size and remote nature of the monument, it is difficult to explore it in its entirety without a considerable amount of time and effort. Some of the more accessible places are highlighted here; further exploration is up to your individual desires and preparedness.

The Sand Canyon Pueblo is accessible by a paved road, although this is a bit of a convoluted route; get a map and directions from the Heritage Center. From the Heritage Center in Dolores take CO 184 west

Painted Hand Pueblo, named for the hand imprint on the rock wall.

to its junction with US 491 and go south to CR P and turn west. Follow this for approximately 9 miles, turn south on CR 17 and follow this as it turns into CR N. The trailhead for the ruins is on the left off CR N. The ruins are not restored, but by following the trail you'll be able to view much of the site marked by signs. Here there were 420 rooms, 90 kivas, and 14 towers. Centered around a spring, it is estimated that as many as 750 people lived here during the Pueblo's peak. By 1300 CE the area had been abandoned, as were many other pueblo sites in the Colorado region. The total hiking distance is less than 2.0 miles round-trip on a good trail and takes one to two hours.

Continuing on CR N past the ruins leads to BLM Road 4728 on the left. This road leads to the edge of the canyon with dispersed campsites along the way and an impressive view of Sleeping Ute Mountain to the south. A wet road will be difficult, if not impossible, to travel.

To explore sites a bit off the main road, visit the Painted Hand Pueblo north of Hovenweep National Monument Visitor Center on CR 10. The turn-off is about 8.5 miles from the visitor center on Hovenweep Road/CR 10; turn onto BLM Road 4531 and continue for 1.0 mile to the trailhead. Under dry

Given that this is an undeveloped/unrestored area, the remnants you'll see will be much like this foundation wall.

conditions the road is passable by most 2WD vehicles, but under wet conditions even the best 4WD vehicles will likely not make it to the trailhead. Parking at the turnoff and walking is an option if conditions are wet, although you'll likely get muddy along the way. Dispersed camping can be found here as well. From the trailhead it's about 0.5 mile to the tower-like ruins where the Painted Hand petroglyph can be found. The tower is remarkably intact given its age and materials (sandstone). It also shows the meticulous detail in construction methods of these early craftsmen.

One mile from the turnoff on BLM Road 4531 is the trailhead for Cutthroat Castle, part of Hovenweep National Monument. While you can drive close to these ruins, the moderate 0.8-mile hike is more pleasant. You'll be able to see the surrounding landscape more intimately and observe the skilled construction of the Ancestral Puebloan people. There are several sites for dispersed camping along the 2.0-mile road, some with impressive views of the canyons below. As always, use existing sites, build fires only in fire rings and when safe, and minimize your impact.

Another easily reached site is the Lowry Pueblo on the northern boundary of the monument. This is one of the most complete and developed sites within the monument. It was restored in 1965. Access is north from Dolores on CO 491 to CR CC at Pleasant View. Turn west here and continue for 8.6 miles on a paved road,

USEFUL CONTACTS:

Canyons of the Ancients National Monument
Visitor Center and Museum
27501 Highway 184
Dolores, CO 81323
970-882-5600

blm.gov/programs/national
 -conservation-lands/colorado
 /canyons-of-the-ancients

mesaverdecountry.com/things-to-do
 /culture-arts/canyons-of-the-ancients

except for the last few miles. Signs direct you to a parking area with restrooms and an information kiosk. A short walk on the wheelchair-accessible trail leads to the ruins where you can explore a forty-room dwelling and eight kivas, including the Great Kiva. Built during the Great Pueblo period from 1100 through 1300 CE, the structures here

The Great Kiva with the covered Lowry Pueblo in the background.

reflect an increased sophistication in construction methods and the ability to build as high as three stories. A visit here takes about an hour, depending on your level of curiosity.

GETTING THERE:

A visit to the Canyons of the Ancients Visitor Center and Museum in Dolores is especially useful as the drive can be confusing with many turns onto country roads. Some of the more popular sites to visit have directions below.

Sand Canyon Pueblo: From the visitor center in Dolores, take CO 184 west to its junction with US Highway 491, go south to County Road P, and turn west. Follow County Road P for approximately 9 miles, turn south on County Road 17, and follow this as it turns into County Road N. The marked trailhead for the ruins is on your left. This is also the trailhead for the northern access to Sand Canyon Trail.

Sand Canyon Trail: The south trailhead is accessed from County Road G, about 12.0 miles west of Cortez, CO.

FACILITIES:

There are no developed campgrounds within the monument, but there are several options in the surrounding communities. The thirty-one-site campground at nearby Hovenweep National Monument is available on a first-come, first-served basis. There are a couple of sites that can accommodate RVs up to 35 feet, but most are designed for tent camping. There is also a developed campground at McPhee Reservoir outside of Dolores. There is camping at Mesa Verde National Park, which, if you're touring the area's attractions, is a must-see.

19. Hovenweep National Monument

NEAREST TOWN:	Aneth, UT
SIZE:	400 acres
BEST SEASON(S):	Year-round, weather permitting
NOTABLE ACTIVITIES:	Archaeological site viewing, hiking, birding, wildlife and plant viewing, photography, astronomy, solitude, Ancestral Puebloan culture

THE MONUMENT:

A modest 400 acres in size, Hovenweep was nonetheless proclaimed a national monument by President Warren G. Harding on March 2, 1923, in recognition of the need to protect its five prehistoric Ancestral Puebloan sites. The monument was designated before modern-day techniques for archaeological investigation had been developed, so many artifacts were lost to faraway museums or sold to private collectors without regard to their cultural significance. Hovenweep means "deserted valley" in the Paiute/Ute language.

Evidence of human presence within this area dates back 10,000 years to when nomadic Paleoindians used the area for hunting and gathering. While theirs was a transient population for many centuries, people began to settle this area around 900 CE, growing crops and creating a community for nearly 2,500 people. The towers themselves, built by Ancestral Puebloans, were constructed primarily between 1200 and 1300 CE. While the true function of many of these structures remains unknown, it is thought that some were designed with celestial observation in mind. It has been shown that a solar calendar was created around the alignment of the structure known as Hovenweep Castle. Light falls into the building through specific openings, marking the summer and winter solstices, as well as both the spring and fall equinoxes. The architecture and construction is notable as well, not only for its design but also for its ability to withstand the elements over the centuries. The inhabitants did not remain long; the majority left for greener pastures by the end of the 1200s. Most of these peoples settled in the Rio Grande Valley in New Mexico and the Little Colorado River Basin in Arizona.

The Cutthroat Castle Unit, accessed by a short hike, shows a community of multi-storied structures located near a water source and land suitable for cultivation.

The monument sits astride the Colorado-Utah border in the southwestern part of Colorado known as the Four Corners, about 40 miles west of Cortez, CO. It lies adjacent on three sides to Canyons of the Ancients National Monument, although these are managed by different agencies. This is a remote monument and the sign at the visitor center—tow charges begin at $500—says it all. You must fill up on gas, food, and water in Cortez, CO, in Monticello, UT, or in Bluff, UT. There are no services at all in or around the monument and cell service is unreliable.

One interesting insect here is the tarantula hawk, a large wasp that can sting and paralyze a tarantula, drag it into a burrow, and then lay an egg on its abdomen, providing a food source for the grub that will soon hatch. Be careful though, the sting of this wasp is both venomous and painful!

THINGS TO DO:
Explore the visitor center and speak with the helpful National Park Service staff. They can give you detailed information on the five communities that once thrived in this area. They will also work with you to create the best visit based on your interests, experience, and time.

The Square Tower Unit with Sleeping Ute Mountain in the background.

The Square Tower Unit, behind the visitor center, is a great place to start your exploration of the monument. There is a moderate 2.0-mile self-guided loop with close-up views of several structures within the unit. This is also the largest and most accessible collection of archaeological remains in the monument. Visitors typically spend one to two hours exploring this area.

Like many other monuments of the West, Hovenweep has some of the darkest skies in the country. The monument was designated the 17th International Dark Sky Park. None of these ruins are accessible after sunset, so stargazing must take place in the parking lot, the campground, or on nearby BLM lands.

THINGS TO SEE:

If you have limited time but want to see ancient ruins, the Square Tower Unit is the best choice. It's close to the loop trail and allows you to easily return to your vehicle at a time of your choosing.

The Horseshoe Group along Hackberry Canyon is another short 1.0-mile round-trip trail. Here you'll find excellent examples of the precise stonework the Ancestral Puebloans used. Their construction methods are on par with work by today's craftsmen. Extend your walk a bit farther to reach the Holly Group. There is no evidence of the use of outside scaffolding of the Holly Tower; building occurred from inside the tower, one floor at a time. As with similar sites, these structures are located adjacent to a seep or spring.

With more time, there are several other sites to visit. About 8.5 miles from the visitor center on Hovenweep Road/CR 10 the ruins of Cutthroat Castle can be found. Turn right onto BLM Road 4531 and drive about 2.0 miles to the trailhead and a road dropping into the drainage below. This road requires a high-clearance vehicle but, alternatively, it's a good 0.8-mile one-way hike to the ruins. If it's wet, don't drive along this road as you'll likely get stuck. An added benefit of this outing is that 1 mile down BLM Road 4531 you'll come to the marked trailhead for the Painted Hand Pueblo, an interesting and intact tower. This is on BLM land, so there is dispersed camping at a few sites along the road and near the trailhead. This site is part of the Canyons of the Ancients National Monument, also discussed in this guide.

GETTING THERE:
From Cortez, CO, take US Highway 160 south of town to the junction with County Road G, also known as Ismay Trading Post Road. Follow this for approximately 40 miles to the junction with Hovenweep Road and turn north toward Cajon.

Another more direct route leaves Pleasant View, CO, on County Road CC or BB, which joins CO Highway 10 and heads southwest for about 20.0

Looking across the landscape near the trailhead for the Cutthroat Castle Unit.

Sleeping Ute Mountain, 9,984 feet, at sunset.

miles to the visitor center. Be forewarned that the unpaved portion of this road is often impassable when wet.

From Bluff, UT, take US Highway 191 north for 9.0 miles to UT Highway 262, which is also known as Trail of the Ancients. Follow this approximately 25.0 miles to the visitor center.

FACILITIES:

As mentioned earlier, there are no services in the area of the monument. There is a thirty-one-site campground near the visitor center with vault toilets and water. It can accommodate only a few RVs up to 35 feet in pull-through sites, but most of the sites are designed for tent camping. Drinking water is available only during the summer months. Dispersed camping can be found on the BLM lands surrounding Hovenweep National Monument, including Canyons of the Ancients. Stop at the Heritage Center in Dolores for help finding these areas. Otherwise, ask the staff at the visitor center. There is also developed camping at McPhee Reservoir outside of Dolores and at Mesa Verde National Park, a must-see if you're touring the area.

Other services can be found in Cortez or Dolores, as well as Blanding, UT, or Bluff, UT, where you can find food, lodging, gas, and anything else you need for your travels.

USEFUL CONTACTS:

Hovenweep National Monument
McElmo Route
Cortez, CO 81321
970-562-4282 ext. 5

nps.gov/hove

20. Yucca House National Monument

NEAREST TOWN:	Towaoc, CO
SIZE:	34 acres
BEST SEASON(S):	Year-round
NOTABLE ACTIVITIES:	Archaeological site viewing, hiking (limited), birding, wildlife and plant viewing, Ancestral Puebloan culture

THE MONUMENT:

Yucca House stood largely untouched and unnoticed for 800 years. This small site was built around 1150 CE due to the nearby availability of water. It was a center of activity for the Ancestral Puebloan people of the Montezuma Valley. Today it is surrounded by private land, and while it is open to the public, access can be tricky. There is a driving guide on the website with specific driving directions, or you can pick up a brochure from nearby Mesa Verde National Park Visitor Center. Parking is adjacent to a working ranch house, so be respectful; do not park in the driveway or on the grass, and do not move the parking logs. The trailhead is a short walk along a boardwalk from the parking area.

Remnants of the boundaries of the structures here are all that is visible in this undeveloped monument.

This monument was established by President Woodrow Wilson on December 19, 1919, and is currently managed by the National Park Service. This monument resulted from a collaboration of public and private interests. On July 2, 1919, Henry Van Kleeck donated the original 9.6 acres of land that are now a part of the monument's total 34 acres. There are three perennial springs close by as well as the Navajo Wash to the east.

THINGS TO DO:

If you're coming through Cortez, stop at the welcome center on 928 E. Main Street for information on this monument and advice on the region. You can plan your trip to specific sites most effectively without spending needless time searching as you drive around.

There was no established trail at the time of this writing, but several social trails lead through and around the various ruins. Most of the ruins are hard to distinguish from the surrounding landscape, but if you look closely, you'll see evidence of a structured layout with grand views of the valley below and easy access to farmlands and water. There are two distinct centers here: the Lower House and the West Complex. The Lower House has an L-shaped portion that contained eight one-story ruins and possibly several two-story portions as well. If you've visited nearby Sand Canyon Pueblo in Canyons of the Ancients, you'll see a remarkable similarity between the two sites. This is not surprising given that many cultures traveled freely between sites for trade and, likely, just out of curiosity. The larger West Complex is horseshoe-shaped and contains as many as 600 rooms along with 100 kivas.

This region is rich in public lands and national monuments, including Canyons of the Ancients, Hovenweep, Chimney Rock, Canyon de Chelly, and Aztec Ruins as well as Chaco Culture National Historic Park and Mesa Verde National Park. Visits to these sites provide a better understanding of the breadth of early Ancestral Puebloan settlements.

What appears to be a marine fossil embedded in the soft sandstone is evidence that at one time this was likely an inland sea.

THINGS TO SEE:

The presence of a perennial spring allows many wildlife species to live here. There are 125 bird and 69 mammalian species documented here. It's not unusual to see bald eagles during the winter months. Numerous predatory bird species, including peregrine falcons, are found here as the landscape favors their style of hunting and offers suitable habitat for nesting. Pronghorn, elk, and mule deer are some of the larger mammal species in the area.

A sage thrasher, common throughout Colorado, is identified by the yellow eyes, short bill, and bold streaking on its underside.

GETTING THERE:

From the junction of US Highways 160 and 491 in Cortez, CO, drive approximately 8 miles to MC County Road B and turn west. Continue for 0.8 miles, crossing MC County Road 21, to a dirt road on the right just before a farmhouse. Cross the yellow cattle guard and proceed 1.4 miles toward a white ranch house with a red roof to the west. Park on the left side of the driveway without blocking the owner's access.

USEFUL CONTACTS:

Yucca House
National Monument
P.O. Box 8
Mesa Verde, CO 81330
970-529-4465
nps.gov/yuho

colorado.com/colorado-official
 -state-welcome-center
 /colorado-welcome-center-cortez

FACILITIES:

None exist within the monument. Nearby Cortez, 8.0 miles to the north, can supply food, fuel, and lodging needs. The Ute Mountain Travel Center in Towaoc, CO, offers food, fuel, and lodging in their casino as well as an RV park with full hookups, laundry, and showers.

21. Chimney Rock
National Monument

NEAREST TOWNS:	Pagosa Springs and Bayfield, CO
SIZE:	4,726 acres
BEST SEASON(S):	Mid-May to late September; closed November to mid-May
NOTABLE ACTIVITIES:	Archaeological site viewing, hiking, birding, wildlife and plant viewing, photography, geology, unique astronomy, history

THE MONUMENT:

At 7,000 feet, Chimney Rock National Monument is the highest of all Ancestral Puebloan sites and covers 4,726 acres. President Barack Obama declared Chimney Rock a national monument on September 21, 2012. The actual rock formation known as Chimney Rock is 315 feet tall and dominates 1,000 acres of the monument. Roughly 2,000 people occupied this site, based on the 200 rooms excavated here. The site is managed by the US Forest Service. Currently there is no visitor center, but the Chimney Rock Interpretive Association (CRIA) provides guided tours of the site and runs a small visitors cabin/bookstore at the road's end. This group is the best contact for additional or on-site information.

View from the top of the ridge showing the valley below, likely a place for the inhabitants to grow seasonal crops.

There are generally four seasons here with highs in the low 40s during the winter and in the 70s to 80s during summer. Lows can reach single digits in winter and average in the 40s during

The rising sun highlights the prominent Chimney Rock.

summer. The area receives about 18 inches of precipitation annually and four feet of snow.

THINGS TO DO:

This is a seasonal monument and is only open to the public from mid-May until the end of September, from 9:00 a.m. to 4:30 p.m. CRIA offers 2.5-hour guided tours along a paved walkway to the site of unexcavated ruins and on to the Great Kiva and up-close views of Chimney Rock itself. Once you sign up for a tour and pay the fee, you drive about 2.5 miles up a steep gravel road to a parking area at about 7,400 feet. No trailers or large RVs are allowed. Here you'll join your group and an interpretive guide for the tour. You can also choose the Kiva Audio-Guided Tour that allows you to set your own pace. There is no shade, therefore drinking plenty of water is necessary to adjust to the high altitude. CRIA also offers special tours focused on the full moon, the night sky, or sunrise/sunset. In addition, there is a Dance of the Ancients Tour that allows you to observe Native American dance rituals. This is conducted near the visitors' cabin once a year in late May at 10:00 a.m. and 1:00 p.m. Reservations are strongly recommended for all special tours.

A young male broad-tailed hummingbird.

Evening clouds over nearby Navajo Reservoir, a great place to camp during your visit.

THINGS TO SEE:

Every 18.6 years a major astronomical event is visible from the monument, which may explain why the Chacoan people built the Great House near Chimney Rock. This event, a Major Lunar Standstill (MLS), is related to the natural north-south oscillation of the moon during its orbit. Every 18.6 years it pauses for about three years, the MLS, and during this time from the right vantage point it's possible to see the moon rising between the spires of Chimney Rock and its neighbor, Companion Rock. The winter solstice is the best time for viewing a full moon between the spires at sunset and photographing the event, but the view from the Great House Pueblo only allows a brief 15-minute window to observe this phenomenon. It has been calculated that the construction of the Great House between 1076 CE and 1093 CE coincided with an MLS. The next MLS is calculated to begin in 2021.

USEFUL CONTACTS:

Chimney Rock Interpretive Association
P.O. Box 1662
Pagosa Springs, CO 81147
970-731-7133

USFS Camping Information
forestcamping.com/dow/rockymtn/sanj

GETTING THERE:

Drive west from Pagosa Springs on US Highway 160 for 16 miles, then turn left onto CO

Highway 151 and continue for a few miles to the entrance.

From Durango, drive 43 miles east on US Highway 160, then turn right onto CO Highway 151 and continue for a few miles to the entrance.

FACILITIES:

There are no facilities within the monument for camping and only a small bookstore with snacks and water. Nearby there are numerous opportunities for camping within the San Juan National Forest. The seasonal Lower Piedra Campground just west of the monument on US 160 offers seventeen sites near the Piedra River in a high-altitude forest setting. Five are RV pull-through sites, but there are no hookups or services. Middle Mountain, Pine Point, and Graham Creek Campgrounds are

Rabbitbrush and Chimney Rock.

similar and located along the shores of Vallecito Lake. Reservations are encouraged. Twenty miles to the south on CO Highway 151 the 2,100-acre Navajo State Park has 138 sites and three cabins, access to the Navajo Reservoir for boating and other water sports, and is a great spot for birding. There are flush toilets, showers, a nearby laundry, and thirty-nine RV sites with full hookups. Nearby Carracas and Rosa Campgrounds also offer RV sites with hookups. Windsurf Beach and Arboles Point are primitive campgrounds open year-round and can accommodate small RVs but have no hookups.

Pagosa Springs (east on US 160) and Durango (west on US 160) each offer a range of food, lodging, fuel and RV parks. Pagosa Springs also has hot springs. Durango has the famous Durango and Silverton Railroad if you'd like to tour the Rocky Mountains from the comfort of an old-style narrow-gauge train. Fall is a great time for this while the aspens change colors.

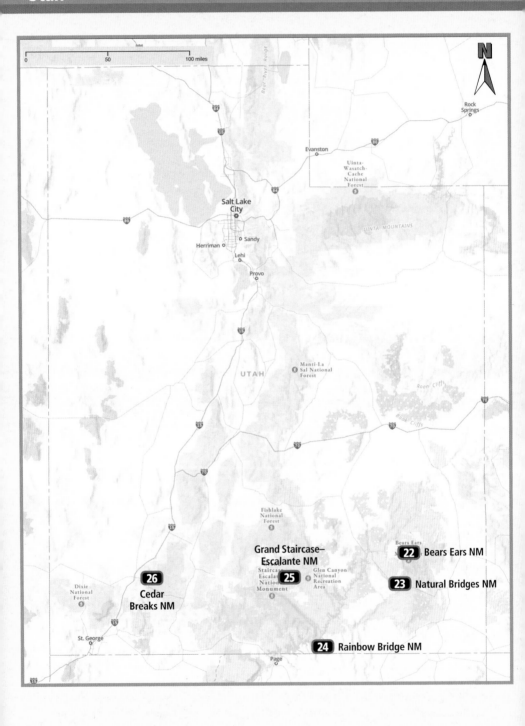

22 Bears Ears NM

23 Natural Bridges NM

24 Rainbow Bridge NM

25 Grand Staircase–Escalante NM

26 Cedar Breaks NM

22. Bears Ears
National Monument

NEAREST TOWNS:	Bluff, Blanding, and Monticello, UT
SIZE:	Presently 201,876 acres
BEST SEASON(S):	Fall through spring; the ranger station is closed during the summer due to extreme heat
NOTABLE ACTIVITIES:	Archaeological site viewing, hiking, birding, wildlife, photography, geology, astronomy, solitude, mountain biking, world-class rock climbing, history

THE MONUMENT:

Established on December 28, 2016, by President Barack Obama, Bears Ears is a consolidation of 1,351,849 acres of land previously managed by the Bureau of Land Management and US Forest Service. Currently, the monument is co-managed by these agencies along with a partnership of five local Native American tribes: the Navajo Nation, Hopi, Ute Mountain Ute, Ute Indian Tribe of the Uintah and Ouray Reservation, and the Pueblo of Zuni. With over 100,000 archaeological sites, the area embodies substantial cultural significance for many of the region's Native Americans.

Unfortunately, 85 percent of the monument was temporarily removed from monument status on December 4, 2017, by President Trump, despite

Sunset on the "Bears Ears" from nearby
Natural Bridges National Monument

The "Big Crane" of Butler Wash.

Pictograph of a hunter on horseback shooting a mule deer with a bow and arrow at Newspaper Rock.

"The Citadel," a long and very defensible isthmus of land with ruins just below the top.

overwhelming support for the original boundaries to remain intact during a public review process. As of this writing, the reversal is under legal review. However, much of the original monument lands remain publicly accessible.

The weather here can be harsh, particularly during the summer. Highs of over 100 degrees are common and are often higher in the canyons. Summer rains from late July through early September produce flash floods that inundate a drainage very quickly and become a risk to hikers. Winter temperatures are often below zero, and ice poses a unique hazard within this desert environment.

THINGS TO DO:

A popular activity here is to search for petroglyphs and archaeological sites. Bears Ears has the largest single collection of such artifacts within the American West. A favorite visit is the Wolfman Panel in Butler Wash, easily accessed off UT 163 west of Bluff and just north of the sign for the local airport. This is also the start of the 22.0-mile drive along Butler Wash to UT 95 to the north. At the start of the drive there is a gate. Once you go through the gate (be sure you close it behind you), drive 1.0 mile to a kiosk alongside a fence. Turn left at the kiosk and follow a track to a small parking area. A short walk toward the gulch on a well-marked trail leads to a panel of petroglyphs, while across the drainage you can see remnants of an old archaeological site. Other sites within Butler Wash include the Procession Panel and the Monarch Ruins. The Monarch Ruins can be reached by a short 1.0-mile hike along a well-marked trail.

House on Fire in Mule Canyon, a short and easy 2.2-mile roundtrip hike alongside a stream bed.

Monarch Ruins along Butler Wash, a short, 1.6-mile roundtrip hike from Utah County Road 262/Lower Butler Wash Road.

An equally popular and easily accessible site is the House on Fire Ruins in the Mule Canyon area. To reach this area, travel on UT 95 to 0.5 mile east of the Mule Canyon Indian Ruins. Turn on Texas Flat Road and continue for about 1.0 mile to the trailhead on the left (west) side of the road. Given its popularity, parking may be at a premium, especially on weekends, so you may need to park farther along the road in various pullouts. This mostly level trail follows the drainage in a westerly direction and is clearly marked and well-traveled. Look for the ruins at about 1.0 mile to the right and slightly uphill. The ridges above the ruins have the appearance of flames when light strikes them.

Two other interesting hikes are the Seven Kivas and The Citadel, both toward the end of Cigarette Springs Road. Do not drive to the end of Cigarette Springs Road without a high-clearance 4WD vehicle. Drive approximately 6 miles to a broad rocky road on your left (high clearance needed) and follow it 0.8 mile to its end and the trailheads for both hikes. Camping is allowed; there are a few sites with spectacular views. The marked trailhead for the Seven Kivas Trail is on the north side of the parking area. The trail drops to a bench that traverses below the parking area and then drops into the canyon. The Citadel Trail begins at the south side of the parking area and heads east along a broad mesa, which ends at The Citadel. Gaining The Citadel requires a bit of scrambling, but it is manageable for those in good health.

Indian Creek, in the northern part of the monument, features truly unique, world-renowned splitter cracks for those interested in climbing. Although it's located within Canyonlands National Park, Indian Creek falls within the boundaries of Bears Ears. To get there, take UT 211 west for

An ash-throated flycatcher in a brief moment of inactivity while scanning for flying insects.

Camping is widely dispersed, with few rules and even fewer neighbors, although you need to stay on marked roads and use existing sites.

roughly 27 miles, stopping at the Newspaper Rock along the way. There's camping at Creek Pasture and Super Bowl Campgrounds, but there is no water, cell service, food, or gas, so bring what you need! Spring and fall are the best times here as summer can be hot, which limits climbing to the shade in the morning or late afternoons.

Another excellent site is Natural Bridges National Monument, which has unique natural bridges formed by centuries of erosion.

THINGS TO SEE:

Canyons and vistas; too many to document within the scope of this guidebook! Visit the BLM Ranger Station at Kane Gulch to get information on different areas, day hikes, backpacking, and weather. An excellent guidebook specific to the Bears Ears is *The Best Bears Ears National Monument Hikes* by Morgan Sjogren, which has detailed information on how to fully enjoy and appreciate this region.

For stunning views, one of the best and easily accessible viewpoints is Muley Point at the end of a 5-mile gravel road off UT 261 near its junction with UT 163. Here you'll be treated to an immense vista stretching for miles to the south and west. Take in views of Monument Valley and Valley of the Gods, 20 miles away, and colorful cliffs and buttes. The nearby Goosenecks State Park

USEFUL CONTACTS:

Bureau of Land Management Monticello Field Office
365 North Main
Monticello, UT 84535
435-587-1510
blm.gov/office
  /monticello-field-office

bluffutah.org/lodging

fs.usda.gov/visit
  /bears-ears-national-monument

is spectacular for the double turn the San Juan River makes as it wends its way to the Colorado River.

Leftover from the last Ice Age is a stand of genetically related aspens about 1.5 miles from the Kane Gulch Ranger Station. Aspens are typically found at higher elevations and often do poorly at lower altitudes. Seeds were left here from glaciers that moved across this landscape and these hardy trees took hold and thrived. It has been determined that this line of trees has been growing in this location for the past 10,000 years, all from the same original stock.

GETTING THERE:

From Blanding, UT, take UT Highway 95 west for 32.0 miles to its junction with UT Highway 261. Turn south and drive about 4.0 miles to the

Sunrise on a sandstone tower in the nearby Valley of the Gods.

Kane Gulch Ranger Station. Here you can find additional information on accessing the entries to the monument as well as current road conditions.

FACILITIES:

Note that the ranger station is only open from March 1 through June 15 and from September 1 through October 31.

Dispersed camping is allowed in parts of the monument, along the Butler and Comb Wash Roads, the Valley of the Gods, and on Cedar Mesa. You are required to stay on previously disturbed areas and off-road vehicle travel is prohibited. Overnight backpack trips require a permit from the BLM. You can call their office at the number in the "Useful Contacts" section to make reservations.

There are developed campgrounds at Indian Creek and nearby at the Needles Outpost and Windwhistle Campgrounds. Near Monticello there are the Nizhoni, Buckboard, and Dalton Springs Campgrounds, while Devils Canyon Campground is near Blanding. Close to Bluff, and along the San Juan River, is the Sand Island Campground, which also holds the impressive Sand Island Petroglyph Panel. This is the best quality petroglyph site you will find with easy access, a few feet from where you park! The Goosenecks State Park Campground is on the south side of the monument and close to the junction of US 163 and UT 261.

23. Natural Bridges
National Monument

NEAREST TOWNS:	Bluff and Blanding, UT
SIZE:	7,636 acres
BEST SEASON(S):	Year-round
NOTABLE ACTIVITIES:	Archaeological site viewing, hiking, birding, wildlife and plant viewing, photography, unique geology, astronomy, solitude, mountain biking, history

THE MONUMENT:

President Theodore Roosevelt established this monument, Utah's first, on April 16, 1908. It protects an area of unique natural rock bridges and evidence of centuries of human habitation. The area was used by early hunter-gatherers around 7,000 BCE and more recently by Ancestral Puebloans who found it suitable for a farming lifestyle. Today, the Hopi continue to make this area their home. Many ruins attest to the early inhabitants and their eye for fertile ground, with plentiful water and shelter in an otherwise harsh desert landscape.

A short hike on a marked trail to the drainage below the bridge will give you an up-close sense of the immensity of the Ochoyama Bridge.

Ochoyama Bridge with sunburst.　　　Sipapu Bridge at sunset.

As part of the Colorado Plateau, the monument has a high desert climate, with temperatures fluctuating as much as 40 degrees in a single day. Summers are hot, often exceeding 100 degrees, while winter temperatures are in the 30s to 50s. Rainfall averages nine inches annually, with most falling during the spring and fall. Very little snow falls here, except occasionally in the nearby higher mountains, although even a little snow or ice can make roads and trails impassable.

THINGS TO DO:

Exploring the monument can be as easy as driving the 9.0-mile, one-way counterclockwise paved loop. Or be more adventurous and hike into one of the drainages below the monument's three bridges.

While the landscape is intriguing, most people come here to see the bridges. Bridges differ from arches in how they are formed. Arches are typically found on the skyline while bridges form in the bottoms of deep canyons. Arches result from erosion on the surrounding rock mass, while bridges are primarily formed from water cutting into the layers of sandstone, eventually working through and creating a bridge.

The bridges in the monument represent three age groups: young, such as the Kachina bridge; middle-aged, as shown by Sipapu Bridge; and old, as represented by Owachomo Bridge. The names of the bridges have changed over the years, but the current name Kachina is for the rock art found on the bridge; Sipapu, for "the place of emergence"; and Owachomo, or "rock mound," for a feature on the east side of the bridge. Early inhabitants of the area, the Paiute, referred to the bridges as mah-vah-talk-tump, or "under the horse's belly."

A tree on Sipapu Bridge, demonstrating the critical value of tinajas for plants and wildlife, is barely visible in the sunlight on the bridge.

Hiking to the base of any of the bridges is easy. Be mindful about straying off the marked trails as there are dropoffs, and the terrain can be quite dangerous. There is no cell phone service here.

At only 0.6 mile on level ground, one of the easiest trails is to the Horse Collar Ruin Overlook. It has views of Ancient Pueblo ruins across the drainage as well as Sipapu Bridge, the longest span of the bridges here. The trail to the drainage under Owachomo Bridge is moderately strenuous, especially on the way back, which is all uphill. But being underneath the 106-foot-tall span is well worth the effort. Viewing Kachina Bridge is best accomplished from below because while it is visible from the pullout, the orientation of the bridge and its small size make it difficult to see.

USEFUL CONTACTS:

Natural Bridges
National Monument
HC-60 Box 1
Lake Powell, UT 84533-0001
435-692-1234 x616

nps.gov/nabr

bluffutah.org

The unmaintained Loop Trail connects all the bridges. On this trail you can visit all three bridges or just two as this trail intersects with the individual trails for each bridge and leads back to the parking area. The Loop Trail is 8.6 miles and involves some bushwhacking, so this is an all-day effort. Start early to avoid the heat of the day, and if there have been recent rains, you may be pleasantly surprised to find small waterfalls and pools along the way.

THINGS TO SEE:

The bridges, of course, but also consider ruins in the area. Along with the Horse Collar Ruins, there are other sites with Ancestral Puebloan pictographs and historic and protected structures, dating back thousands of years.

This is canyon country, and these dominant landscape features can be appreciated at Hovenweep National Monument, Canyonlands National Park, Arches National Park, Capitol Reef National Park, and Grand Staircase-Escalante National Monument, among other places. One could easily spend weeks exploring the public lands of southern Utah.

Much of the soil in this area is a fragile cryptobiotic crust made up of fungi, lichens, algae, and bacteria. This "living soil" contributes to the local ecology by fixing both nitrogen and carbon for use by plants. Typically found in more arid regions of the world and in places where plant cover is limited and widely space, cryptobiotic soil also contributes to soil stability. This crust is easily damaged and can take many years to recover. Be mindful of where you step and stay on marked trails.

Something you won't see here is light pollution. The monument is designated as an International Dark Sky Place. You can fully appreciate the night sky overhead, often seeing the Milky Way and beautiful star formations, or even a meteor shower such as the predictable Perseids Meteor. The Perseids routinely show up from mid-July through the third week of August annually and peak on August 12 or 13.

GETTING THERE:

From Blanding, UT, take UT Highway 95 for 34 miles to the junction with Natural Bridges National Park Road. Drive another 4 miles to the monument entrance.

From Hanksville, UT, drive 90 miles south on UT Highway 95 to the Natural Bridges National Park Road, turn left, and continue for another 4 miles.

Mule deer after a heavy snowfall, browsing for food.

Driving south on UT State Highway 261 from the monument you'll be faced with this descent into Monument Valley, Arizona.

FACILITIES:

This remote monument has no services nearby, so an overnight trip takes some planning. The closest town of note is Blanding, about 40 miles to the east. Cell phone service is not available within the monument.

Camping within the monument is at a first-come, first-served, thirteen-site campground that accommodates vehicles up to 26 feet. The campsites have a table, fire grill, and tent pad but no electricity or hookups. There are vault toilets, and water is available year-round at the visitor center. There is also dispersed primitive camping in the surrounding BLM lands.

Heading south from the monument on UT 261, a good place to stop is Goosenecks State Park, about 30 miles away. Here you can view a unique double bend of the San Juan River as it flows toward the Colorado River and, ultimately, the Grand Canyon. Primitive camping is available here with vault toilets but no water or electricity. The views are incredible, especially on a clear night.

Nearby Blanding, population 3,670, offers several options for lodging and dining.

Also, there is an International Balloon Festival in January in Bluff.

24. Rainbow Bridge
National Monument

NEAREST TOWN:	Page, AZ
SIZE:	160 acres
BEST SEASON(S):	Winter, but open year-round
NOTABLE ACTIVITIES:	Hiking, birding, wildlife and plant viewing, photography, geology, astronomy, solitude, mountain biking, Navajo culture

THE MONUMENT:

President Taft designated Rainbow Bridge National Monument on May 30, 1910, to protect the long-standing cultural value of this geological feature. It had not likely been seen by colonial settlers until the 1909 expedition led by Byron Cummings and William Douglass. Without their Paiute guides, Nasja Begay and Jim Mike, it's doubtful they would have been able to find this remarkable feature. Rising 290 feet above its namesake creek and spanning 275 feet, it's one of the largest natural bridges in the world. The immensity of the bridge dwarfs the size of the monument, a mere 160 square acres.

The massive Rainbow Bridge is one of the world's largest known natural bridges.

The white-tailed antelope squirrel, whose home range can be as large as fifteen acres, feeds primarily on vegetation, although it will eat lizards and rodents.

Horseshoe Bend, just south of Page, Arizona—this bend in the Colorado River can show impressive colors under the right light.

The drainage over which the arch spans, Bridge Canyon, has long been used by Indigenous peoples, dating back 10,000 years. Some settled here, growing crops and establishing communities. Had it not been for the creation of Lake Powell, it's possible that most people would have remained unaware of its existence. With the creation of the Glen Canyon Dam and the rising waters of the Colorado River, Rainbow Bridge was under threat of being inundated, which led to a vocal outcry from the Diné (Navajo) to preserve this sacred site. The dam has been controversial since its inception, offending not only Indigenous people but those concerned for the environment and the loss of irreplaceable archaeological treasures as the canyons filled with water. Lake Powell has been called "the world's largest bathtub," and Western writer Edward Abbey has called it many names, most of which are unprintable.

At an altitude of 4,000 feet, this is another dry, high-altitude desert environment. Drinking sufficient water, even if you don't feel thirsty, is essential. There are over 750 different species of plants within the Lake Powell region. This is remarkable given the poor quality of the soil and paucity of rainfall, less than seven inches annually. Wildlife, while present, may not be seen during a typical day tour as most desert creatures prefer to avoid the heat. Regardless, desert bighorn sheep, coyotes, black-tailed jackrabbits, and mule deer all manage to eke out a living here. Roadrunners, bald eagles, peregrine falcons, and northern harriers are among the sixty-two species of birds that have been seen here, either as permanent residents or, more likely, passing migrants.

Moonrise at sunset over a sandstone formation in Lake Powell.

A black-tailed jackrabbit, also known as the American desert hare, is common to this region.

THINGS TO DO:

As noted, this is a small monument, and much of it remains protected to respect Indigenous peoples. Hike the mile or so from the boat and simply gaze at this awesome site. Consider why this site is sacred to Indigenous peoples and think about the geological forces that shaped this feature.

Another option for getting to the monument involves a cross-country hike of up to 17 miles. Permission is required from the Navajo Nation as the route is entirely on their land, beginning near Navajo Mountain. Note that this is not an easy trek and involves route-finding with a topographic map and compass as well as traveling through several canyons. The trail is not marked except for an occasional cairn, which can be washed away during floods. Add to this the extreme weather and minimal water sources in the off-season and you have all the ingredients for a disaster if you fail to prepare properly.

THINGS TO SEE:

The bridge, of course! Nearly all of the 100,000 annual visitors arrive by a scenic 52-mile, five-hour boat ride. Most of the boats offer a topside viewing deck with seating. Tour operators allow visitors about 90 minutes to hike to the bridge and back. The boat ride offers many opportunities for photography of the sandstone scenery, much of which was long-ago swallowed by the Glen Canyon Dam.

Just a few miles south of mile markers 544 and 545, you can access the parking area for Horseshoe Bend on the west side. This is an impressive

The boat ride in from the Lake Powell Marina can provide some interesting photography if you remain aware.

"incised meander" of the Colorado River where it has cut through 1,000 feet of sandstone. The site is open daily from sunrise to sunset.

Another unique attraction is the sandstone slot canyons that exist here. Many are open to the public via concessions authorized by the Navajo Nation.

GETTING THERE:
Page, AZ, is your destination by vehicle. You'll need to enter Glen Canyon National Recreation Area to board the boat, however.

Page is located on the AZ/UT border and can be accessed from the west through Fredonia, AZ, on US Highway ALT 89, a scenic 115.0-mile drive east and north.

From Flagstaff to the south, take US Highway 89 north for 142.0 miles.

FACILITIES:
There are no facilities within the monument, so you must bring anything you wish to eat or drink during the boat tour and at the monument. Some tour operators provide snacks and beverages, and there are toilets at the dock by the monument.

USEFUL CONTACTS:

Rainbow Bridge National Monument
c/o Glen Canyon National Recreation Area
691 Scenic View Drive
Page, AZ 86040
928-608-6200
nps.gov/robr

Navajo Nation Parks and Recreation Department
navajonationparks.org

25. Grand Staircase–Escalante National Monument

NEAREST TOWN:	Escalante, UT
SIZE:	Presently 1,003,863 acres
BEST SEASON(S):	Year-round, weather permitting
NOTABLE ACTIVITIES:	Archaeological site viewing, hiking, birding, wildlife and plant viewing, photography, unique geology, astronomy, solitude, mountain biking

THE MONUMENT:

Grand Staircase–Escalante National Monument was established on September 18, 1996, by President Bill Clinton. It was the first monument designated on BLM lands, and the last area of the continental United States to be mapped. This is a large and remote monument, comprising over one million acres of landscape dominated by vast plateaus, endless multicolored cliffs, rock formations, and deeply cut canyons.

As with Bears Ears, this monument was also temporarily reduced in size on December 4, 2017, by President Trump. This 47 percent reduction has been challenged in court by different user groups and is under legal review.

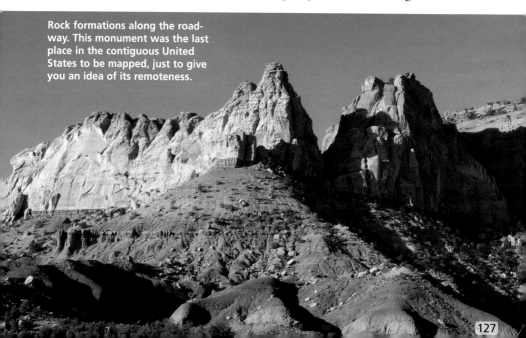

Rock formations along the roadway. This monument was the last place in the contiguous United States to be mapped, just to give you an idea of its remoteness.

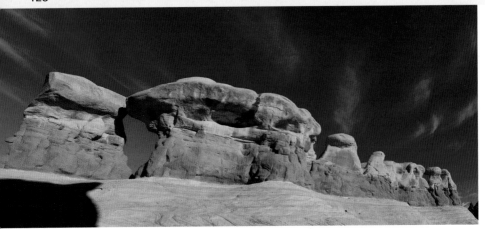

Hoodoos at Devils Garden, 13 miles down Hole in the Rock Road.

While there are several roads suitable for passenger cars, much of the monument can be accessed only via rough 4WD tracks or on foot. You must stay on existing roadways; no off-road driving is permitted by vehicles or bicycles. There are no services in the monument, nor is water available. Be prepared with a full tank of gas, good tires, a full-size spare, and plenty of food and water for everyone in your group. It is wise to plan what you would do if you had to spend the night out here. That said, there are several car trips that provide a sense of the monument and its geological history.

This is a high-altitude desert with summer temperatures exceeding 100 degrees. Winters are cooler with temperatures in the 40s and 50s and up to 26 inches of snow, which can make the roads impassable. Annual rainfall totals 10 inches, with most falling from July to October.

The monument's ecology ranges from low-lying desert shrub to high altitude coniferous forests. Wildlife corresponds to these different habitats; you can find bears, desert bighorn sheep, and, rarely, mountain lions as well as 200 different bird species including bald eagles and peregrine falcons. As always, most birds can be found along the riparian zones of the Paria and Escalante Rivers. Dinosaur fossils are common within the boundaries; 20 new species have been discovered here since 2000.

THINGS TO DO:

Stop at one of the four visitor centers located at Big Water to the south on US 89, Kanab to the southwest on US 89, Cannonville to the north on UT 12, or the Interagency Visitor Center in Escalante, also on UT 12. These centers provide you with current road conditions, weather forecasts, and ideas about how to maximize your visit.

There is a popular drive on a paved road, the Burr Trail Road, which heads generally east out of Boulder Town on UT 12. This leads to the border with Capitol Reef National Park at mile 31 where you can enjoy spectacular views of the park's Waterpocket Fold. This is a great late afternoon drive; time it so you arrive at the border of the monument just before sunset to enjoy the gorgeous colors the high desert is famous for. Along the way you'll pass through a 7-mile canyon with towering 400-foot cliffs of rust-colored sandstone. Dispersed camping can be found off the paved road on established dirt tracks or at Deer Creek Campground. If you're pressed for time, 11 miles down this road there is a small pullout on the north side where you can park. Look across the wash and find Long Canyon Slot, also known as "Singing Canyon." It is a 15-minute walk to the slot and a chance to explore this short, typical slot canyon.

The 45-mile Hell's Backbone Road connecting Boulder and Escalante offers expansive views and a look into the Box-Death Hollow Wilderness Area. Built by the Civilian Conservation Corps in 1933, this was the first road to connect the two communities. The Hell's Backbone Bridge is a good place to stop and take in the scenery.

Another common drive is the 57-mile Hole in the Rock Road #200. Starting about 5 miles east of Escalante, this road leads into the Glen Canyon Recreation Area to the road's namesake,

The 126-foot Lower Calf Creek Falls, an easy 6-mile roundtrip that follows the creek upstream.

Pictographs can be seen on the high cliff across Calf Creek as you hike toward the falls.

Desert Bighorn Sheep are difficult to spot as they occupy high, rocky terrain that's typically inaccessible for most people.

Dark-eyed juncos gather together in large flocks during the winter and often include sub-species such as this pink-sided junco.

A flowering prickly pear cactus, native only to the Americas.

Hole in the Rock. Named for a rock formation, the 180-mile route was the trail for the last major wagon train on the American frontier. It was built in 1879 by the San Juan Mission of Mormon pioneers so they could descend to the Colorado River and continue to the area of Bluff, Utah. Note that this road is a long way from anywhere and while it's a good gravel/dirt track, it can have a significant amount of washboard after the first 7 miles or so. Four-wheel drive is required for the last 7 miles.

THINGS TO SEE:
Drive a portion of the Cottonwood Road south of Cannonville to Kodachrome State Park and on to Grosvenor Arch for a half-day outing. The entire 46-mile road is suitable for passenger vehicles under dry conditions and leads to Highway 89 to the south or Highway 12, if you're traveling north. There is camping at each end of the drive, at Kodachrome State Park and at White House Campground.

Hole in the Rock Road brings you to two areas that contain aboveground slot canyons. When you cross the third cattle guard on this road, travel for 7.8 miles to a parking area on the west side of the road. The first slot canyon is Zebra Slot, named for its horizontal striping on the rock walls. There is a social trail here; after following it for about 2.0 miles you'll enter Harris Wash. Here you may lose the trail, but make a note of your surroundings and press on upstream (left) for about

0.25 mile. Zebra Canyon will be the first canyon on your right. If you feel you might have missed it, backtrack to the beginning of Harris Wash and try again. There are plenty of side canyons in Harris Wash so it's not uncommon for people to become confused. Once in the canyon feel free to explore as much as you wish, but keep an eye on the time and the weather.

At 13 miles down Hole in the Rock Road, you'll find the turnoff for the Devils Garden, a collection of sandstone hoodoos within 100 feet of the parking area. This is a great place for families as kids can run around and burn off some of that stuck-in-the-car energy. It's also a good opportunity for teaching about hoodoos and the layering of rock over time. While there are a number of these formations scattered around, the majority lie within an acre or two adjacent of the parking area. Sunset here is stunning as the light warms the already rust-colored tones of the sandstone. Try your hand at nighttime photography and a technique known as "painting with light," the use of artificial light to illuminate a subject at night.

You can drive 1.3 miles farther and turn right on Collet Top Road. Follow this road for 2.3 miles to a small wilderness area that contains dinosaur tracks embedded in the sandstone. Use caution at the wash crossing; it's better to walk the remaining distance than to get stuck. This is another good teaching opportunity for children or adults. The tracks can be found on the upper level of

Camping at Kodachrome Basin State Park is both quiet and picturesque, offering amenities such as showers and a seasonal laundry.

A Hoodoo at Devils Garden, photographed at night with a 10-second exposure and using a headlamp to "paint" the rock with light for a more balanced image.

the grey sandstone to the north. It takes a little searching and perseverance, but they are there! As many as 800 footprints have been located in this area. These are irreplaceable remnants of earth's history and should be treated with the utmost respect and care.

The second slot canyon area, Dry Fork Narrows, is accessed at 26 miles. Take the Dry Fork turnoff and continue for 1.7 miles to Dry Fork Wash. From here, hike downstream for about 100 yards of the Dry Fork Narrows to Peek-A-Boo Gulch; a 12-foot climb is required to enter the canyon. If that seems too daunting, consider Spooky Gulch, 0.5 mile farther downstream. It is more accessible than Peek-A-Boo but has its own challenges. The task here is to believe that you can squeeze through these narrows, in some places only about 10 inches wide! If you can manage the tight embrace of the canyon walls, you'll be able to go about halfway up the canyon before encountering the first of two mandatory climbs. For some this is a good turnaround point. Enjoy your visit but be mindful of human waste, a problem in this area. Use the facilities at Devils Garden as needed, as there are none in this area.

USEFUL CONTACTS:

Escalante Interagency Visitor Center
755 W. Main Street
Escalante, UT 84726
435-826-5499
blm.gov/visit
    /escalante-interagency-visitor-center

Grand Staircase–Escalante National Monument
745 E. Highway 89
Kanab, UT 84741
435-644-1300
blm.gov/programs
    /national-conservation-lands/utah
    /grand-staircase-escalante-national-monument

Grand Staircase Escalante Partners
gsenm.org

GETTING THERE:

Escalante, and its Interagency Visitor Center, should be a first stop for orientation and information on closures and road conditions.

From Pangulch on US Highway 89, drive 7 miles south to the junction with UT Highway 12. Drive an additional 59 miles to Escalante.

From Lao to the north drive, drive 16 miles on UT Highway 24 to the junction with UT Highway 12, then another 55 miles south to Escalante.

FACILITIES:

Aside from the small communities that surround the monument, there are no services within. It is essential that you bring what you may need in the event of an emergency or vehicle breakdown. Cell service is scattered to nonexistent.

Camping can be found at Deer Creek on Burr Trail Road in the northeast part of the monument. There are six sites here, vehicle size is restricted to 20 feet, and no trailers are allowed because there is no room to turn one around. However, there is a large pullout on the side of the road just before Deer Creek where trailers can be parked or turned around. There are no hookups or water but there is a vault toilet. Flash flooding is a risk here as the sites are close to the Deer Creek level.

Grosvenor Arch, a unique 150-foot double arch made up of sandstone that lies at the end of an easy, 0.25-mile paved trail.

Additional camping can be found off UT 12 at Calf Creek Recreation Area. This is a great choice if you plan to hike to Lower Calf Creek Falls. There are thirteen sites. None have electricity but water is available during the warmer months. Seven of the sites are across Calf Creek, which can easily be forded by a passenger car unless the water is high, in which case crossing by any vehicle should be avoided. You can also access these seven sites via a short walk on foot over a suspension bridge. Given the proximity of the campsites to the creek, caution should be exercised if there is a chance of rainfall and flash flooding.

There is a State Park Campground at Kodachrome Basin just south of Cannonville and Henrieville on the north side of the monument. Named for its colorful sandstone formations, it's a destination for many, especially photographers. It offers forty-seven sites for RVs up to 45 feet but has no hookups, although there is a dump station. There are year-round showers and a seasonal laundry.

Pick up a brochure at the Interagency Visitor Center in Escalante for information on outfitters, guides, and other services in the area.

26. Cedar Breaks National Monument

NEAREST TOWNS:	Brian Head and Parowan, UT
SIZE:	6,150 acres
BEST SEASON(S):	Year-round, weather permitting
NOTABLE ACTIVITIES:	Hiking, birding, wildlife and plant viewing, photography, geology, astronomy, solitude, mountain biking, cross-country skiing

A Bristlecone Pine along the rim of the amphitheater. These trees can live to 4,800 years of age and are capable of withstanding marginal soils and extreme weather.

THE MONUMENT:

Cedar Breaks is a natural amphitheater that sweeps for three miles from edge to edge. Over 2,000 feet deep, the rim sits at over 10,000 feet altitude, which provides a stunning setting for the iconic red and orange sandstone formations of the monument. The geology rivals Bryce Canyon National Park, but it is more compact and has fewer visitors given its remote location. Although its 6,150 acres may seem small compared to other monuments, its grandeur is impressive. The monument was declared by President Franklin D. Roosevelt on August 22, 1933.

Given its high altitude, it has four seasons and is snow-covered in winter, when access to the area is closed. Operating season is from late May to mid-October, with the weather determining the dates of closure. Summers are mild with highs in the low 60s and lows drop-

View looking westward across part of the amphitheater: pinnacles and walls of iron oxide–impregnated sandstone, formed by weathering and erosion, provide a magnificent display of color and form.

ping to the 40s. Winters are cold with temperatures, on average, staying in the 20s during the day and lower teens at night. Annual snowfall, which occurs in all months except July and August, amounts to 245 inches with an average depth of 27 inches. On one visit in late May, there was still snow on the ground. At this elevation it is important to take precautions against the high levels of UV light that can damage your skin.

The monument was formed by deposits of shale, limestone, and sandstone in Lake Claron about 60 million years ago. These layers were then uplifted and began the erosion process, which continues today at a rate of approximately two inches every five years. A volcanic rock, rhyolite tuff, covers much of the plateau, and originated from volcanic eruptions 28 million years ago. Deposits of iron and manganese create the vivid colors of the breaks, leading Southern Paiute peoples to name it "un-cap-i-un-ump" or "The Circle of Painted Cliffs." Iron oxides reveal themselves in red, orange, and yellow, while manganese oxides provide the various shades of purple. Early settlers called this topography, "badlands" or "breaks" and considered them an obstacle rather than beautiful scenery. The name "Cedar Break" is misleading because it originally referred to the trees that grow in this area, which are junipers.

Lightning, resulting from fast-moving storms that frequent high-altitude regions, is best avoided by being inside during these events.

THINGS TO DO:

Photography is a popular activity, day or night. The contrasting colors are eye candy for photographers, painters, or those who want to immerse themselves in this spectacle. If you wish to photograph the monument, don't overlook sunset, when the setting sun illuminates the hoodoos and other rock formations with a warm alpenglow. Scout a location earlier in the day and then go on a hike, have a picnic, or take a nap; just be back at your location before the sun sets. Stay 30 minutes after the sun has gone down and watch as the colors of the sky and rocks change. Often, some of the most remarkable light shows itself during this time. A tripod is necessary for the best possible photographs. When shooting the night sky, pay close attention to your surroundings as the cliffs can be abrupt and unforgiving. Carry a headlamp with spare batteries and a map, and let someone know where you'll be and when to expect you back.

During the winter months when UT 148 is closed, you can access the monument via skis, snowshoes, or snow machine. There is a warming hut open to the public on the weekends in January and February. Rangers are present in the Winter Warming Yurt, which does double duty as a winter ranger station. The winter parking area is at the junction of UT 143 and UT 148, about 3 miles south of Brian Head. It's a 1-mile ski, snowshoe, or snow machine ride from there to the yurt. You can rent gear in nearby Brian Head. Ranger-led snowshoe walks on Saturdays in January and February allow you to go with an experienced ranger if you're uncomfortable solo. Some feel winter is the best time to visit with the brilliant colors of the rocks highlighted by a blanket of white snow and a blue sky. There is also skiing at nearby Brian Head Resort. With 650 acres, 71 runs, three terrain parks, eight lifts, and over 360 inches of snow annually at 9,600 feet, you're sure to find something worth making turns on.

A 17-minute photo exposure over the amphitheater at night creates star trails across the southwestern sky.

There are several hiking trails within the monument that are easy, although altitude should be factored in. A short, level walk at sea level becomes noticeably more difficult for many people at 10,000 feet.

The 2-mile round-trip Sunset Trail, on a paved and accessible track, leaves the Campground Trail, goes past the Point Supreme picnic area, and ends at Sunset Overlook. Here you'll enjoy spectacular sunset views with minimal effort.

The 2-mile Alpine Pond Trail is a win-win. You'll see striking views of the breaks in one direction and on the return, wander through a spruce-fir-aspen forest and alongside meadows of colorful wildflowers. The pond is fed from a natural spring, which fills what was originally a sinkhole.

For the more adventurous or those seeking more solitude, the Rattle-snake Creek Trail is a round-trip 9.8-mile trail that drops 2,500 feet in 4 miles, plunging into the drainage of Ashdown Creek, within the boundaries of Ashdown Gorge Wilderness. Choose to go upstream into Cedar Breaks or downstream to the 7-mile marker on UT 14. For this trail you should be competent with map and compass, self-sufficient, ready to get wet, and mindful of the private property tracts along the route. Flash floods are a definite hazard here.

Monument staff offer activities for visitors. There are discussions of the origins of Cedar Breaks, a laser guided tour of the night sky, an annual Wildflower Festival and the Plein Air Festival, both in July. The latter festival features artists who paint outdoors and make their work available for

Possibly a female plateau fence lizard heading for shelter to enjoy her midday meal.

sale to the public at the Southern Utah Museum of Art. Cedar Breaks is one of several notable sites that participate in the event, drawing attention to the uniqueness of America's public lands.

THINGS TO SEE:

The visitor center is worthwhile to appreciate the architecture of the log cabin structure. Built by the Civilian Conservation Corps in 1927, it rests on the threshold of Point Supreme, seeming to hang on the edge as if suspended in air. It is now on the National Register of Historic Places, despite being threatened with destruction in the 1970s.

The wildflowers here during the summer months are outstanding for their brilliant colors and variety. The alpine meadows host Colorado columbine, bluebell, fireweed, Parry primrose, and subalpine larkspur. Bristlecone pine trees also make this area their home and can be found on walks around the area.

USEFUL CONTACTS:

Cedar Breaks
National Monument
2390 West Highway 56
Suite #11
Cedar City, UT 84720
435-986-7120

nps.gov/cebr

utah.com/cedar-city

GETTING THERE:

From Parowan, UT, on I-15, take UT Highway 143 approximately 15 miles south to the entrance, following the signage along the way.

FACILITIES:

The Point Supreme Campground is open when the monument is officially open. There are twenty-five sites available for tents and RVs, ten of which can be reserved at recreation.gov while the others are first-come, first-served. The restrooms have showers, and water is available, although there is no dump station. There are also RV parks and campgrounds in nearby Brian Head and Cedar City as well as more conventional lodging.

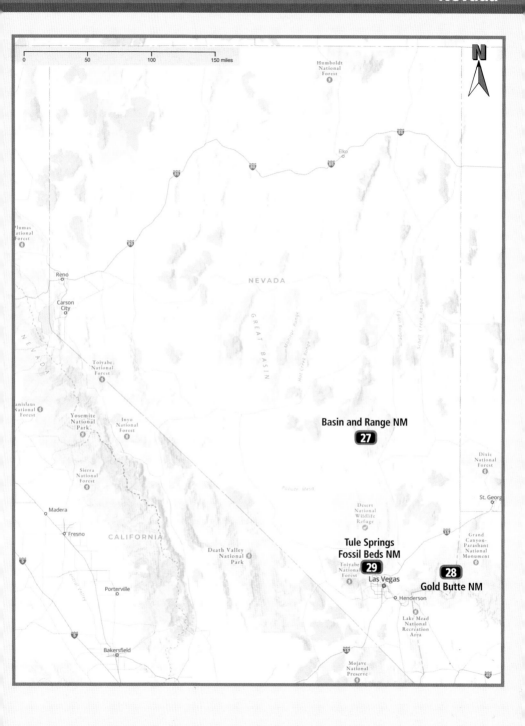

27. Basin and Range
National Monument

NEAREST TOWNS:	Ash Springs, Preston, and Warm Springs, NV
SIZE:	700,000 acres
BEST SEASON(S):	Year-round, weather permitting
NOTABLE ACTIVITIES:	Archaeological site viewing, hiking, birding, wildlife and plant viewing, photography, geology, astronomy, solitude, mountain biking

THE MONUMENT:

Basin and Range National Monument was designated on July 10, 2015, by President Barack Obama. Located about 93 miles north of Las Vegas on US 93 and NV 318, this 700,000-plus acre monument is a great place to take a break from the hustle and bustle of the big city. Paved roads around the borders of the monument allow you to take one or several days circumnavigating the area, adding forays into the monument for further exploration.

The weather is high desert and quite warm in the summer with little precipitation and temperatures in the upper 90s. Winter temperatures are in the 50s during the day and in the 20s at night, with occasional snow, especially at the higher altitudes. Annual precipitation is a meager nine and a half inches of rainfall. As with similar environments, the best times to visit are spring or fall when you can enjoy moderate temperatures both day and

This is a big, open place, leaving one with a sense of a world beyond human interference.

The creativity of the artist is shown here by selecting a natural feature from which to display their work.

A red-tailed hawk perched on an old fencepost, looking for prey.

night. You can see desert plants flowering in the spring when there has been enough rainfall.

THINGS TO DO:

Logan Canyon Road is an easy and accessible drive north of Alamo. Follow NV 318 north from Crystal Springs for 2.5 miles, just past a pullout for Nesbitt Lake on the east side of the highway. Look for an unmarked dirt road on the west side of NV 318 with a barbed wire gate, which you need to close after you pass through. Follow this gravel road for about 7 miles to the Archaeological District of the monument. Within the next 2.5 miles there are well-known petroglyph sites, some are marked and some aren't. This route crosses a few washes, so use good judgment if you're driving a passenger car or a 4WD vehicle if the road is wet. Walking is a better option than trying to get assistance and allows you to wander around to see what unmarked treasures you can find. This is a great place to let kids loose and challenge them to find as many petroglyphs as they can.

The Timber Mountain route heading west over Timber Mountain Pass has exceptional vistas. The unmarked turnoff is on NV 318 about 8 miles north of Crystal Springs and about 0.2 mile before the signs marking the boundary between Lincoln and Nye Counties. The well-maintained gravel/dirt road runs 23 miles west to a three-way intersection known as Water Gap. Here there are several options: Seaman Wash Road, which brings you back to NV 318, turns south here. Cherry Creek Road continues straight and offers options for traveling through the monument, exits to the west or the south. Signage is nearly nonexistent in the monument and there are confusing side roads, but you can use dead reckoning to identify key landmarks with a good topographic map. Following the most well-traveled road is a good guideline but not a guarantee. The road is suitable for 2WD vehicles unless it's wet, when some of the washes it runs across will be challenging. Whichever route you select, you won't be disappointed as the landscape is stunning, with north-south running mountain ranges separated by enormous basins. Hence the monument's name!

A pleasant drive from the south leaves from Rachel on NV 375, also known as the "Extraterrestrial Highway" for its ties to the infamous Area 51. Look for a gravel operation on the north side of the highway before reaching Rachel. Turn north here and follow the main road past an old homestead and up valley, trending to the east as you enter the monument.

THINGS TO SEE:

The broad and very open vistas of the West are well represented here as is solitude and quiet, especially if you've recently spent time in Las Vegas.

An attraction (not yet open as of spring 2021) is a work of earth art called "Heizer's City" just west of Water Gap on Timber Mountain Road within Garden Valley. This massive piece of artwork began in 1972 and will be the largest in the world once completed. The size approximates the National Mall in Washington, D.C., measuring 1.25 by 0.25 miles. Some of the structures reach as high as 80 feet, although much of the work is below ground level and not readily visible. Its estimated cost will exceed $25 million. The work is an effort to incorporate various ancient monuments, minimalism, and industrial technology. Some photos can be found on the Internet by photographers allowed to visit and document the progress. Note that Heizer's City is located on Michael Heizer's private land and trespassers are not welcome.

USEFUL CONTACTS:

Ely District (BLM)
Caliente Office
1400 Front Street
Caliente, NV 89008
775-726-8100
blm.gov/office
 /caliente-field-office

cityofcaliente.com

GETTING THERE:

Take I-15 north from Las Vegas to the junction with US Highway 93. Follow this and US Highway 318 north for about 95 miles to the unmarked Timber Mountain Road on the left, just 0.2 mile south of the Lincoln and Nye County line.

From Rachel on NV Highway 375 on the southern boundary of the monument, find the gravel operation and a

The massive "City," an earth art sculpture on private land in Garden Valley, is one of the largest sculptures ever created. Created by Michael Heizer, its opening is delayed indefinitely as of this writing.

dirt road that leads north up the valley. Take this road and head east to eventually connect with NV Highway 318.

FACILITIES:

There are no facilities within the monument, limited cell service, and no fuel. Dispersed camping is allowed, but you should use previously established sites and do not drive anywhere off the main roadways. There is camping at the Pahranagat National Wildlife Refuge about 3 miles south of Alamo. There are sixteen sites, many of which are suitable for small to medium-sized RVs. There are neither hookups nor water, but there are well-spaced vault toilets. The real draw here is that the sites, including the picnic areas, are located along the shore of the lake with great views. There are a number of birds here, with the season determining which species are present.

The Silver State OHV trail system located off NV 318 about 17 miles north of the junction of US 93 and NV 318 on the east side of the road also has undeveloped camping.

Alamo has fuel, lodging, and limited restaurant options. There is also a well-stocked general store at the Sinclair Station. Rachel, a small community on NV 375 along the monument's southern border has a quaint little diner but no fuel or lodging.

28. Gold Butte
National Monument

NEAREST TOWN:	Mesquite, NV
SIZE:	300,000 acres
BEST SEASON(S):	Year-round
NOTABLE ACTIVITIES:	Archaeological site viewing, hiking, birding, wildlife and plant viewing, photography, geology, astronomy, solitude, mountain biking, 4WD trails

THE MONUMENT:

Founded by President Barack Obama on December 28, 2016, Gold Butte National Monument totals nearly 300,000 acres of wild and remote western landscape, within a three-hour drive of Las Vegas. Once you've had your fill of the bright lights and big city, head to Gold Butte for an alternative Western American experience.

The Lime Canyon Wilderness Area and the Jumbo Springs Wilderness Area both offer unmatched solitude for those who are properly prepared to hike in and explore; however, these areas have additional protections and don't allow mechanized travel.

A lone Joshua Tree stands atop a tall hill overlooking a vast landscape of valleys and peaks reaching to 5,013 feet.

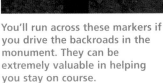

You'll run across these markers if you drive the backroads in the monument. They can be extremely valuable in helping you stay on course.

The silhouette of a J-Tree at sunset. It's hard to imagine that Las Vegas is just a couple hours away to the west.

This is a dry and hot region with summer highs over 100 degrees, cooling off to the upper 70s at night. Winters are more welcoming, with highs in the 60s and 70s and nighttime lows in the 30s. Precipitation averages nine inches annually with no recorded snowfall.

THINGS TO DO:

There is no visitor center in this monument. The best first stop is the Interagency Visitor Center in St. George about 40 miles to the east on I-15.

A popular drive is to Gold Butte, the monument's namesake. It's approximately 20.0 miles on a rough but decent gravel road. At its peak in the early 1900s, this mining town had a population of 2,000 and a post office. By 1909, the town site was abandoned; little is left of it today. The drive is a National Backcountry Byway with stops along the way noted by markers and GPS posts. The first part of the drive from Mesquite is on a paved road that deteriorates to rough exposed aggregate and finally to gravel at Whitney Pockets. This is a good turnaround if you don't wish to go farther, but it's also a great place to explore. The Whitney Pockets are a group of contrasting red- and light-colored sandstone formations that hide an old Civilian Conservation Corps–constructed dam back in the recesses of the rocks.

If your vehicle is capable or if you wish to hike or bike, a jeep trail begins 0.2 mile north of the First Rock Camp to a site of petroglyphs. From the turnoff, it's about 2 miles to the petroglyph area. This outing is great way to experience the area, so pack a lunch and take your time exploring the crags.

Phainopepla, a silky flycatcher with striking red eyes against a pure black head. White wing patches are visible while in flight.

A trio of burros, likely left here after miners abandoned the area. Apparently, the habitat suits them as they've not only survived but propagated widely as well.

Diamond Peak, one of the higher peaks in the monument, at sunset.

The Whitney Pockets Overlook Trail is another area hike that is a bit longer. It begins at the First Rock Camp area and heads 3.2 miles across the desert and onto a ridge that affords excellent views of the Pocket to the east. You'll pass Indigenous peoples' dwellings, the original residents and caretakers of this land, as well as petroglyphs along the way.

There is no end of Jeep trails throughout the monument. A search for "jeep tours" in Mesquite, NV; St. George, UT; or Gold Butte National Monument should get you in touch with folks who are knowledgeable about these activities.

THINGS TO SEE:

The monument exhibits the wide-open expanse quintessential to the American West: grand vistas, clear skies, and few people. The area is part of the Mojave Desert Scrub, a mix of plants that flourish despite harsh conditions such as the creosote bush and Joshua tree. There are also many species of yucca, including the Utah agave, which when grouped together send up a long, slender stalk of flowers in the spring that attract birds and flying insects, after which the individual plant dies.

Devil's Throat, a large sinkhole 100 feet across by 125 feet deep, is a popular and accessible landmark. It's fenced to keep the unwary from venturing too close to the unstable edge of the sink. Devil's Throat is about 7 miles down the main roadway from Whitney Pocket and then another 0.25 mile west to the site. There is ample parking and a short walk to the fence. The sink was formed by either limestone or gypsum pockets that were dissolved by underground water, causing the overlying alluvium layer to collapse.

Little Finland, named for the sandstone rock formations of the area, requires good judgment and a capable 4WD vehicle. Mud Wash North Road is one route to this area. It starts about 4 miles from Whitney Pocket and follows Mud Wash downstream for 5 miles. Do not attempt this route in the rainy season as you could find yourself stuck in mud or wet, loose river gravel. Even when dry, the loose river gravel and sand that collects along the wash can bring your forward progress to an abrupt halt. This road joins the Mud Wash Road after about 3 miles. An alternative approach is to take Mud Wash Road northwest from near Devil's Throat and enter the wash in about 3 miles. From here, conditions allowing, you can hike or drive about 2 miles to the red sandstone formations. Take some time to explore this area. The best time for photography is from mid-afternoon until sunset, as the formations face mostly west. There is an area of petroglyphs along the red sandstone walls in the wash as you drive in and a USGS survey marker.

GETTING THERE:

While there are several rough and lengthy approaches from the east, most

One of many unique sandstone formations in Little Finland.

The Falling Man petroglyph suggests an unfortunate outcome for a man climbing on the cliffs above.

Little Finland, a modest-sized area of weathered red sandstone, at the end of the drive along Mud Wash streambed.

visitors opt for the more convenient access right off I-15 at Exit 112. This is commonly known as the "Backcountry Byway," and heads south for about 40 miles. From Exit 112, drive to Riverside and head south on Gold Butte Road into the monument.

FACILITIES:

There are no services within the boundaries of the monument and no cell phone service. You must be self-sufficient and carry enough food and water for your group. If your vehicle breaks down on the main route, it's likely that someone will come by eventually to assist you. If you're on a side road the chance for meeting someone else decreases. As always, be prepared to spend the night out.

Camping is dispersed throughout the monument, but you must use existing sites and campfires; charcoal fires are not allowed. There is another campground off I-15 just west of Mesquite at the Virgin River Recreation Area. It has seventy-seven sites that can accommodate pull-through RVs and tents. There is water but no hookups or showers. Although it is a short distance from the Interstate, you can hardly hear the traffic, which drops off after dark.

The closest town with services is Mesquite. It has lodging, restaurants, food, and fuel.

USEFUL CONTACTS:

Gold Butte National Monument
blm.gov/programs
  /national-conservation-lands
  /nevada/gold-butte

visitmesquite.com

29. Tule Springs Fossil Beds
National Monument

NEAREST TOWN:	Las Vegas, NV
SIZE:	22,650 acres
BEST SEASON(S):	Year-round
NOTABLE ACTIVITIES:	Fossil viewing, hiking, birding, wildlife and plant viewing, photography, geology

THE MONUMENT:

Currently administered by the National Park Service, the monument was established on December 19, 2014, by President Barack Obama to protect significant paleontological artifacts and fossils dating back to the Ice Age. Protection for many parts of the monument was overdue with encroachment by off-road vehicles, particularly along the southern boundary, which also borders the expanding suburbs of northern Las Vegas. At 22,650 acres it's not a large monument, but it has a long history of paleontological research and exploration. This is one of few monuments not established solely by Executive Order. Both houses of Congress passed legislation in support of

Looking across the monument toward the Desert National Wildlife Refuge (DNWR) area. This is a great place to let the kids go exploring.

The high peaks of the DNWR, accessed by a rough dirt/gravel road, offer a through-route to US Highway 95, a pleasant way to escape the desert heat for a few days.

protecting the natural resources of this area. Much of the awareness and support came from local organizations that recognized the monument's value.

Weather here is typical of the high desert, hot and dry summers with cool and dry winters. June through August temperatures can exceed 100 degrees, while in mid-winter they can be in the upper 60s with nighttime lows in the 40s. Precipitation is limited to just over four inches per year. Elevation ranges from 2,200 feet to over 9,000 feet at the top of Hayward Peak. This vast difference results in a wide range of plant and animal species that thrive at different elevations. It also provides an escape from the sweltering temperatures of the lower area during the hot summer months.

A major archaeological dig occurred here in 1962. The "Big Dig," led by C. Vance Haynes, Jr., searched for evidence that man existed alongside the exotic creatures of the Ice Age. No such evidence was found, and the site was largely abandoned in 1963 after 200,000 tons of earth had been moved. There is still evidence of this excavation, such as large trenches up to a kilometer in length, but the Dig's efforts produced thousands of fossils dating back 7,500 to 250,000 years. Species found from the Pleistocene era (the Ice Age) include Columbian mammoths, bison, American lions, horses, and camelops. This area was a large, moist riparian ecosystem when these creatures existed, unlike the harsh desert landscape of today. There is still ongoing archaeological research. Visits to these sites may be arranged through the Protectors of Tule Springs, a local advocacy group.

In addition to numerous desert animals and reptiles, the monument holds several patches of the rare Las Vegas bear poppy, *arctomecon californica*. This plant has blue-gray leaves and produces a stalk up to 20 feet, the end of which displays the yellow flowers that typically bloom from March to May, water dependent. It is a protected species and is under consideration for additional protection under the Endangered Species Act. The usual desert wildlife shows up here, typically at night when it's cooler. You might find tracks of the kangaroo rat, the uncommon desert tortoise, lizards, and bird species that are year-round residents, such as northern mockingbirds, sharp-shined hawks, or house finches. Nearby Corn Creek, at the Desert National Wildlife Refuge Visitor Center, may be the best location for bird-watching in southern Nevada.

The one challenge is the lack of facilities or development, even within the strict guidelines of the National Park Service. There are no trails and virtually no signage. There is no visitor center, and finding entry to the monument can be challenging. Popular access points are at the T intersection of Durango Drive and Moccasin Road from the southern end, or off Corn Creek Road to the north. The benefit of taking the latter approach is that it's also the entrance point for the Desert National Wildlife Refuge, the largest in the lower forty-eight states. The Refuge is primarily focused on protecting desert bighorn sheep and their habitat.

THINGS TO DO:

Stop at the Desert National Wildlife Refuge Visitor Center north of town and east of US 95 north to get information on the monument and the Refuge.

Hike around on your own with the time you have available. The proximity to the hustle and bustle of Las Vegas makes this a welcome and quiet reprieve from that busyness.

A variety of cacti can be found on the northern side of the monument. They often have a symbiotic relationship with other plants, such as the mesquite found here at the base of this cactus.

THINGS TO SEE:

Fossils abound and can be seen by walking around, especially in the exposed mud formations of the monument to the south. It takes some effort and time to spot them. If you have kids who are budding paleontologists or rock hounds, this is a good place to let them out for a few hours to explore.

Desert bighorn sheep, the primary focus of protection in the DNWR.

GETTING THERE:

To access the southern portion of the North Unit, exit US Highway 95 at Kyle Canyon Road. Stay on the eastern frontage road, North Sky Pointe Drive, and go north, curving east onto West Moccasin Road for about 3 miles to the junction with North Durango Drive. A parking area will be on your left (north).

To go to the North Unit directly, drive north on US Highway 95 for about 15 miles, turn right onto Corn Creek Road, and drive another 5 miles to the visitor center for the Desert National Wildlife Refuge.

FACILITIES:

There are no facilities within the monument, but the monument's location at the northern edge of Las Vegas means there is no end of dining and lodging options as well as entertainment choices.

There is a campground on Mormon Well Road within the Refuge just north of the main area of the monument. It has an excellent visitor center where you can get information on road conditions, wildlife viewing, and weather updates.

The Refuge allows camping, but the drive to the camping area is over roughly 15 miles of an irregular dirt and rock road. There are also dispersed sites along the way.

USEFUL CONTACTS:

Tule Springs Fossil Beds National Monument
601 Nevada Way
Boulder City, NV 89005
702-293-8853
nps.gov/tusk

protectorsoftulesprings.org

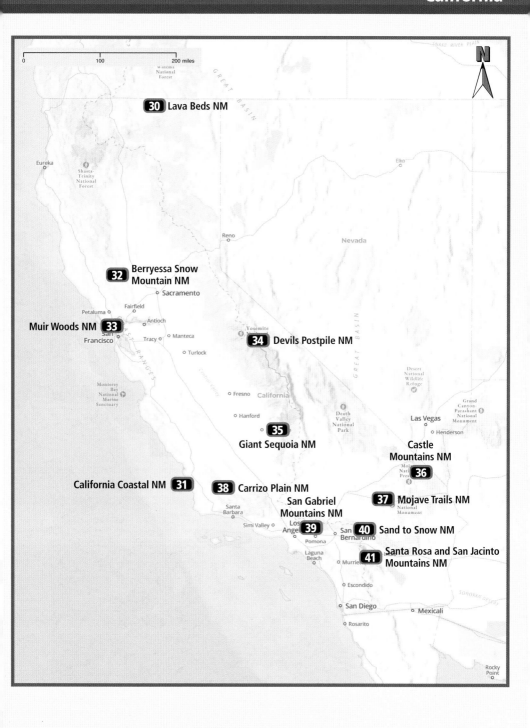

30. Lava Beds National Monument

NEAREST TOWN:	Tulelake, CA
SIZE:	46,000 acres
BEST SEASON(S):	Year-round
NOTABLE ACTIVITIES:	Hiking, birding, wildlife and plant viewing, photography, unique geology, astronomy

THE MONUMENT:

Located in north-central California east of the Cascade Mountain Range, Lava Beds was officially designated a national monument on November 21, 1929, by President Calvin Coolidge. It consists of more than 46,000 acres and represents the largest total area covered by a volcano in the Cascade Range. Within this landscape lies a textbook catalog of volcanic formations such as lava tube caves, fumaroles, cinder cones, spatter cones, pit craters, hornitos, maars, lava flows, and volcanic fields. A series of small earthquakes in 1988 attest to the ongoing underground activity in this region. Much of these

A Lava Cave, more of a lava tube that's been exposed to the outside, offers an opportunity for exploration, once you've checked with the visitor center to see which are open and the precautions you need to take.

A rainbow forms over the extensive lava flows of the monument.

formations and activity originate in the nearby Medicine Lake Volcano, southwest of the monument.

Being a semi-arid, high-altitude desert environment, the monument receives 14.8 inches of annual precipitation, including 44 feet of snowfall, which can close local roads temporarily. Call (530) 667-8113 for current road conditions. Average temperatures range from 31.5 degrees in December to 68 degrees in the summer months, with highs of up to 90 degrees.

THINGS TO DO:

There are numerous caves throughout the monument, over 700 at last count, two dozen of which have developed entrances and trails. The Cave Loop Road allows you to drive close to the entrance of a few caves just south of the visitor center. Entering these caves require a permit from the visitor center where the staff will also sanitize your shoes if necessary. Any clothing or equipment used in other caves in the United States, Canada, or Europe must also be cleaned or not brought into the caves. The presence of white-nose syndrome requires this extra precaution. White-nose syndrome is spread to bats by a fungus and is fatal. Taking a few preventative steps before visiting these caves will help protect fragile bat populations.

Nearby Tule Lake National Wildlife Refuge is a major wintering area for a host of waterfowl and worth a visit. Many bald eagles spend the winter here. It's not unusual to spot forty or fifty of these birds spread out across the frozen waters. Wildlife species found within the monument include the American pika, mule deer, rock wrens, California quails, and several migratory bird species.

Petroglyphs at the nearby Petroglyph Point, a protected and sacred site for those of Modoc-Klamath heritage.

Alpenglow on Mount Shasta, 14,180 feet, from the Indian Well Campground. This is a popular volcano for mountaineers and is certainly skiable under the right conditions.

A Cooper's hawk, a very adept avian predator in this region.

THINGS TO SEE:

Nearby Petroglyph Point holds one of the largest panels of Native American rock art in the United States and is easily accessible from the roadside. It contains over 5,000 separate carvings, some dating back as far as 1,500 years. Most of these petroglyphs are a geometric style as opposed to the human and animal forms found in other locations. This entire area remains a sacred landscape for those of Modoc-Klamath heritage and as such, defacing these sites is not only disrespectful but illegal.

The hulking mass of nearby 14,179-foot Mount Shasta can often be seen, weather permitting, to the southwest of the monument. Mount Shasta is another example of the intense volcanic history of this area.

There are thirteen hiking trails that range from short and easy to long day hikes into the adjacent Black Lava Flow Wilderness Area. These trails provide a grand view of the monument, displaying the extensive nature of the lava flows and craters and cinder cones.

GETTING THERE:

From the town of Tulelake, follow the Volcanic Legacy Scenic Byway west for 4.0 miles to Hill Road. Turn left and continue to follow the scenic byway for another 18.6 miles, then turn left onto Road 10 to the visitor center.

FACILITIES:

The nearest towns are Tionesta and Tulelake, CA, and Merrill, OR, roughly 20 to

A A female yellow-rumped warbler, AKA "Butterbutt" for the prominent yellow patch at the base of its tail. **B** A trio of bald eagles, each of a different age based on their coloration, with the youngest, on the left, hiding a scrap of fish that he's bound to lose to the dark-colored adult bird about to land. **C** Male and female mule deer, a buck and a doe, joined together for the annual rut. **D** California quail, distinguished by the brown-colored crown, versus chestnut color of a Gambel's quail.

40 minutes from the monument. Merrill is likely your best bet for finding food, lodging, and fuel. Camping is available at Indian Well Campground, which has forty-three sites and can accommodate RVs up to 30 feet. Water and vault toilets are available. Additional dispersed camping can easily be found in the surrounding Modoc National Forest, particularly to the south. There are picnic and day-use areas at Fleener Chimneys and Captain Jack's Stronghold.

USEFUL CONTACTS:

Lava Beds
National Monument
P.O. Box 1240
Tulelake, CA 96134
530-667-8113

nps.gov/labe

visittulelakecalifornia.com

klamath.org/visitors

31. California Coastal National Monument

NEAREST TOWN:	Multiple
SIZE:	7,924 land-based acres
BEST SEASON(S):	Year-round
NOTABLE ACTIVITIES:	Hiking, birding, wildlife and plant viewing, photography, coastal geology, marine life viewing

THE MONUMENT:

Established on January 11, 2000, by President Bill Clinton, this is the longest monument, stretching over 1,100 miles along the entire California coast. It includes at least 20,000 islets, reefs, and rock outcroppings within its 13.8-mile seaside boundary. On March 11, 2014, President Obama added 1,665 acres of public land onshore at Point Arena, the Stornetta Public Lands Unit.

There are five regulated gateways to access the monument: Trinidad, Point Arena, Pigeon Point, Piedras Blancas-San Simeon, and Palos Verdes Peninsula. The nearby communities help manage the monument through local community groups, governments, conservation organizations, and concerned citizens. This is a unique collaboration within the BLM for managing its lands.

With ample winds from the Pacific Ocean and numerous bluffs from which to launch, the Pacific coast is a playground for hang gliders.

A pounding surf along with sea stacks that provide a protected site for numerous sea birds along the coast.

The Point Arena Lighthouse at the Point Arena-Stornetta unit, the only land-based portion of the monument where the public is allowed limited access.

The climate varies from the northern portion of the monument, where it can be cooler, to the mild temperatures of the southern coast. Eureka, in the north, has average year-round daytime highs in the upper 50s and lower 60s with nighttime lows in the 40s. This area also receives 40 inches of rain annually. June through September are the driest months. Morro Bay, to the south, has slightly warmer temperatures and receives half the amount of rain the north does. There is no snow along the coast.

THINGS TO DO:

Whale watching is a popular activity along the coastline. Tour outfitters can bring you close to these magnificent mammals, especially the common gray whales. These whales make an incredible 6,000-mile excursion from the icy waters of the Bering Sea, near Alaska, to their winter breeding and calving grounds in the temperate waters of Baja California, Mexico. This migration occurs from mid-December through mid-March. While a tour offers the best opportunity to see whales, it's not impossible to view them from the shoreline. The link in the "Useful Contacts" section identifies dozens of land-based sites where you can look for marine life and eight different areas that are popular for whale watching. Binoculars or a spotting scope are highly recommended. Other marine mammals that may be seen include orcas, humpback and blue whales, porpoises, and dolphins.

Elephant seals can be found at a popular pullout 1.5 miles south of Point Piedras Blancas or 5 miles north of San Simeon, which offers close-ups of the seals. They come here twice a year for breeding, birthing, and resting after eight to ten months in the open sea.

The black oystercatcher, distinguished from the American oystercatcher by its all-dark body, often feeds in small, noisy flocks along the beaches and mudflats.

Bull elephant seals battle with one another as the females largely ignore their displays near San Simeon.

THINGS TO SEE:

Given the monument's length, there is virtually no end to the number of unique experiences available. Starting at the Oregon border, US 101 heads south along the coast with fantastic opportunities to view giant redwoods alongside the grandeur of the Pacific Ocean. These massive trees, the largest in the world, can only exist in the unique ecosystem of the Pacific Coast. During dry summer months their needles can absorb up to 200 gallons of water from the ever-present fog, thus ensuring their survival through even the driest of years.

Turn onto CA 1 in Leggett to begin your journey south to the Mexico border. The highway hugs the Pacific Coast shoreline all the way to the bor-

The Western Gull is a common resident of the Pacific beaches.

der. Some areas restrict large RV travel for short distances. You'll traverse the bluffs high above the ocean on a narrow winding roadway and pass natural attractions along the way. One of the more interesting is the elephant seal haul-out near San Simeon, south of San Jose.

GETTING THERE:

Given that the monument runs along California's coastline, you can enter anywhere there is public

The waters here can be unforgiving, as evidenced by this vessel, washed up and aground along the beach.

A surfer at Patrick's Point State Park. The use of a long telephoto lens compresses the subject, making everything look close together.

access to the land-based portion of the monument. There are six regulated gateways into the monument.

Trinidad Head: Near Trinidad. Access is restricted, but this entry point is open the first Saturday of each month and for special events.

Point Arena: Adjacent to Point Arena. Open for day-use only. Motorized vehicles and hang-gliding are prohibited. Dogs must be leashed.

Fort Bragg–Mendocino: Located in Fort Bragg.

Pigeon Point: Five miles south of Pescadero. Lighthouse tours have been closed since December 2001 due to the deteriorating brickwork. A youth hostel and overnight lodging are available on-site as well as an outdoor hot tub.

Piedras Blancas–San Simeon: About 5.0 miles from San Simeon. Access to the light station grounds by guided tour only. Water activities such as kayaking and diving are allowed unless otherwise restricted. An elephant seal rookery is located 6.0 miles north of the Hearst Castle.

Palos Verdes Peninsula Gateways: Located in the South Bay region of southwestern Los Angeles County. Torrance borders the monument to the north.

FACILITIES:
There is no public camping within the monument. However, given that it parallels the California coastline from Oregon to Mexico, there is no short-

A fifteen-second exposure along with a small aperture, f32, gives the waves a fog-like appearance at sunset.

age of camping and other lodging facilities in the communities along the way. There are roughly thirty-five state and federal campgrounds within a short drive of the coast along the monument's 1,100-mile course. Some of these are open seasonally, while others are extremely popular and close to large urban centers, so plan ahead. See the "Useful Contacts" section for a list of all California state parks.

If you find yourself traveling through one of California's major cities, note that California permits motorcyclists to use lane sharing or lane splitting. This allows motorcycles to pass stationary or moving vehicles in the space between the vehicles, so look twice when changing lanes.

USEFUL CONTACTS:

California Coastal National Monument
Bureau of Land Management
940 2nd Ave.
Marina, CA 93933-6009
831-582-2200

blm.gov/programs/national
-conservation-lands/california
/california-coastal

visitcalifornia.com/in/feature
/8-top-places-whale-watching

elephantseal.org

parks.ca.gov

32. Berryessa Snow Mountain National Monument

NEAREST TOWNS:	Winters, St. Helena, and Hidden Valley Lake, CA
SIZE:	330,000 acres
BEST SEASON(S):	Year-round
NOTABLE ACTIVITIES:	Hiking, birding, wildlife and plant (lots of poppies) viewing, photography, geology, astronomy

THE MONUMENT:

Established on July 10, 2015, by President Barack Obama, these 330,000 acres have a diverse world of wildlife and plants well-suited to such a trying environment. The monument is jointly managed by the Bureau of Land Management and the US Forest Service. As a result, there is much private land interspersed within and around the monument boundaries, so take care to not cross onto private lands. The establishment of this monument was contentious; it took over ten years of effort by local groups working alongside other interests to create it. Compromises had to be made, so hunting is still allowed, as are historic water activities such as motorized boating and fishing and off-road vehicle recreation.

Tule elk at sunrise.

Looking over Berryessa Lake from a high point on the Blue Ridge Trail.

A waterfall along M10, about 3 miles from the Bear Creek Campground.

There are two wilderness areas within the monument, Cache Creek and Cedar Roughs. They can only be accessed by foot or on horseback.

The climate here is mild, although it can be quite warm in July and August with highs in the 90s and little precipitation. Winters are cool with daytime highs in the 50s and 60s and nighttime lows in the 30s. Most of the annual precipitation falls as rain from December through March, totaling 31 inches.

THINGS TO DO:

There is a BLM visitor center about 7.0 miles off CA 128 on Knoxville Road at the southern end of the lake that has limited information about the monument and the surrounding area.

If you're on the southern end of the monument near the Stebbins Cold Canyon Reserve, the 5.0-mile Blue Ridge Loop Trail is a must. The appropriately named mountains resemble the Blue Ridge Mountains of the eastern United States. To reach the trailhead, take CA 128 west. Before the dam, look for a hairpin turn and follow the signed trail into the Cold Creek drainage, where you'll see two large culverts that go under the highway. Go up through the one on the left and regain the trail as you exit. Don't enter this drainage when there is high water flowing, you can always come back another day. Starting at an elevation of 200 feet, the trail tops out at 1,535 feet. You can go in either direction but going counterclockwise provides a steep gain of 1,275 feet in just 1.75 miles. You'll be rewarded with views of the southern tip of Berryessa

An expansive view looking east from the top of M3 at mile 17, 6,300 feet in elevation.

Lake much sooner and have the option of retracing your steps downhill back to the car if you don't wish to go any farther. This part of the trail can be muddy, so if it's rained recently you may wish to consider another hike or heading clockwise on the loop. Poison oak is common here so be careful of the foliage you touch.

Another option is to hike 1.0 mile up the Homestead Trail from the same starting point, over moderately easy ground to the Vlahos Homestead. Here you can stroll around the remains of what used to be an active goat ranch and cheese farm in the 1930s. From here you can continue on the Blue Ridge Loop, reaching a high point of nearly 1,700 feet before returning to the parking area.

Other hiking opportunities in the southern area include Putah Creek (easy), Smittle Creek Trail (moderate), and Berryessa Peak Trail (hard). Stop at the visitor center for more specific information about these areas.

CA 20 from either Clear Lake on the west or Williams on the east provides access to Walker Ridge Road, a gravel/dirt road suitable for all passenger vehicles. Along the drive you may encounter great blue herons, American kestrels, and northern harriers. At the intersection with Bartlett Springs Road you can go west for 5 miles to Indian Valley Reservoir, but the downhill portion of this road after the four-way junction and 2 miles east of the reservoir is steep and one lane with only a few pullouts. Gorgeous views of the reservoir, fishing, and quiet camping reward those who choose this path. If you continue on this road it leads back to CA 20 near the northern shore of Clear Lake.

If you choose to return to Walker Ridge Road, continue to drive north up the valley, gaining the Lodoga-Stonyford Road after a few miles.

On the northern end you can choose from several US Forest Service roads that lead into the monument. Some are well traveled and maintained, while others are more rough. For example, US Forest Service Road 24N07 just west of Elk Creek on the east side of the monument is a bit steep in places. The descent on the west side is narrow and steep and has several areas that would become difficult to negotiate in wet conditions.

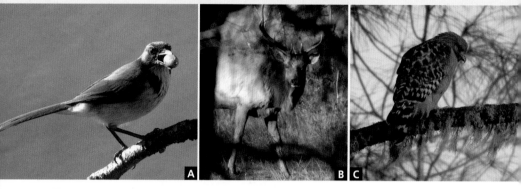

A A western scrub jay with the day's prize, a big, fat acorn. **B** A bull Tule elk peering through the bushes, always wary. **C** A red-shouldered hawk, *Buteo lineatus*, looking annoyed just before taking off to search for a meal.

Dispersed camping and campgrounds can be found along the way, and there is an excellent overlook at about mile 17 with grand views to the south. At about 35 miles, Lower Nye Dispersed Campground is a nice place to stop before heading back out to civilization.

Fishing and other water sports and activities are popular, especially on Berryessa Lake. You can find the California chinook salmon and Northern California steelhead in the monument's waterways. Whitewater kayaking is popular along Cache Creek in the southern portion of the monument. In spring, you can find vast fields of California poppies and Indian paintbrush. The serpentine soil, distinctive to this region, allows for growth of unique and specialized plants such as the adobe lily. A world-class off-road vehicle network lies adjacent to the monument and within the Mendocino National Forest. Fouts Springs within the Grindstone Ranger District is a gateway for further exploration of the area by ORV. There are even launch points for hang gliding alongside and within the monument.

THINGS TO SEE:

While Lake Berryessa is not an actual part of the monument, viewing it from a high point is undoubtedly a huge attraction for visitors. In addition to the Blue Ridge Loop Trail, there are numerous viewpoints and camp-grounds that offer this opportunity.

The medium-sized Tule elk, *Cervus canadensis nannodes*, can often be seen in the area around Pillsbury Lake in the northern portion of the monu-ment. At one point in the late 1800s they were thought to be extinct, so today's population of about 5,700 individuals across California represents a strong comeback for these large mammals. They can only be found in Cali-fornia and should not be mistaken for either the Roosevelt elk of the Pacific

Northwest or the Rocky Mountain elk of their namesake region. Adult males typically weigh 450 to 700 pounds while females range from 375 to 425 pounds and can stand four to five feet at the shoulder.

Other wildlife present in this unique and biologically rich region are the black-tailed deer, northern spotted owl, mountain lions, chinook salmon,

A 17-minute exposure at dusk over Indian Lake Reservoir.

and many different bird species including bald and golden eagles. Two old-growth forests within the monument support this wildlife diversity.

GETTING THERE:

Lake Berryessa Park Headquarters: On the west side of the lake.

BLM Field Office, Ukiah: On the southwestern side of Lake Berryessa, about 7.0 miles off CA 128.

The town of Winters: Winters, on the south end of the monument, will be the closest. Distances vary depending on your destination.

USEFUL CONTACTS:

Bureau of Land Management
Ukiah Field Office
2550 North State Street, Unit 2
Ukiah, CA 95482
707-468-4000

clearlakeincalifornia.com

visityolo.com

FACILITIES:

There are plenty of campgrounds within and near the monument. Some are managed by the BLM and US Forest Service while others are state-run or private. There is also dispersed camping within the monument at designated sites. Be mindful of private property though, as there are many inholdings, especially in the Lake Berryessa Recreation Area. A map from one of the visitor centers will help you avoid any confusion.

There are towns around and within the borders of the monument; most offer food, lodging, fuel, and tourist-style activities.

33. Muir Woods National Monument

NEAREST TOWN:	Tamalpais Valley, CA
SIZE:	554 acres
BEST SEASON(S):	Year-round
NOTABLE ACTIVITIES:	Hiking, birding, wildlife and plant viewing, photography, American natural history

THE MONUMENT:

Located alongside Mount Tamalpais and just 12 miles north of San Francisco, Muir Woods is a little gem amid a major metropolitan area. At 554 acres, it is relatively small compared to other monuments, but it provides sanctuary to one of the few remaining stands of old growth coastal redwood forest in the San Francisco area. Some 240 acres consist of these stately

An easy stroll through the redwood forest here is a peaceful respite from the surrounding metropolis of San Francisco.

giants of the littoral forests. Muir Woods is part of the Golden Gate National Recreation Area, which hosts a variety of activities and natural sites. The monument is open daily from 8 a.m. until sunset.

Designated a monument on January 9, 1908, by President Theodore Roosevelt, it originally consisted of just 295 acres of land donated by local philanthropist William Kent. He was adamant that the lands be named after John Muir, in recognition of Muir's tireless efforts to promote the cause of conservation. Kent is also known for introducing the bill to Congress in 1916 that established the National Park Service, when he was a Representative.

The climate of Muir Woods is generally cool and moist year-round. Rainfall, occurring primarily from November through March, amounts to as much as 47 inches in the higher elevations. Temperatures range from the upper 60s in the summer to the 50s during winter. It rarely freezes or snows. There is a considerable amount of humidity and fog throughout the year, which is critical for the redwoods as they obtain much of their water, as much as 200 gallons a day, by absorbing it from the air.

Given its proximity to San Francisco, accessing the monument with the Muir Woods shuttle service is the best option for most visitors. It's best to visit on a weekday rather than a weekend; as many as 6,000 people a day visit the monument during the peak season between April and October, of which 80 percent arrive by their own vehicle. It's also helpful to arrive before 9:30 a.m. or a couple of hours before closing, as most visitors arrive during late morning and through the afternoon.

RVs are allowed on Muir Woods Road, but they must be less than 17 feet long and 8 feet wide as the road is steep and winding. There is no parking for RVs or other over-sized private vehicles. Parking is limited, so you may have to park some distance from the entrance. There is no cell service within the monument.

THINGS TO DO:
The monument has 6 miles of trails. There are three loop trails within the forest that are roughly 30, 60, and 90 minutes in length, depending on your speed of travel. Each loop coincides with a bridge that crosses Redwood Creek, so returning to the entrance is quite easy. The first loop is 0.5 mile and takes you through the Bohemian and Founders Groves for a superb experience of the forest. The second loop, 1.0 mile, goes to Bridge 3 and passes the Cathedral Grove along the way. The last loop, out to Bridge 4 and back, is 2 miles round-trip and allows you to experience the majority of the monument on level ground. The first two loops are on boardwalk and

wheelchair accessible. To gain a higher view of the forest and be closer to the canopy, you can take the Hillside Trail at Bridge 2 and follow it to Bridge 4, or continue farther via the Ben Johnson Trail.

If you're looking for a longer hike, consider a connecting trail with one of the trails in the surrounding Mount Tamalpais State Park lands. Gaining the Ben Johnson Trail after Bridge 4 provides you with 4.0 miles of hiking, typically done in about three hours. This trail affords views of Mount Tamalpais, the Pacific Ocean, and San Francisco. Return via the Dipsea Trail Loop. For a more strenuous outing, consider heading for Stinson Beach via the Dipsea Trail. This trail winds for 10 miles out-and-back through the redwood forest, grasslands, and onto Stinson Beach.

Runners can participate in one of the Dipsea races held each year in June and November. The original 7.5-mile race, established in 1905, is the oldest cross-country trail running event in the United States. The course begins at Mill Valley and ends at Stinson Beach. It is popular: only 1,500 participants are allowed out of thousands of applicants.

If you wish to have your wedding within the monument, you must apply ahead of time for a permit. The same is true of commercial filming and other special events. Visit the National Park Service website, nps.gov, for more information.

If photography is your thing, a tripod is essential. The upper canopy produces considerable shade, preventing light from reaching the forest floor. A tripod allows for the longer shutter speeds necessary to create a good image. Be mindful of others and try to position yourself out of the way. Bracketing your shots can also be useful due to the different amounts of light present in a given composition. You can then combine them, using appropriate software, to produce a more balanced exposure.

USEFUL CONTACTS:

Muir Woods
National Monument
1 Muir Woods Road
Mill Valley, CA 94941
415-561-2850

nps.gov/muwo

parksconservancy.org/visit/tours
  /muir-woods-bus-tours

nps.gov/goga/planyourvisit/permits
  .htm (Golden Gate NRA)

THINGS TO SEE:

For many people, simply viewing the tallest living things on earth, the old-growth coastal redwoods, is enough. The trees can reach up to 250 feet in height and typically attain an age of 500 to 800 years.

The oldest tree in the monument is at least 1,200 years old.

Wildlife viewing is limited within the monument as most of its creatures are nocturnal. You may occasionally see deer and sometimes sea otters, but frequently the chatty western gray squirrel is the only wildlife seen. Spotted owls and pileated woodpeckers breed and nest within the monument, although they are rarely seen. Roughly 50 species of birds have been spotted here, less than one might expect given the setting. This is due to lack of food, primarily insects. The tannin in the redwoods acts as a repellant to the insects, and because of shade produced by the canopy, there is little chance for flowering plants to survive and provide habitat for insects.

Redwood Creek has been a critical corridor for spawning coho salmon, although their numbers have decreased significantly in recent years.

Redwood Creek, working its way through the monument, has long been a critical spawning stream for Coho salmon, although fewer and fewer make the trip each year.

GETTING THERE:

North of the Golden Gate Bridge, take US Highway 101, which turns into CA Highway 1. Drive along this narrow, twisting mountain road for approximately 8 miles to the entrance.

FACILITIES:

There is no camping within the monument, but there are camping opportunities in the surrounding Tamalpais State Park and the Golden Gate National Recreation Area. Reservations for either are encouraged due to the proximity to San Francisco and other popular attractions.

Tamalpais Valley is the nearest town with full services. San Francisco offers no end of lodging and dining opportunities in the surrounding area.

34. Devils Postpile
National Monument

NEAREST TOWN:	Mammoth Lakes, CA
SIZE:	798 acres
BEST SEASON(S):	Spring through fall; winter can have considerable avalanche hazard
NOTABLE ACTIVITIES:	Hiking, birding, wildlife and plant viewing, photography, geology, astronomy, cross-country skiing in winter

THE MONUMENT:

Established on July 6, 1911, by President William H. Taft, Devils Postpile is a small, 798-acre monument. It is enclosed within the boundaries of the Ansel Adams Wilderness and has portions of both the John Muir Trail and the Pacific Crest Trail. Its namesake columns of basalt were formed 100,000 years ago and resemble the rock at Devils Tower in Wyoming, although they are shorter and of a different origin.

A wide-angle view of the Postpile showing the pentagonal basalt columns.
Photo by Getty Images/iStock Photos

Given the heavy snowfall in this region, the monument is not open during winter. Its short season typically runs from mid-June until around mid-October when the winter snows close normal access. In 2017, the monument did not open until July 21, so it's best to check the website for the most up-to-date information. There is a mandatory Reds Meadow Shuttle Bus for all visitors unless you are backpacking into the mountains or camping in the campground. The shuttle bus can be accessed from the Mammoth Mountain Ski Area, near the Main Lodge, where there is also designated vehicle parking.

The weather here is typical of a high mountain environment with snowfall during a large portion of the year. Snowfall for nearby Mammoth Mountain Ski Area averages 20 feet at the Main Lodge (elevation 8,900 feet). The elevation of Devils Postpile is 7,500 feet. Winter temperatures can reach the low 40s during the day and fall to the teens at night. Summers are more pleasant with highs in the 70s and nighttime lows in the mid-40s.

The aptly named Rainbow Falls.
Photo by Getty Images/iStock Photos

THINGS TO DO:

Within the monument, there are roughly eight miles of trails offering a range of opportunities. The most common and easy 0.8-mile round-trip hike to the Postpile is popular and gives great views of the rock formation. It also takes you along the San Joaquin River and a peaceful meadow. You can continue on a 1.7-mile loop that includes going to the top of the Postpile, where you can see the rocks lying in per-

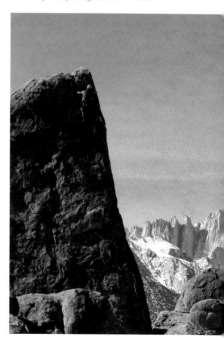

The author on Shark's Fin Arete, 5.7, in Alabama Hills south of the monument. The Mount Whitney massif is in the background.

Nearly horizontal layers of basalt columns that make up the Postpile. Photo by Getty Images/iStock Photos

The pentagonal-shaped tops of the Postpile. Photo by Getty Images/iStock Photos

fect formation just like floor tiles. You can even see the markings left by glaciers traveling over the tops of the rocks.

The somewhat lengthy but easy 2.6-mile loop to Minaret Falls is a pleasant outing suitable for the whole family. The Minaret Falls do not get the same attention as Rainbow Falls, so this trail is likely to have fewer people and more solitude. There's a good spot near the base of the falls for taking a break or enjoying a picnic with a wonderful view.

The John Muir and Pacific Crest Trails merge just as they enter the monument from the north. Either makes for the beginning of a memorable backpacking trip into the surrounding Ansel Adams Wilderness Area or a pleasant day hike to one of the high-altitude lakes nearby.

Dinosaur Falls Trail is a short hike between bus stops 7 and 10, which includes views of Sotcher Lake. It is approximately 1.5 miles one-way and rated easy and, as a bonus, offers a small waterfall.

THINGS TO SEE:

The columns of basalt are the most sought-after views here, although the 101-foot high Rainbow Falls is a close second. Rainbow Falls is a 2.5-mile hike one-way, and it is downhill, so remember the hike back is uphill. It can be warm and dry in the summer months so dress appropriately and bring and drink plenty of water.

To take full advantage of the short summer season, wildflowers, including shooting stars, tend to show their blooms in early June through early July. This is a good time to see Rainbow Falls in its glory as the snowmelt

The High Sierras in the Ansel Adams Wilderness, adjacent to the monument.
Photo by Getty Images/iStock Photos

from up high fills the Middle Fork of the San Joaquin River. There are over 450 species of native plants within the monument. The 0.5-mile self-guided Agnew Meadow Flower Walk is the best place to see wildflowers, depending on the season.

There are 115 species of birds within the monument including bald eagles, great horned owls, Rufous hummingbirds, and the dark-eyed junco. These birds can be found in the monument's montane meadows, wetlands, or coniferous forest. Mammals include black bear, mule deer, pine marten, and ever-present coyote.

Fall is a great time to be in this area as there are many groves of aspen and cottonwood changing colors. The weather can be unpredictable so be prepared for cold and possibly, snow.

USEFUL CONTACTS:

**Devils Postpile
National Monument**
P.O. Box 3999
Mammoth Lakes, CA 93546
760-934-2289
nps.gov/depo

**Eastern Sierra
Avalanche Center**
esavalanche.org

visitmammoth.com

bishopvisitor.com

The nearby Mono Lake is a critical stopover for millions of land birds and waterfowl due to its high salinity that supports trillions of tasty brine shrimp.

GETTING THERE:

From Mammoth Lakes, take CA Highway 203 /Minaret Road for approximately 20.0 miles to the entrance.

FACILITIES:

There is limited camping within the monument on a first-come, first-served basis. Given that July and August are busiest here, have an alternative plan during these times. Campers are exempt from the shuttle system. The overall length of your camping vehicle should not exceed 25 feet, both due to the size of the campsite as well as the two sharp turns needed to get to the campground.

The US Forest Service operates five nearby campgrounds within the Reds Meadow Valley. From north to south these are Upper Soda Springs, Pumice Flat, Pumice Flat Group, Minaret Falls, and Reds Meadow. Only the Pumice Flat Group CG may be reserved through recreation.gov. There is also dispersed camping throughout the Inyo National Forest and on nearby BLM lands. Obtain a map of these lands from the US Forest Service or the BLM to find a spot. Camping anywhere along the Owens River is prohibited, as it is owned by the City of Los Angeles.

Mammoth Lakes is nearby and offers food, fuel, lodging, and is a popular year-round tourist destination. Bishop, farther south, also has food, fuel, and lodging resources.

35. Giant Sequoia National Monument

NEAREST TOWNS:	Fresno, Visalia, and Porterville, CA, from the east, Bakersfield from the south
SIZE:	328,000 acres (both units)
BEST SEASON(S):	Year-round, with winter road closures possible
NOTABLE ACTIVITIES:	Hiking, birding, wildlife and plant viewing, photography

THE MONUMENT:

The big tree is Nature's forest masterpiece, and so far as I know, the greatest of living things. It belongs to an ancient stock . . . and has a strange air of other days about it; a thoroughbred look inherited from the long ago—the Auld Syne of Trees.

—John Muir

Established on April 15, 2000, by President Bill Clinton, this monument protects thirty-eight groves of giant sequoia trees, *Sequoiadendronden giganteum.* These trees are the largest living trees in the world, greater in wood volume than the enormous coastal redwoods. It's hard to imagine that

At 105 pounds, Jake is a pretty good-sized dog, but here he's dwarfed at the base of a giant sequoia.

A The bark of a giant sequoia can be up to 3 feet thick and serves to protect the species from fire and other dangers. **B** Giant sequoia are typically found in small groves in a very specific environment with only sixty-eight known groves in existence.

a seed the size of an oat flake can, over time, grow to over 300 feet in height and weigh as much as 2.7 million pounds! The bark is part of its survival strategy and can be as thick as 3 feet, protecting the core from fires and insects. Little can actually kill one of these trees, short of a chain saw, and most end up toppling over due to a shallow root network. Fire causes the seed cones to open and the seeds to disperse; the new sprouts rely on the ash from burned trees for nutrients as well as the openings in the canopy created by the burning for sunlight.

There is continued controversy surrounding the monument's designation. Most opposition comes from local communities that rely on the timber industry for employment. Many wish to reduce the size of the monument so that the surrounding timber can be logged, under the belief that this would suppress fires. However, logging rarely involves removal of the underbrush that is the primary fuel source for fires, and sequoias depend on fire as the sole method for seed distribution. Additionally, the amount of useable timber from a felled sequoia is limited by the tendency of these trees to shatter when striking the ground. Sequoia are only found in small groves along the western slopes of the Sierra Nevada Mountains in California, typically at between 5,000 and 7,000 feet. This limited distribution and their slow rate of growth before reaching reproductive maturity make them especially vulnerable.

The monument has two units, one to the north and the other to the south, about 25 miles apart and separated by Sequoia National Park. There

The view from one of the pullouts along the road in the Northern Unit.

are sixteen groves within the northern section and twenty-two in the southern section. The northern unit, which is traversed by several well-maintained roads, is more popular with easier access. However, if you're looking for solitude and fewer crowds, especially during summer, head to the southern unit.

The weather here varies with both the season and altitude. Summers, with cool temperatures rarely above the mid-70s in the higher elevations, offer a welcome respite from the sweltering heat and humidity of the lower valleys nearby. Winters can be impressive with as much as 17 feet of snowfall annually, closing many of the roads, at least temporarily. Winter temperatures range from daytime highs of 45 degrees to lows in the teens.

THINGS TO DO:

You can access the northern unit via CA 180 from the Fresno area to the north or via CA 198 from its southern end in Visalia. You can access the southern unit by taking CA 190 from Porterville or the longer approach from the east via CA 178. Either way involves eventually navigating mountain highways that are denoted with an "M." These are paved and well-maintained roadways that are generally open, although there are seasonal snow closures in areas. Check with the Bureau of Land Management office at the number in the "Useful Contacts" section to see which roads are closed.

In the northern unit, CA 180 winds its way up from about 3,000 feet through cool forests to nearly 7,000 feet. A stop at the Grant Grove Visitor Center from the north, or the Foothills Visitor Center from the south, will get you a wealth of information on the road and area, including a video.

A California ground squirrel scans its surroundings from the nearby safety of its burrow.

A young mule deer male, or buck, seems alert for danger but probably is just annoyed at my presence.

There are two national parks adjacent to the monument, Kings Canyon and Sequoia, so allow additional time to explore these as well. The roads in these parks are steep, winding mountain roadways, therefore vehicle length is restricted to 22 feet in several sections.

Driving Ten Mile Road is a great way to see the monument and offers access to several stands of sequoia. This road is often closed during the winter months, so spring, summer, and fall are your best bets for travel here. There are numerous seasonal campsites available along the road.

FS Road 13S98A, a narrow, dirt track best suited for 4WD vehicles, will take you about 0.5 mile to several small stands of sequoia and few other people. You can park at a pullout along the road for the Bearskin Grove and hike the short distance if you lack the appropriate vehicle or conditions are wet. There are other US Forest Service roads within the monument open for exploring with the proper vehicle. Towing is expensive this far from town, so choose wisely.

In the larger southern unit, CA 190 becomes M107 as it winds south through the monument. Near Quaking Aspen Campground there is a turnoff for FS Road 21S05. Take this a few miles to the trailhead for the hike to the Needles Lookout. The hike is a moderate 4-mile round-trip effort that leads you to an active fire lookout with views of the valley and the Needles Rock formation. Late afternoon or sunset provide the best light on these granite spires. At the junction near Holey Meadow Campground you can take M50 west to exit the monument or M50 east to continue traveling through the monument. Before this junction there is a great place to

Looking across the valleys toward Kings Canyon National Park and the Sierra Range.

stop and wander among the sequoias at the Trail of 100 Giants. This paved walkway gives you the chance to walk among the giants. Just after Johnsondale, M50 east turns into M99, still heading east. At Johnsondale Bridge it turns generally south toward Lake Isabella, a large reservoir managed as a US Forest Service (USFS) Recreation Area. Sections of this road are narrow and steep, at times only one lane.

There are hundreds of side roads that can be explored, far too many for this guide. A detailed USFS map of both units from the visitor centers will enable you to negotiate the maze of USFS roads.

THINGS TO SEE:

The overlook just south of Quail Flat provides impressive views across Kings Canyon and east to the high peaks of the Sierras. Another overlook on the north end of Ten Mile Road is located about 2.5 miles east of Hume Junction. The road is narrow, and the dirt pullout is small so take care. Here you can see across a portion of Kings Canyon all the way to the snow-capped Sierra peaks.

A stop at Converse Basin Grove, with its numerous huge stumps, provides a view of the effects of logging. This is also the site of the 269-foot Boole Tree, one of the ten largest sequoias. It is also the largest tree found on land managed by the USFS. Named for Frank Boole, manager for the Sanger Lumber Company in the late 1890s, it is one of the few in this area that managed to dodge the sawyer's

USEFUL CONTACTS:

Giant Sequoia National Monument
1839 S. Newcomb
Porterville, CA 93257
559-920-1588

visitfresnocounty.org

visitvisalia.org

An uprooted and fractured sequoia, possibly fallen from high winds, along the Trail of a Hundred Giants in the Southern Unit, easily accessed from the road.

Given the preponderance of climbers in California, it's likely that these granite slabs and spires have routes on them.

trade. If the seasonal road is open to the trailhead, it's a 2.5-mile moderate loop to the site and back.

GETTING THERE:

From Fresno, take CA Highway 180 for 40.0 miles to the Northern Unit of the monument.

From Porterville, take CA Highway 190 for approximately 15.0 miles to the entrance for the Southern Unit.

FACILITIES:

There are dozens of developed seasonal campgrounds within both units of the monument, and dispersed camping is allowed in areas that have been used previously. These sites can also be found on USFS maps of the area. Driving off-road is strictly prohibited by all vehicles. Winter campgrounds that are open in Sequoia National Park are Azalea in the north and Potwisha in the south. Forest roads often open up to areas that are suitable for dispersed camping as well. Developed campsites are at Buck Rock, Ten Mile, Hume Lake, Stony Creek, Big Meadows, and Horse Camp. All have satisfactory access to the monument. Campfires and the use of propane stoves are highly restricted, if not banned outright, due to elevated fire danger and difficulty fighting fires in these remote areas. Fuel can be found at Hume Lake and at Stony Creek Village in Sequoia National Park and small grocery stores. If you plan on spending several days camping it's best to stock up in the Fresno area, Visalia, or Porterville before heading out. Any of these three cities provides a full range of amenities.

36. Castle Mountains
National Monument

NEAREST TOWNS:	Nipton, CA, from the north; Searchlight, NV, from the east
SIZE:	21,000 acres
BEST SEASON(S):	Year-round
NOTABLE ACTIVITIES:	Hiking, birding, wildlife and plant viewing, photography, geology, astronomy, solitude, mountain biking, 4WD trails

THE MONUMENT:

This modest-sized monument, about 21,000 acres, was established by Executive Order on February 12, 2016, by President Barack Obama. It comprises public lands on the far eastern edge of the Mojave Desert and is managed by the National Park Service. The monument represents a unique landscape of moderately high peaks up to 5,500 feet, desert grasslands, and numerous archaeological sites of early human habitation. It is surrounded on three sides by the Mojave National Preserve.

Sunrise over the Castle Mountains, framed by Joshua trees.

Large cloud formation over Castle Mountains. While it looks like it might hold rain, nothing came of it.

A deer track, very dry and worn, showing little rain for a long time . . .

Large mammals that live here include desert bighorn sheep, mule deer, and mountain lions. Birds sighted in this area include golden eagles, Swainson's hawks, prairie falcons, and Bendire's thrashers. The landscape is harsh and does not support large populations of anything living, short of the pervasive creosote bush and the abundant Joshua tree.

This desert environment is hot and dry in the summer and cool and dry in the winter. There are typically fewer than twenty days of precipitation annually, averaging about seven inches, with most falling from December through March. Temperatures in the summer can exceed 100 degrees with lows in the 70s. Winter brings a bit of relief from the searing heat with average temperatures in the 60s and nighttime lows in the mid-40s.

THINGS TO DO:

Driving into this monument can be a challenge. It is not connected directly to any notable highways and requires travel along rough gravel and dirt roads. If you can manage the conditions, the rewards of solitude, stunning views, and forests of Joshua trees await.

One approach is located 26 miles east of I-15 and 6 miles west of the town of Searchlight, Nevada, off Nevada State Road 164 (Nipton Road). Locate a well-marked sign for Walking Box Ranch Road. Follow this for about 16 miles to a large grey-blue water tank and turn right onto BLM Road 131. At 18 miles the road turns into BLM Road 144, which continues in a westerly direction. It is the most heavily used road in the monument, so it's easy to stay on track. At 25 miles you'll come to an intersection with Ivanpah Road. You can go north (right) back to Nipton or south (left) to Goffs,

An old-style wind-powered well for cattle and wild-life, one of the few sources of water in the area.

A sage sparrow taking flight from a yucca plant.

which is near I-40. The road south changes to Lanfair Road after 43 miles and eventually turns to pavement at about mile 50. Along the way you'll be treated to great views of the Castle Mountains and well-populated forests of Joshua trees. There are numerous Jeep trails, usually marked as BLM roads, that you can explore on foot if you lack an appropriate vehicle.

Reversing this route and getting to Goffs via I-40 Exit 115 is just as scenic, but you don't get to enjoy the smooth pavement after a lengthy trip of being jostled around on rough roads.

The active Castle Mountain Mine is in the area off Walking Box Ranch Road. Actual mining activity has been suspended since 2001 due to the low prices of gold, but the mine holds the rights to resume operations. You may encounter some traffic from the mine.

USEFUL CONTACTS:

**Castle Mountains
National Monument**
2701 Barstow Road
Barstow, CA 92311
760-252-6100

nps.gov/camo

desertusa.com/desert-california
 /goffs-railway-depot

THINGS TO SEE:

There are several old homesteads within the monument that are interesting to visit. There is also an enticing side trip to the outdoor Train Museum at Goffs. The collection of old train components is a reminder of the strong mining history of this area. The rail line was initially built in the late 1800s

Castle Mountains at sunrise with a forest of Joshua trees in the foreground.

to haul ore out of the surrounding mountains, but it didn't last long and soon fell into disrepair.

GETTING THERE:
From Searchlight, take NV Highway 164 west for 6 miles, or take I-15 east to Exit 286. Here you'll find the well-marked sign for Walking Box Ranch Road. Follow this for another 16 miles to a blue-grey water tank. Follow further directions above.

From the south, take I-40 Exit 115 and drive north, through the community of Goffs, for about 50 miles.

FACILITIES:
There are no facilities within the monument, limited cell service, and no fuel. Dispersed camping is allowed, but you should use previously established sites and not drive anywhere off the main roadways.

Food, fuel, and limited lodging can be found in the modest-sized community of Searchlight, Nevada. The town of Nipton, California, is quite small and has little more than one bar and grill, a quaint hotel, and a gift shop, but it's a quiet and pleasant setting to take a break. The nearest fuel off I-40 to the south is in Fenner, at Exit 107. To the north, Exit 1 off I-15 in Nevada has food, fuel, lodging, and casinos. Searchlight also has fuel and food but no obvious lodging. Las Vegas and Laughlin, roughly an hour north or south of Searchlight, respectively, have an abundance of fuel, food, lodging, and entertainment options.

37. Mojave Trails
National Monument

NEAREST TOWNS:	Baker and Mountain Pass, CA, from the north, Amboy from the south
SIZE:	1.6 million acres
BEST SEASON(S):	Year-round, although summers can be hot
NOTABLE ACTIVITIES:	Hiking, birding, wildlife and plant viewing, photography, sand dune geology, astronomy, solitude, mountain biking, 4WD trails, history

THE MONUMENT:

Located in southeastern California between I-10 and I-40, Mojave Trails National Monument surrounds the Mojave National Preserve on three sides and comprises more than 1.6 million acres. It is one of the largest national monuments in the country. Of this acreage, 350,000 acres are further protected by their status as wilderness. President Obama designated this area as a monument on February 12, 2016, to protect the unique qualities of the southwestern desert represented here. The monument includes several mountain ranges rising to over 6,000 feet, prehistoric lava flows, Indige-

The Cadiz Dunes at sunrise. A great place and time for photographing these nearly untracked dunes.

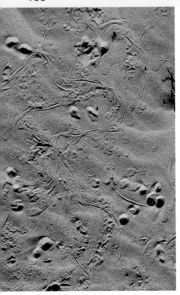

Somebody lives here and they're very busy at night! Morning is a good time to search for signs of wildlife activity.

Sand dune at sunset. Try moving around the edges of the dunes as you search for a photo, that way you minimize the tracks you leave so that others can have the same opportunity.

nous trading routes, and fields of sand dunes that rival those in Colorado's Great Sand Dunes National Park. It also protects the World War II Desert Training Center and the longest remaining intact section of the renowned Route 66.

Weather here is typical of a desert environment: hot summers and mild to cool winters with scant precipitation that mostly falls between November and March, totaling just under seven inches. Summer highs can reach the mid-80s while winters have an average daytime temperature in the mid-30s. Snow does occasionally fall here, but it doesn't stick around for long. It can be windy, with an average annual wind speed of nearly 20 mph. The desert wind rarely drops below 10 mph.

Wildlife includes larger mammals such as mule deer, mountain lions, and bighorn sheep. Animals in the desert may seem absent but most species adapted to this environment conduct much of their activity during the dark. A walk around the desert reveals numerous tracks from coyotes, black-tailed jackrabbits, kangaroo rats, and roadrunners. The black-masked loggerhead shrike can sometimes be seen as it searches for lizards to eat. Ravens are common here, as elsewhere, given their remarkable adaptability to a wide range of environments and a willingness to scavenge for food. Golden eagles inhabit the region but are rarely seen.

Borrego milkvetch is found in the dunes area, a rare and endangered plant species in California.

THINGS TO DO:

Drive the legendary Route 66, the iconic highway that helped give rise to the concept of the Great American Road Trip. Commissioned in 1926 and dubbed the "Mother Road," it con-

The endangered desert tortoise can live to 80 years of age, although they have an extremely low reproductive rate and are vulnerable to predation, disease, and environmental factors. Photo by Garry Harshbarger

An American crow soaring overhead in search of a meal.

nected Chicago with Los Angeles, but only a portion of the route was actually paved. This did not include the section that ran through the Mojave Desert, which wasn't paved until 1938. At the time, in the 1930s, this was the main route used to escape the Dust Bowl of the Midwest for greener pastures along the West Coast. After World War II, it became popularized with the song "Route 66" by Bobby Troup. Route 66 ran 2,448 miles and was quite popular before being largely replaced in the 1950s by the interstate highway system. Only fragments of the original highway remain, and this is one of the best preserved.

A day trip to Afton Canyon, also known as the Grand Canyon of the Mojave, is a highlight. The area is easily accessible to most vehicles, conditions permitting, from I-15 Exit 221 in the northwest corner of the monument, via a 3-mile road. Because it has year-round water, courtesy of the Mojave River, it's also an excellent location for birding and wildlife viewing. There is a campground here as well if you'd like to spend the night in the desert. The Cady Mountains Wilderness, to the south of Afton Canyon, has some of the best habitat in the region for desert bighorn sheep.

If you enjoy OHV riding, two areas are available. One is in the northwest corner of the monument at the Rasor OHV Area, off Highway 15. The other is west of the Marine Corps Air Ground Combat Center off Highway 247 at Johnson Valley OHV Area.

If you have the time and are properly equipped, the Mojave Road is another option. This is one of the original overland routes that brought early American pioneers to the west. It's best left to those with solid experience on rough 4WD trails. It runs 147 miles from the eastern boundary in the north

Some of the original Route 66 runs through part of the monument. This was America's first paved roadway between Chicago and Los Angeles, built in 1926 and spanning 2,448 miles.

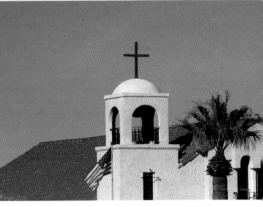

A vestige of earlier Spanish occupation of these lands is evidenced by the many missionaries that can be found throughout the American Southwest.

and crosses the entire Mojave National Preserve to finish on Highway 15 in the northwest. You can also exit at Afton Canyon, or you can head south on better roads about mid-way through the route on Rock Canyon Road. Along the way you'll be treated to the southern border of Castle Mountains National Monument, Government Holes Well, Cinder Cones Lava Bed, Afton Canyon, and an endless desert landscape that you'll likely have all to yourself. About two-thirds of the way across, going east to west, you can gain access to Kelbaker Road, which runs north to Baker or south past the Kelso Depot Visitor Center, alongside the Kelso Dunes and on to I-40.

THINGS TO SEE:

A visit to the Cadiz Sand Dunes in the southern portion of the monument is particularly worthwhile, especially from the north off I-40. Contact the monument office, the California Department of Transportation, or the State Patrol for current road conditions. You may have to drive to CA Highway 62 and go north on a dirt access road. This road begins about 7 miles east of the Iron Mountain Pumping Station and is marked by a barrel and a Bureau of Land Management sign. Starting here, it is 35 miles to the Cadiz Dunes Road and another 2 miles west down a sandy track to the trailhead. You'll pass a salt mining operation to the east at about mile 16. Approaching from the north, it's about 15 miles from Cadiz. Note that high winds may cover parts of the road with drifted sand. The dunes are formed by prevailing winds from the north, carrying sand particles from Cadiz Dry Lake until these winds lose energy and deposit the sand, forming the dunes over time. The area is designated as wilderness, and no OHVs are allowed. This means

Reconstructed Camp Iron Mountain Church, built for the millions of troops that trained here in preparation for the African Campaign of WWII.

Lava flows along the trail to Amboy Crater make walking off-trail here a difficult task.

that you get to experience the dunes as they've existed for centuries, in their natural and pristine state. The best times to visit are sunrise or sunset.

Camp Iron Mountain is a short side trip on the southern end of the monument. It is located 1 mile west of the restricted entrance to the Iron Mountain Pumping Station. There are roadside plaques on both sides of Highway 62: one for Camp Granite to the south, and the other for Camp Iron Mountain to the north. The best-preserved site is Iron Mountain, which you can approach with a high-clearance vehicle by driving uphill for about 1.5 miles to the fence that encloses and protects the site. Be wary of soft sand. There are turnstiles placed along the fence line for access by foot. This area, originally known as the Desert Training Center, was intended to train troops for combat with the German Army in North Africa. Major General George S. Patton was the center's first commanding general, and nearly 1 million men and women trained here between 1942 and 1944. Walking the enclosed area offers a glimpse into the lives of the troops that lived here before deploying to either Europe or the Pacific.

The Amboy Crater gives you a sense of the volcanic

USEFUL CONTACTS:

Mojave Trails National Monument
Needles Field Office
1303 S. Highway 95
Needles, CA 92363
760-326-7000

blm.gov/programs
  /national-conservation-lands/california
  /mojave-trails-national-monument

barstowchamber.com

A rising moon over the Amboy Crater lava fields at sunset.

activity that once ran rampant in this region. The crater itself is one of the youngest in North America, reaching about 250 feet high. There is a 3-mile round-trip trail that leads to the top of the cinder cone and grand views of the surrounding lava fields. West of Ludlow you can stop at the Pisgah Crater Lava Flow, one of the most studied areas in North America for the impact volcanism has had on evolution during our continent's history.

GETTING THERE:
Exits 72, 100, 107, and 115 off I-40 will all put you on dirt roads leading north into the monument.

Leaving I-15 at Exits 246 (Baker), 272, or 286 will give you access to the northern portion of the monument via dirt roads.

FACILITIES:
Aside from the campground at Afton Canyon, there are no facilities within the monument. Cell service is limited. Dispersed camping is allowed only on previously established sites. Driving anywhere off the main roadways is prohibited. Always practice Leave No Trace ethics, even for your pets.

You can get fuel and food in Amboy, "the ghost town that ain't dead yet," but no lodging. It also has Route 66 root beer and souvenirs. Food and fuel are also available at Ludlow and Fenner, both off I-40. Needles, Barstow, Baker, Bullhead City, and Twentynine Palms all have food, fuel, restaurants, and lodging.

Formal camping can be found at Afton Canyon, which has nineteen large individual sites and one group site. There are pit toilets, some shade, and a water spigot. There is also first-come, first-served camping at nearby Joshua Tree National Park.

38. Carrizo Plain National Monument

NEAREST TOWN:	Taft, CA
SIZE:	204,107 acres
BEST SEASON(S):	Year-round
NOTABLE ACTIVITIES:	Hiking, birding, wildlife and plant viewing, photography, San Andreas Fault geology, astronomy, solitude, mountain biking

THE MONUMENT:

With peaks rising to over 5,100 feet from the lower plains, Carrizo Plain National Monument is the largest single native grassland remaining in California. The 204,107-acre monument was further protected as a National Historic Landmark in 2012 for its archaeological importance. Bordered by the San Andreas Fault on the east, the Tremblor Range to the northeast, and the Caliente Range to the southwest, Carrizo Plain National Monument is largely an enclosed basin. Soda Lake collects the runoff from both sides of the basin. President Bill Clinton designated the monument on January 17, 2001, although efforts to protect this area began in 1988.

The Tremblor Range of mountains run along the monument's eastern border, with the San Andreas Fault lying along their western base.

Grasslands alongside Soda Lake, the most dominant feature within the monument, and which hosts seasonal migrations of thousands of birds.

Weather here is typical of semi-arid grassland at these elevations. Summer highs exceed 100 degrees, while winter lows can dip below freezing. Precipitation is limited to an annual amount of just nine inches, with most of that falling as rain from December through March. An abundance of sunshine and clear skies makes it a good place for stargazing, despite its proximity to Los Angeles. The sunshine, along with adequate water, can produce a "superbloom" that covers entire hillsides in wildflowers.

The Bureau of Land Management, the California Department of Fish and Wildlife, and The Nature Conservancy manage the monument jointly, a unique collaboration within the national monument system. Much of their efforts are directed at restoring the native ecosystems to protect rare and endangered plant and animal species. You'll notice a significant difference in the grasslands between the northern and southern sections. The northern portion looks healthier and contains more original grasslands, while the southern portion appears to be overgrazed and shows little in the way of native grasses. Although controversial, the use of cattle to control non-native species is part of the monument's range management plan. The idea is that invasive species emerge earlier than native grasses and therefore will be eaten by the cattle and not allowed to propagate. The cattle are then removed when native plants begin to appear.

Oil is a big business in this part of the country, and the nearby Midway-Sunset Oil Field is the third largest in the United States. The industry enjoys considerable local support, as it represents long-term employment for many residents. No commercially viable deposits have been found within the monument, and it is believed that the area's geology does not favor petroleum deposits underground. But Vintage Production, a subsidiary of Occidental Petroleum, has held the mineral rights to 30,000 acres within the

This 425-foot offset channel in Wallace Creek is due to movement of the San Andreas Fault. Even today, the fault is slowly moving toward San Francisco at a rate of about 1.3 inches per year, about as fast as your fingernail grows.

monument since before its designation by President Clinton and it can still exercise those rights.

THINGS TO DO:

The visitor center is inside the Goodwin Education Center toward the northern end of the monument. It is only open from December through May, from 9 a.m. to 4 p.m. Thursday through Sunday. You can pick up a useful map and guide to the monument at a kiosk on the southern end of Soda Lake Road, the primary route through the monument, or at the visitor center to the north.

The Soda Lake Road from the south off of CA 166 is poorly maintained wash-boarded gravel and dirt for 24 miles, with only a few short stretches of pavement. The 45 mph posted speed limit is almost laughable, as the road conditions don't allow vehicles to travel at such speeds. Motorcycles might do better, but it's still a bumpy ride. This road is suitable for all vehicles except when wet, when it becomes impassable in places. The northern half of the road is paved and makes for a much more enjoyable drive. It will also take you to most of the must-see destinations within the monument, particularly if you have limited time.

That said, driving the road is a great way to experience the vastness of the area. It's approximately 45 miles from CA Highway 166 along the south-

The Western meadowlark, a denizen of the desert grasslands of the American West, has a very distinctive and pleasing call.

With a wingspan of over 7 feet, the Golden Eagle can easily soar in search of its prey—typically small mammals, reptiles, and birds.

ern border to CA Highway 58 on the northern boundary, so plan accordingly with your time, fuel, food, and water.

THINGS TO SEE:

Painted Rock archaeological site is a popular location to learn about the history of the Indigenous peoples who inhabited this region. It represents some of the most noteworthy examples of rock art in the world. Access is limited to July 16 through February 28 by permit only, available at recreation.gov or by calling 877-444-6777. Guided tours are offered from March through May, again by permit. Horses and pets are not allowed on the Painted Rock Trail or in the parking area. The trail is 0.5-mile one-way from the parking lot. There are picnic tables and a toilet at the visitor center but no water.

Soda Lake Overlook, just a few miles from the northern boundary of the monument, offers grand views of the plains below, Soda Lake, and the Tremblor Range to

USEFUL CONTACTS:

Carrizo Plain National Monument
17495 Soda Lake Road
Santa Margarita, CA 93453
805-475-2131
blm.gov/programs/national-conservation-lands
/california/carrizo-plain-national-monument

Goodwin Education Center
blm.gov/visit/goodwin-education-center

visitkern.com/lodging-maricopa

visitcentralvalley.com/visitor-guides

the east. Soda Lake itself teems with waterfowl when water is present and serves as an important staging area for many migratory birds. This is an excellent place to be at sunrise or sunset for an unforgettable view.

The Wallace Creek Trail leads to a remarkable view of a creek bed offset from the movement of the nearby San Andreas Fault. As of this writing, the creek bed has been altered by about 425 feet, most recently from the 1857 Fort Tejon earthquake, which moved it nearly 23 feet. The upstream portion, part of the North American Plate, is moving slowly southeasterly while the Pacific Plate on the downstream side moves northwesterly. The trail is about 0.5 mile over moderate terrain. While there are other locations to view offsets of the fault, this is certainly the most impressive. To get here, take Seven-Mile Road for 6 miles, then turn right onto Elkhorn Road and follow it for 4 miles to the parking area and trailhead.

Carrizo Plain is also home to a diverse collection of wildlife, including Tule elk, pronghorn, sandhill cranes, and the critically endangered giant kangaroo rat. The endangered California condor has been reintroduced on nearby land, and it is hoped they will find the plains here attractive for permanent habitation. The western meadowlark is common and it's always a pleasure to hear its melodious song in the morning as the sun rises and a new day begins.

There are several old homesteads within the monument that provide a glimpse of how ranching and farming were accomplished in the late 1800s.

GETTING THERE:
Take Exit 257 off I-5 at Buttonwillow and follow CA Highway 58 for about 28 miles to the northern access road.

To access Soda Lake Road from the south, take CA Highway 166 from Maricopa for about 12 miles.

FACILITIES:
There are no services within the boundaries of the monument. There is limited cell service and no fuel. Two primitive campgrounds have vault toilets but no water. Selby Campground is 5 miles from the main road and has ten sites, with one able to accommodate groups. There is also a small corral for horses. KCL Campground is much closer to the main road and is one of the few areas with trees. It has eight sites with a vault toilet and corral for horses. Dispersed camping is allowed only in certain areas within the monument and not along the valley floor.

39. San Gabriel Mountains National Monument

NEAREST TOWNS:	Los Angeles from the south, Palmdale, CA, from the north
SIZE:	350,000 acres
BEST SEASON(S):	Year-round
NOTABLE ACTIVITIES:	Hiking, birding, wildlife and plant viewing, photography, mountain biking

THE MONUMENT:

Only 90 minutes from Los Angeles, San Gabriel Mountains National Monument provides an outdoor opportunity for many city dwellers. It covers nearly 350,000 acres, including four wilderness areas and parts of the San Andreas Fault. It has 600 archaeological sites and a rare Mediterranean ecosystem, as well as 300 species of native California plants that grow only here.

The establishment of this monument on October 10, 2014, by President Barack Obama ensures that the millions of residents of the Los Angeles Basin, as well as future generations, have a place to experience the outdoors. More than 4 million people visit this area annually. Due to its recent designation, at the time of this writing, little has been done to identify this as a monument other than a few signs.

View looking down the Bear Creek Canyon while 15 million people live just beyond the distant mountains.

Mount San Antonio (Baldy), 10,064 feet, offers the adventurous a 9.2-mile loop with an elevation gain of nearly 4,000 feet.

Weather here varies with both the season and the altitude. In Wrightwood, summer highs barely reach 80 degrees, while winter lows can be in the low 20s. This area, on the northeast edge of the monument, also receives about 22 inches of precipitation a year, including over 5 feet of snow. Closer to Los Angeles, temperatures in the monument are in the mid-70s for much of the year, with lows in the 50s to 60s at night. This area gets about 18 inches of rain annually and no snow. The rainiest months are during winter.

THINGS TO DO:
There are dozens of hiking trails, ranging from easy to quite hard. Perhaps the hardest thing to do here is choosing which trail to hike. Many of the trails are multi-use, with visitors on horseback, bicycles, and even off-road vehicles. An Adventure Pass, $5 per day or $30 annually, is required to access or park at many of the trailheads. A small sampling of the many potential hikes are listed here. Many of these trails double as excellent birding walks to search for mountain quail, acorn woodpeckers, mountain chickadees, or dusky flycatchers.

The Sturtevant Falls Trail leads to a gorgeous 50-foot waterfall with little effort. It's 3 miles out-and-back and gains only 650 feet, although the last 0.5 mile back to the parking area is uphill.

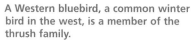
A Western bluebird, a common winter bird in the west, is a member of the thrush family.

A type of ground squirrel found on the eastern side of the monument.

A much tougher trail takes you to the 10,064-foot summit of Mount San Antonio (Baldy), which requires hiking a 9.2-mile loop with an elevation gain of nearly 4,000 feet. This is a doable day hike only an hour or so from northern Los Angeles, but it's definitely not for beginners. This trail often has snow into June. Microspikes or crampons can be useful. This peak is one of the SoCal Six-Pack of Peaks Challenge and offers excellent training for higher peaks. There are stone shelters at the summit.

For bicyclists, the West Fork National Scenic Bikeway is a 14-mile round-trip route that follows the San Gabriel River for 7 gorgeous and serene miles. It's shared by hikers and walkers, but because it's a paved utility access road, it remains gated and free of motor vehicles. The first few miles can be busy, but after that you may only encounter the occasional fisherman. The Glenn Campground is about 7 miles up the trail if you wish to stay overnight. You'll need an Adventure Pass to park at the trailhead. Pick one up at the San Gabriel Entrance Station, which you'll pass on the way in. To reach the Bikeway, drive north on CA Highway 39 (San Gabriel Canyon Road) out of Azusa for about 8.5 miles to where the road crosses the West Fork of the San Gabriel River. Park here and start your adventure from the south side of the bridge.

The drive to the monument starts near sea level and can take you as high as almost 10,000 feet, so take precautions to make sure your visit isn't complicated by altitude illness. Drink plenty of non-alcoholic, non-caffeinated liquids; don't overexert yourself; and be mindful of the stronger sun at higher altitudes.

There are fourteen official trails within the monument, including the Pacific Coast Trail. Maps can be obtained at the visitor center.

THINGS TO SEE:

The cosmos can be seen from the nearby Mount Wilson Observatory. From April through November, you can take a self-guided tour during the week or a guided tour on the weekends. Harlow Shapley, who measured the size of the Milky Way, and Edwin Hubble, who proved the existence of distant galaxies similar to our own, both worked here in the early 1900s.

GETTING THERE:

There are several access roads and byways. The most frequently used is the Angeles Crest Highway (CA Route 2), which is accessible from I-210 at Exit 20 to the south or from Wrightwood to the north.

USEFUL CONTACTS:

San Gabriel Mountains
National Monument
110 N. Wabash Avenue
Glendora, CA 91741
626-335-1251

Angeles National Forest
710 N. Santa Anita Avenue
Arcadia, CA 91006
626-574-1613

Chilao Visitor Center
1 Moccasin Trail
Palmdale, CA 93550
626-796-5541

Grassy Hollow Visitor Center
Angeles Crest Highway (Route 2)
Valyermo, CA 93563
626-821-6737

Mount Baldy Visitor Center
6778 Mount Baldy Road
Mount Baldy, CA 91759
909-982-2829

Clear Creek Information Center
Angeles Crest Highway (Route 2)
La Cañada Flintridge, CA 91011
626-821-6764

Big Pines Visitor Center
24537 Angeles Crest Highway
(Route 2)
Wrightwood, CA 92397
760-249-3504

San Gabriel Canyon Gateway
Center
N 1960 San Gabriel Canyon Rd.
Azusa, CA 91702
626-969-1012

Crystal Lake Campgrounds
crystallake.name/index.htm

Camping
fs.usda.gov/activity/angeles
/recreation/camping-cabins

Mount Wilson Observatory
mtwilson.edu

▲ View looking east over the Mojave Desert.

An acorn woodpecker, easily identified by its striking facial markings and prominent eyes. It's typically found in woodlands and is fond of drilling holes in trees to pound a nut into for the winter.

FACILITIES:

There are sixteen campgrounds within the monument and many more in the surrounding national forest. A few can handle RVs. Individual campsites are first-come, first-served, while group camps, some accommodating up to 300 people, need to be reserved through recreation.gov. Some campgrounds may be closed during winter. Look for Coldbrook, Manker, and Los Alamos campgrounds at the website listed in the "Useful Contacts" section.

There are nine first-come, first-served campgrounds at Crystal Lake, as well as lodging, fuel, food, and a visitor center. The visitor center is staffed by volunteers, so it has irregular hours except for Saturdays.

There is virtually no end to the options for food, fuel, lodging, and entertainment in nearby Los Angeles or San Bernardino, not to mention the dozens of surrounding communities, many of which cater to tourists.

40. Sand to Snow National Monument

NEAREST TOWN:	Big Bear Lake, CA, on the north side
SIZE:	154,000 acres
BEST SEASON(S):	Year-round
NOTABLE ACTIVITIES:	Hiking, birding, wildlife and plant viewing, photography, geology, mountain biking

THE MONUMENT:
Located in San Bernardino County in south-central California, Sand to Snow National Monument represents a uniquely complex and diverse landscape ranging from the floor of the Sonoran Desert to the 11,503-foot summit of San Gorgonio Mountain. The Monument's 154,000 acres are co-managed by the Bureau of Land Management and the US Forest Service. Recognizing this as a rare opportunity to protect such a diverse landscape, President Barack Obama declared this a national monument on February 11, 2016. Given its proximity to southern California's large population, the goal was to preserve critical wildlife corridors and habitat alongside a growing demand for

View looking toward San Gorgonio Mountain, 11,503 feet, the "snow" in the Sand to Snow National Monument.

203

A common raven perched atop a dead yucca, the highest point around. Note the very large, thick bill that distinguishes it from the similar American crow.

A "Super Blue Blood Moon" lunar eclipse in the early hours of January 31, 2018. This is a combination of the moon being its closest to Earth, the second moon in a single month, and a total lunar eclipse.

outdoor recreation. San Gorgonio Mountain has long been a sacred place to the Native Americans of this region, including the Serrano, Cahuilla, and Luiseno. Twelve threatened or endangered animal species live here, as well as over 240 species of birds.

Weather here varies with the altitude and the season. At the lower elevations, summer temperatures can be as high as 100 degrees or more during the day, while nighttime lows generally remain in the 70s. The winter months bring some relief, as highs typically stay in the 70s with lows in the mid-40s. Rainfall amounts to less than 5 inches annually. Temperatures at higher altitudes, such as around Big Bear Lake, are a more comfortable 80 degrees in the summer with lows in the 40s. Winter highs are in the upper 40s with lows into the 20s. Snowfall is common, with an annual average of over 60 inches.

THINGS TO DO:

Many trails crisscross the monument's rugged terrain. A unique standout among the abundant options is the punishing "Nine Peaks Challenge," a 27-mile one-day sufferfest that includes 8,300 feet of elevation gain as you ascend nine separate peaks. It's helpful to be familiar with the area beforehand, as you'll likely start and finish in the dark.

The Pacific Crest Trail runs for roughly 30 miles within the monument's borders. This section passes just east of Big Bear Lake and travels south through the monument to I-10.

Swiss Canyon Trail, the Joshua Tree Short Loop, and Blind Canyon Trail are three of the most popular hikes in the area. They are rated easy, moder-

The cedar waxwing is a fairly common winter visitor to Big Morongo Canyon Preserve, a great place for birding with 263 species having been documented there.

A stream with fall colors—it's nice to see bright colors in an otherwise largely monochromatic landscape.

ate, and hard, respectively. Swiss Canyon Trail is very well maintained, about 2 miles round-trip with roughly 500 feet of elevation gain. Access is from Verbena Drive on the southern side of the monument, north of I-10. Joshua Tree Short Loop is 6.2 miles in total length and gains about 700 feet overall. Time it for spring wildflower blooms. It starts at 3,900 feet and can be cooler than other outings in the area. It's accessed from Campground Road south of Yucca Valley. The trailhead for Blind Canyon Trail is just north of Desert Hot Springs at the end of Santa Cruz Road. This is a single trail, but you can do a 3.9-mile loop, and there are numerous side trails that can make this an enjoyable adventure or a frustrating exercise. Either way, given the nearly 1,000 feet of gain, you'll get a good workout with great views along the way. It's also one of the most important avian habitats in California, so you'll likely see a good number of birds along the way. There are many other hikes in the region to choose from, and this is only a small sampling.

The hike to the top of San Gorgonio Mountain is something of a rite of passage for many hikers in California, given that it's the highest peak south of the Sierras. At 11,503 feet, it's visible for some distance, even from Mount Whitney 190 miles to the north. This is a difficult undertaking, given the ascent of nearly 5,400 feet over about 10.0 miles of trail, one way. It's mostly uphill, and while many do it as a very long day hike, there are some camping options. High Creek Camp at 9,440 feet is probably the most popular and has water. No wilderness permits are needed for day hikes, but they are required for overnight stays. The effort required, the high altitude, and the unpredictable weather all combine to make this an outing only for experienced hikers and climbers.

A waterfall along the Forest Falls Trail on the northern side of the monument.

An old cedar tree, weathering the harsh environment of the monument.

If you visit during the winter months, which can have more agreeable temperatures, you also have the chance to ski in the vicinity of Big Bear Lake. There are two lift-served ski areas: Snow Summit and Bear Mountain. Snow Summit is a modest 8,300-foot peak with mostly beginner and intermediate terrain overlooking Big Bear Lake. Bear Mountain is also good for beginners and intermediates, as 70 percent of its terrain is rated as such. The two areas share a common owner and lift tickets are interchangeable. Both rely heavily on artificial snow, as do many other Southern California ski areas.

Nearby Joshua Tree National Park offers world-class rock climbing along with a chance to explore a unique desert ecosystem.

THINGS TO SEE:

Watch the birds, especially at the 31,000-acre Big Morongo Canyon Preserve on the eastern side of the monument, adjacent to Joshua Tree National Park. Here you have the best chance of seeing some of the more than 240 species that nest or pass through this area. Designated an Important Bird Area, the preserve sits on the Pacific Flyway and is home to one of only ten large cottonwood and willow riparian habitats in all of California. Golden eagles, western bluebirds, phainopepla, verdin, and the brilliantly colored vermilion flycatcher are all known to nest here during the spring. You might also catch a glimpse of some of the larger mammals that come here for water during dry periods. Mule deer, desert bighorns, numerous bat species, the occasional black bear, and the common desert kangaroo rat are all found here at various times.

There are several access points to the monument. Angelus Oaks is on the west side, Whitewater and Mission Creek Preserves are on the south, and Big Morongo Canyon Preserve is in the eastern portion. Pioneertown Pipes Canyon Road leads into the isolated segment of Black Lava Butte north of Yucca Valley.

The drive along CA Highway 38 on the north side of the monument provides excellent views of San Gorgonio Mountain as it takes you over a high pass and down to Big Bear Lake. Along the way you can take the short side road east leading to the Forest Falls Trailhead. This trail follows a delightful stream with a small waterfall at its head. This area also has picnic sites, camping, and leads to the Vivian Creek Trailhead. Vivian Creek Trail continues on for those wishing to slog the 8.5 miles to the summit of San Gorgonio. This is also a good place to find some of the monument's snow during winter. You can access CA Highway 38 from I-10 at the Yucaipa exit.

Whitewater Canyon Road leads to the Whitewater Canyon Trailhead. To reach it, take I-10 for about 5 miles west of Palm Springs. Continue north on Whitewater Canyon Road for 5 miles to the trailhead. Here you can stroll up the typically dry riverbed for a few miles to the

USEFUL CONTACTS:

Palm Springs-South Coast Field Office (BLM)
1201 Bird Center Drive
Palm Springs, CA 92262
760-833-7100

Barstow Field Office (BLM)
2601 Barstow Road
Barstow, CA 92311
760-252-6000

San Bernardino National Forest
602 S. Tippecanoe Avenue
San Bernardino, CA 92408
909-382-2600

San Gorgonio Wilderness Association
34701 Mill Creek Road
Mentone, CA 92359
909-382-2906
sgwa.org

Mill Creek Visitor Center
34701 Mill Creek Road
Mentone, CA 92359
909-382-2882

visitpalmsprings.com

bigbear.com/travel-tools
  /visitor-center/

pcta.org

bigmorongo.org

mojavemonuments.org/sand-to-snow

Thirty miles of the Pacific Coast Trail lie within the monument's boundaries, although it will cost you 7,000 feet of elevation gain.

A climber on the Hobbit Roof, a 5.9 climb at Joshua Tree National Park. Sand to Snow National Monument links its boundaries with those of the national park, expanding the area's protection for wildlife and recreation.

top of Red Dome, a remnant of previous volcanic activity. Or take the Canyon View Loop Trail, a more difficult hike with 1,000 feet of gain, which brings you to a high point with excellent views of the surrounding landscape. You can also access the Santa Ana River, Southern California's longest.

GETTING THERE:

From the east, one access point is Big Morongo Canyon Road off CA Highway 62/29 (Palms Highway).

From the south, take Cottonwood Road, just west of the junction of I-10 and CA Highway 111.

CA Highway 38 from the Bear Lake area provides access to several trailheads on the northern and western boundaries of the monument.

FACILITIES:

No services of any type are found within the monument's boundaries. However, there is no shortage of camping, lodging, food, and fuel in the many communities surrounding the monument. Campgrounds can be found at Barton Flats and Mile High Pines in the north and Mountain Home along the western border. Reserved camping can be found at Joshua Tree National Park as well.

41. Santa Rosa and San Jacinto Mountains
National Monument

NEAREST TOWN:	Palm Desert, CA
SIZE:	280,071 acres
BEST SEASON(S):	Year-round
NOTABLE ACTIVITIES:	Hiking, birding, wildlife and plant viewing, photography, desert geology, mountain biking

THE MONUMENT:

The Santa Rosa and San Jacinto mountains have long been protected as public lands, beginning in the late 1800s. The monument includes state reserves and game refuges as well as the San Jacinto Wilderness Area of 32,248 acres, with peaks as high as 8,922 feet. The monument is co-managed by the Bureau of Land Management, the US Forest Service, and the Cahuilla people, who own a considerable portion of the monument.

The landscape here, especially at the higher altitudes, can be quite harsh and exposed. Make sure you're prepared for this if you choose to go out hiking and let someone know where you're going and when you expect to return.

The Cahuilla (ʔívillúqaletem or Ivilyuqaletem) and their ancestors have occupied this region for over 3,000 years. Peaks such as Santa Rosa Mountain and Tahquitz Peak are sacred to them. Their villages were often near the mouths of canyons or in the valley, with different habitation sites for summer and winter. All of these facts must be taken into consideration when visiting the monument, as each stakeholder may have different rules for the use and management of various areas. Much like Sand to Snow National Monument, the terrain here varies from the desert floor of the Coachella Valley to the summit of Mount San Jacinto at 10,834 feet. To protect the unique geological, biological, cultural, and scientific features of this region, the area was designated a national monument by Congress on October 24, 2000.

The weather here varies with the location and altitude. The mountains are often described as a "humid island" above the surrounding desert. The coastal side of the range can receive 15 inches of precipitation annually, the eastern side gets only 6 inches, and the higher elevations above 5,500 feet can receive as much as 30 inches. Temperatures range from highs in the triple-digits in the lower altitudes to as cold as the teens or single digits in the winter at higher altitudes. In the lower elevations, expect summer temperatures as high as 100 degrees or more during the day while nighttime lows generally remain in the 70s. The winter months bring some relief, as highs typically stay in the 70s with lows in the mid-40s.

Bladderpod, a hardy, foul-smelling plant native to California, flowers for most of the year and is often used in home gardens for its drought tolerance and color.

THINGS TO DO:

The first stop should be the visitor center on CA Highway 74, about 4 miles south of the intersection with CA Highway 111 in Palm Desert. Here you can watch an informative documentary, look over interpretive displays, pick up maps or other useful guides to the area, and get information on current trail conditions.

Sunrise falls on some of the mountainous terrain found in the monument.

The visitor center has a 0.2-mile loop, the Ed Hastey Garden Trail, which will introduce you to many of the plants common to this area. You can also see a number of different bird species, particularly Anna's and black-chinned hummingbirds, phainopepla, and the California quail.

A longer and more difficult trail, the Randall Henderson Trail, can range from a 1.0-mile loop to a 2.5-mile loop, starting and ending at the southern parking lot. Hiking lower elevation trails is best from November through April, while May through October is typically the peak time to hike the higher trails.

There are two noteworthy trails at nearby San Jacinto State Park. The moderate Deer Springs to Suicide Rock Trail is a 3.3-mile (one-way) hike that gains 1,700 feet. The views from Suicide Rock of the valleys below are impressive. A more strenuous outing involves 8.1 miles of hiking from Devil's Slide to the summit of Mount San Jacinto, with 4,400 feet of elevation gain. Big views and a great aerobic workout await.

The easier way to the top of Mount San Jacinto is the Palm Springs Aerial Tramway, which takes you to 2,643 feet, leaving a hike of only 2,400 feet to the 10,834-foot summit. For a more challenging and rewarding ascent, take the Marion Mountain Trail out of Idyllwild or try the grueling Cactus to Clouds Trail, a true sufferfest that ascends 10,700 feet from Palm Springs to the summit. Note that there is no water until you reach 8,500 feet, and

The black-throated sparrow, a fairly common bird in the south-west desert, is easily identified by its conspicuous black throat.

Gambel's quail can often be found near a water source in the scrubland of the desert, usually in large coveys in the fall and winter. Its chestnut-colored crown distinguishes it from the California quail's brown crown.

Brittlebrush, a member of the sunflower family, has brittle branches that produce a fragrant resin, presumably to attract pollinators.

you can easily encounter a 40-degree or more change in temperature. There is an emergency stone shelter near the summit that was built in 1935 by the Civilian Conservation Corps.

THINGS TO SEE:

The largest collection of native fan palm oases in the United States is at the Indian Canyons, at the base of Mount San Jacinto. Many of the monument's more than 200 species of birds may be found in the oases. You'll also find the pleasant Andreas Canyon Loop Trail. At 2.9 miles and with only 442 feet of elevation change, this is an easy way to experience the canyon without a lot of effort.

The flora and fauna of the monument are elevation- and temperature-dependent. There are large swaths of California black oak and Coulter pine along the valley floor, while the higher forests have ponderosa pine, red fir, and deciduous oak. Unique to California, and to this area in particular, there is a grove of giant sequoia on the northeast slope of Mount San Jacinto. These trees were planted as saplings by the USFS in the 1970s and are now a healthy and viable population separate from the other groves within the state. Wildlife that may be seen, especially around water sources in the mornings and evenings, include bighorn sheep, white-tailed jackrabbit, coyote, and the rare badger. Greater roadrunners are common throughout the monument, but they don't stick around for long. There are rattlesnakes here as well, so don't poke your hands or feet into places you can't see. Look for them along the trails, where they often sun themselves.

The visitor center for Joshua Tree National Park in Twenty-Nine Palms has an excellent paved walkway for easy strolling and birding. The Oasis of Mora, along which you can see numerous species of birds among the palm trees, is also a great place for sunrise or sunset.

GETTING THERE:
From the junction of CA Highway 74 and CA Highway 111 in Palm Desert, drive south on CA Highway 74 for about 4.0 miles to the visitor center for more detailed road information.

FACILITIES:
No services of any type exist within the monument. There is

USEFUL CONTACTS:

Santa Rosa and San Jacinto National Monument Visitor Center
51-500 Highway 74
Palm Desert, CA 92260
760-862-9984

visitpalmsprings.com

no shortage of camping, lodging, food, and fuel in the many surrounding communities. Pinyon Flat has eighteen first-come, first-served campsites with potable water, toilets, and picnic tables, managed by the USFS. There is a horse camp at Ribbonwood Equestrian with tables, toilets, potable water, corrals, and showers. These sites can be reserved through recreation.gov.

Dispersed camping is allowed on all BLM lands within the monument, but it's restricted to existing sites with a limit of fourteen days. The USFS also allows dispersed camping except where expressly prohibited. No off-road driving is permitted to access a campsite or for other purposes. Camping within the San Jacinto Wilderness Area requires an overnight permit. Fires, always a hazard in this region, must be carefully managed and never left unattended, if allowed at all, and a permit is required from either the BLM or the USFS.

San Jacinto State Park, centrally located within the monument, offers camping at Idyllwild and Stone Creek campgrounds. There are RV sites with hookups, restrooms, showers, and potable water. Vehicle length is restricted to 24 feet. There are thirty-three sites at Idyllwild, three of which have hookups and four with electricity only. Stone Creek has forty-eight sites including six with electricity. Both are open year-round, although tire chains are recommended in the winter months.

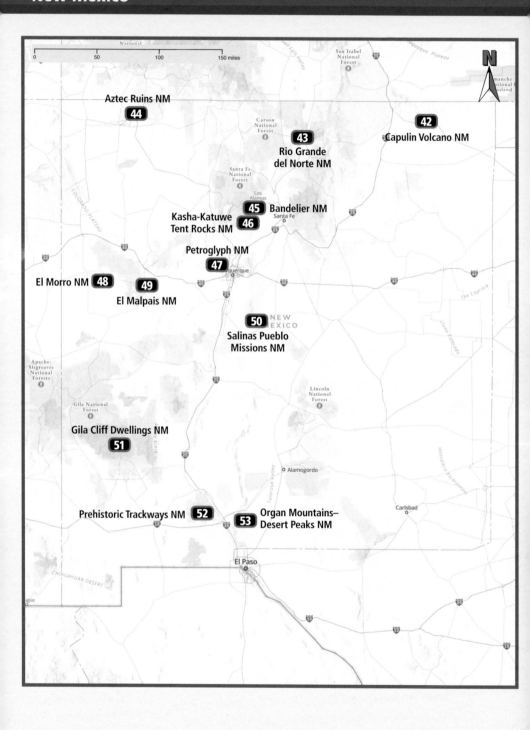

Aztec Ruins NM **44**

Capulin Volcano NM **42**

Rio Grande
del Norte NM **43**

Kasha-Katuwe
Tent Rocks NM **46** **45** Bandelier NM

Petroglyph NM **47**

El Morro NM **48** **49**
El Malpais NM

50
Salinas Pueblo
Missions NM

Gila Cliff Dwellings NM
51

Prehistoric Trackways NM **52** **53** Organ Mountains–
Desert Peaks NM

42. Capulin Volcano
National Monument

NEAREST TOWN:	Raton, NM
SIZE:	768 acres
BEST SEASON(S):	Year-round
NOTABLE ACTIVITIES:	Hiking, birding, wildlife and plant viewing, photography, volcanic geology, astronomy, solitude

THE MONUMENT:

Capulin Volcano is part of the Raton-Clayton Volcanic Field in northeast New Mexico. The name Capulin is derived from the Spanish word for a prevalent shrub, the chokecherry. President Woodrow Wilson established this national monument on August 9, 1916. It is administered by the National Park Service.

Although it covers only 1.2 square miles (768 acres), the monument is home to one of the most significant archaeological discoveries in history. In nearby Folsom, a fluted projectile point was found buried between the ribs of a bison species that had been extinct for 10,000 years. This evi-

A winding road ascends Capulin Volcano to just below the top, from where you can hike the remaining distance to the 8,182-foot summit.

USEFUL CONTACTS:

Capulin Volcano
National Monument
P.O. Box 40
Des Moines, NM 88418
575-278-2201

nps.gov/cavo

ratonnm.gov

dence showed that Paleoindians traveled through this area as far back as 10,000 years ago and significantly pushed back the date at which humans were believed to inhabit North America. Capulin Volcano reaches an elevation of 8,182 feet and sits at the center of the 7,500-square mile Raton-Clayton Field, which encompasses over 100 volcanoes dating back nine million years. From the top of the crater it is possible to see into New Mexico, Colorado, Texas, Kansas, and Oklahoma.

The climate here is warm in the summers with highs in the low 80s and a comfortable 50 degrees at night. Winters get colder with highs reaching the 40s and 50s, and nighttime lows dip into the 20s.

THINGS TO DO:
Drive to the crater rim at the end of the spiral road. There is ample parking and numerous informative signs about the volcano and the surrounding landscape. This area is on the west rim, about 600 feet above the visitor center and roughly 300 feet below the highest point of the crater on the east rim. A steep 1-mile trail heads to the summit through pinyon and ponderosa pine trees and juniper shrubs that cover the volcano's sides. Growth here is limited by a lack of water and the generally poor quality of the soil. The trail circles the rim and leads back to the parking area. The views from along the rim are truly impressive; to the west, you can even see the Great Plains rising up to meet the Sangre de Cristo Mountains. There's also evidence of hundreds of smaller volcanoes and flows. The Lava Flow Trail, a less strenuous hike, can be accessed near the visitor center. Although it's 2 miles round-trip, it's relatively flat, so the hike is a bit easier than on the crater rim.

The museum in nearby Folsom, while not always open, is an interesting side trip to learn more about the Folsom Man site.

THINGS TO SEE:
Find a quiet spot near the volcano and simply enjoy the breathtaking views, the silence, and the solitude. This is a great opportunity to observe, first-hand, ten million years of geological history laid out before you.

Ten million years of volcanic activity await your viewing from the summit, where you can see as far as five states.

GETTING THERE:

Take I-25 Exit 452 at Raton and drive east on US Highway 87 for 27 miles to the entrance.

FACILITIES:

There are no camping facilities within the monument but camping and lodging are available nearby. For campers, Sugarite Canyon State Park is a good choice that is about 30 minutes west on NM Highway 72. It's home to the Lake Alice Campground, which is open year-round and has twelve sites; four are tent only. Other campsites in the state park offer full hookups and can accommodate vehicles up to 45 feet. Soda Pocket Campground is only open during the warmer, snow-free months. It offers fourteen sites, but the road up to the campground is steep and not suitable for all RVs. There is no water at this location, but you can fill up at Lake Alice.

Nearby Raton has food, fuel, and lodging.

43. Rio Grande del Norte National Monument

NEAREST TOWNS:	Antonito, CO, to the north; Questa, NM, to the east; and Taos, NM, to the south
SIZE:	250,000 acres
BEST SEASON(S):	Year-round
NOTABLE ACTIVITIES:	Hiking, birding, wildlife and plant viewing, photography, geology, astronomy, solitude, mountain biking, rock climbing, rafting and kayaking, fishing, hunting

THE MONUMENT:

This monument sits within a wide-open plain with an average elevation of 7,000 feet. Its rugged landscape is beautiful in its starkness, which is punctuated by tall volcanic cones reaching to over 10,000 feet. It has gorges as deep as 800 feet, cut by the Rio Grande into the volcanic basalt. Around 10,000 BCE, early Meso-Indian inhabitants found an agreeable landscape here with easily accessible food, water, and shelter. Over time they were followed by the Jicarilla Apache, Utes, and the peoples of Taos Pueblo and Picuris Pueblo. Eventually these people moved on to more fertile valleys in the region. European settlement was also sparse and short-lived; a few World War I veterans arrived in the early 1900s but were mostly gone by the 1930s.

The monument is nearly a quarter-million acres in size and was designated on March 25, 2013, by President Barack Obama. The Bureau of Land Management oversees the monument.

Weather here is typical for the region and altitude, with summer highs in the upper 70s and nighttime lows in the upper 40s. Winters are dry and noticeably cooler with daytime highs in the 30s to 40s. Nighttime lows can drop to the teens or even single digits. Precipitation is about 13 inches annually including 2 feet of snowfall.

THINGS TO DO:

There is something for everyone in this outdoor playground, with numerous opportunities for wildlife viewing, hiking, photography, paddling, rock-climbing, biking, hunting, and fishing. It can be a bit inconvenient to access

View looking north of the Rio Grande and the narrow chasm it created over a period of millions of years.

from the north. The Rio Grande Gorge Visitor Center in Pilar offers information on activities within the monument and the nearby Orilla Recreation Area. It's located at the intersection of NM Highway 570 and NM Highway 68. The Wild Rivers Visitor Center is in Cerro, to the east of the monument, with up-to-date information on hiking and camping.

La Vista Verde Trail, "The Green View," is a 1.25-mile (one-way) hike to the edge of the Rio Grande. It has remarkable views, and bighorn sheep are often seen here.

If you're drawn by high peaks, hike to the summit of 10,093-foot Ute Mountain. There are no established trails to the top, but you can generally ascend a ridge on the southwest side. The slopes are open but filled with cacti and other prickly things, as well as rattlesnakes, so take care. To

A mature rocky mountain bighorn sheep ram primed for the fall rut.

A pair of female common goldeneye ducks, prevalent throughout the western United States.

Dispersed camping can be found wherever the dirt tracks, and an appropriate vehicle, take you. Here, one can enjoy views of the distant Sangre de Cristo Mountains in northern New Mexico to the east.

reach Ute Mountain, follow NM Highway 552 north out of Questa for about 10.0 miles to the turnoff for Sunshine Valley Road. Turn left (west) on Sunshine Valley Road and continue for 4.0 miles to an unmarked dirt road on the right. Continue straight on this road along the rim of the Rio Grande Gorge. Turn right at the next intersection and drive about 0.3 mile to a left turn onto TP 235. Follow TP 235 for about 4.5 miles and turn right onto an unmarked dirt road. Continue about 2.5 miles to a parking area at roughly 8,300 feet. This last part can be rough and requires a high-clearance vehicle.

Rock climbing is available at a small crag along the Old Stagecoach Road where it crosses the river on the John Dunn Bridge. The approach is less than ten minutes and puts you at the base of basalt outcrops with trad and sport routes from 5.5 to 5.11. There are five walls with routes about 40 feet high, and the anchors can be accessed from above. Watch for bighorn sheep in the area. *Taos Rock Climbs & Boulders of Northern New Mexico* by Jay Foley is the best guide for this crag and others in the area.

Whitewater enthusiasts will find challenging waters in the monument, with up to Class V rapids. The Rio Grande Wild and Scenic River journeys 74 miles through the monument. The Red River is also a Wild and Scenic River, with numerous Class IV rapids. The John Dunn Bridge, one of just a few drivable access points to the river within the monument, is a popular put-in for rafters and kayakers on the Rio Grande.

There are numerous mountain bike trails within the monument, many of which follow Jeep trails that can be rough.

The Black Rock Hot Springs are near John Dunn Bridge. To reach them, cross John Dunn Bridge and hike up to the left for a short distance past the first switchback. The temperature of the spring is a steady 97 degrees. This is a great place to soak after climbing or hiking, but note that it's clothing optional. The Manby Hot Springs are another option. The trailhead can be reached from Taos by taking NM Highway 522 to B-007. Just before B-007 turns sharply to the right, turn left on a very rough road. Take a left at the Dobson House sign and stay to the right until you reach the parking area. Consistent 97-degree water and clothing-optional bathing awaits after a short 15-minute walk.

Looking east over the vast landscape, this track will take you in the direction of 10,093-foot Ute Mountain but is barred by the deep Rio Grande canyon.

The climate here allows for year-round exploration. Snow is rare, though the temperatures can get cold in the winter. Nearby Taos Ski Valley, as well as Red River and Eagle Nest ski areas, offer good snow and plenty of family fun.

THINGS TO SEE:

Elk, mule deer, pronghorn antelope, black bear, and bighorn sheep all call this area home, although many of them are migratory. Located on the central flyway of North America, the Rio Grande Gorge is an Audubon Important Bird Area, which means that you have the chance to see a variety of rare and interesting avians in this region. Golden eagles and peregrine falcons nest here along the cliffs, while Virginia's warbler can be found in the monument's riparian areas. Over 100 bird species may be viewed here at different times of the year.

If you're driving on US Highway 285 and searching for a grand vista, check out Taos Plateau Road. It's on the east side of NM Highway 285 about 1.0 mile south of the Colorado-New Mexico border, just east of prominent 10,908-foot San Antonio Mountain. A 3-mile drive east on TP 121, a rough track, leads to an enormous view of 10,093-foot Ute Mountain and the sweeping plateau before it. You can continue on TP 121 for another 17 miles to the Rio Grande at the foot of Ute Mountain. Either destination is a quiet and peaceful location. Excellent campsites can be found along this track.

USEFUL CONTACTS:

BLM Taos Field Office
226 Cruz Alta Road
Taos, NM 87571
575-758-8851

Rio Grande Gorge
Visitor Center
2873 NM 68
Taos, NM 87571
575-751-4899

Wild Rivers Visitor Center
1120 NM 378
Questa, NM 87556
575-586-1150

taos.org

newmexico.org/places-to-go
 /regions-cities/northcentral/questa

GETTING THERE:
Take US Highway 285 for a few miles from either the north or the south from Tres Piedras, NM, or Antonito, CO, respectively to reach the western border of the monument. There are several entryways along this highway.

Questa, along the eastern border, is only a few miles from the monument on NM Highway 522.

FACILITIES:
Most of the monument that's accessible by vehicle has dispersed camping. You are expected to use existing sites, and campfires are discouraged, if not prohibited, due to the remote nature of the monument and generally dry conditions. Do not drive off-road, as the vegetation is fragile and will take years to recover.

Both the Orilla Verde Recreation Area and Wild Rivers Recreation Area offer several developed campgrounds—seven and five sites, respectively—but getting to them may be a bit challenging, especially for larger vehicles. It's best to check with the local visitor center or BLM office for the most current information.

44. Aztec Ruins
National Monument

NEAREST TOWN:	Aztec, NM
SIZE:	318 acres
BEST SEASON(S):	Year-round
NOTABLE ACTIVITIES:	Birding, wildlife and plant viewing, history, photography

THE MONUMENT:

Located in northwestern New Mexico in the small town of Aztec, these ruins offer a unique opportunity to see and explore 900-year-old Ancestral Puebloan structures. The significance of the site was recognized on January 24, 1923, when Congress declared it a national monument. Managed by the National Park Service, it was also listed on the National Register of Historic Places in 1966 and designated a World Heritage Site in 1987.

The Aztec Ruins were built between 800 and 1,000 years ago by Ancestral Puebloans. It is thought that the site originally supported activities in

The ruins here demonstrated the high quality of craftsmanship that the Ancestral Puebloans possessed.

Looking at the Great Kiva from the outside, this represents a significant religious and spiritual structure for the Ancestral Puebloans.

the regional hub of Chaco Canyon 50 miles farther south, although it could have been its own distinct cultural center. The Animas River, originating in the Rocky Mountains of present-day southwest Colorado, was the primary source of water for farming and daily living for these peoples.

Many Indigenous Americans and descendants of the Ancestral Puebloans maintain a cultural and spiritual connection with this site. Please be respectful of this, and as with all historical sites, do not disturb or remove any artifacts.

Weather is typical of a high-desert environment. Summer highs can reach 90 degrees, with a significant drop to the 50s at night. Winter is cold and dry with highs in the 40s and lows down to the teens. Annual precipitation is less than 11 inches, of which about 15 inches falls as snow.

THINGS TO DO:

It's necessary to go through the visitor center before entering the ruins. Take the time to tour the museum and its ancient artifacts, as well as watch a 15-minute introductory video.

Exploring the site is simple. A map, with pictures and explanations, is available to guide you through the area. The walk around the ruins is an easy 0.5-mile, 45-minute effort suitable for most people. The highlight is entering the restored Great Kiva, an unusual opportunity to see the inside of an intact structure nearly 900 years old. It was used for ceremonial purposes,

Original wood beams can still be seen as support structures, likely for a roof or awning.

This region represents breeding territory for the yellow-headed blackbird, often found in freshwater marshes of the nearby Animas River.

and it's easy to imagine the sacred nature of this structure from within. The West Ruin had over 500 separate rooms, some as high as three stories. Some of the original wood used in the construction is still visible.

There is a short "Native Plants" walk outside the visitor center that will introduce you to some of the indigenous plants that people relied upon to live. A 4-mile round-trip hike to the Animas River along the Old Spanish National Historic Trail is a pleasant way to get to historic downtown Aztec for lunch or shopping.

This region is rich in public lands and preserved areas, including Canyons of the Ancients National Monument, Hovenweep National Monument, Chimney Rock National Monument, Canyon de Chelly National Monument, Yucca House National Monument, Chaco Culture National Historic Park, and Mesa Verde National Park.

THINGS TO SEE:

The ruins themselves are the center of this small national monument, with the Great Kiva as the highlight. The early artifacts uncovered here are similar to those found at Chaco Canyon to the south, while later discoveries reflect a style more common to the San Juan Basin area after 1200 CE.

USEFUL CONTACTS:

Aztec Ruins
National Monument
725 Ruins Road
Aztec, NM 87410
505-334-6174
nps.gov/azru

newmexico.org/listing
   /aztec-visitor-center/2004

farmingtonnm.org

durango.org

The restored interior of the Great Kiva showing some of the exceptional architecture and design of the period.

Earl's House, the former home of archaeologist Earl H. Morris, now serves as the monument's visitor center. Morris, sponsored by the New York Museum of Natural History, began the first official dig here in 1916. In the 1930s, he oversaw the restoration of the Great Kiva. Before Morris arrived and the site was designated a national monument, looting had occurred, and many irreplaceable artifacts were lost forever.

Despite the monument's diminutive size, as many as sixty-three different bird species have been identified here, including such rarities as the yellow-billed cuckoo, Cassin's kingbird, and the lazuli bunting.

GETTING THERE:
From Farmington, drive east on US Highway 64 for a few miles to the junction with NM Highway 516. Take this north for 14 miles to Aztec. Follow signage for the monument, which is just off the main thoroughfare. From Durango, CO, take US Highway 550 for 35.0 miles to Aztec and follow signage for the monument.

FACILITIES:
There is no camping in the monument, but there are numerous options nearby in Farmington, NM, and Durango, CO.

45. Bandelier National Monument

NEAREST TOWN:	Los Alamos, NM
SIZE:	33,677 acres
BEST SEASON(S):	Year-round
NOTABLE ACTIVITIES:	Hiking, birding, wildlife and plant viewing, photography, American history

THE MONUMENT:

Comprising 33,677 acres, Bandelier National Monument was established on February 11, 1916, by President Woodrow Wilson. Though officially a unit of the National Park Service, it's managed by local pueblos and other state and federal agencies.

The monument was named for Adolph F. A. Bandelier, a Swiss-born businessman whose passion for anthropology led him to the American

View overlooking Bandelier Canyon, where the ruins are located alongside Frijoles Creek, a valuable source of water for people and crops.

A northern flicker doing a little spring house-cleaning for its prospective mate.

The wooden stairs leading 140 feet up to the Alcove House.

Southwest in 1880, with sponsorship from the Archaeological Institute of America. His pioneering efforts were key to the preservation of these ancestral homes of the local Cochiti Pueblo peoples. His book, *The Delight Makers*, is still in print.

Ancestral Puebloans resided primarily in Frijoles Canyon, a place that offered a moderate climate, a year-round stream, and ground rich enough to grow crops of maize, beans, squash, and cotton. Their diet was supplemented by local game such as rabbit, deer, and turkey. The Ancestral Puebloans used numerous alcoves in the neighboring volcanic cliffs to create living areas. Some of the villages consisted of as many as 600 rooms as the local population grew.

Several fires have impacted the land here, most recently in 1977, 1996, and 2011. Over 60 percent of the monument lands have been burned, mostly due to an overgrown forest resulting from years of fire suppression. The upside to this is the emergence of stands of aspen trees, which are favored by a variety of wildlife.

During the very busy summer season, May 14 through October, access is limited to a shuttle bus service from 9 a.m. until 3 p.m. The free bus is available at the White Rock Visitor Center along NM State Road 4. You may drive your own vehicle in during these times if you have a handicapped parking tag, are camping in Juniper Campground, or are going on an overnight trip.

Given the geology of the area, rainstorms can cause flash floods, especially from July through September. If you are caught near a flash flood, immediately head for higher ground. Never attempt to cross a flooded stream, as the depth and strength of the water are very deceptive. Afternoon thunderstorms are common in July, August, and September. Plan your activities to be finished by early afternoon at the latest. Temperatures within the monument boundaries vary based on the elevation. Summer temperatures are in the 80s during the day with nighttime lows in the 50s. Winter brings considerable snowfall, especially at the higher elevations, with daytime highs in the 40s and lows reaching down to the mid-teens.

Upper Falls of Frijoles Creek, a pleasant walk from the parking area.

THINGS TO DO:

While most monuments in this guide have fairly reasonable vehicle access, Bandelier is unique in that it's virtually roadless. There are only 3 miles of public roads within the monument, yet some 70 miles of trails are available for hiking and backpacking. While some of the hikes are strenuous, there are several close to the visitor center that have up-close views of the Ancestral Puebloan dwellings, some of which can be entered.

It's a good idea to explore the visitor center and talk to one of the rangers or volunteer staff. The 1.2-mile Main Loop Trail, which can be done in about an hour, travels close to some cliff dwellings and structures along Frijoles Creek.

You can also walk a bit farther upstream to the Alcove House. The trailhead is about halfway through the Main Loop Trail, and it's 0.5 mile to the cave. This site, with a reconstructed kiva, is easily seen from below alongside Frijoles Creek. For a bit of adventure, you can work your way up 140 feet of ladders and narrow steps to the alcove itself. The view from this height is

Spring is in the air as a male wild turkey attempts to impress an apparently uninterested hen.

worth the ascent, although a bit dizzying. Return to the visitor center the way you came.

Overnight backpacking trips lead to areas that see little modern human activity. Roughly 70 percent of the monument is within a designated wilderness area and protected as such. Depending on the length of your outing, you may find remote petroglyphs or historic sites, as well as wildlife that is not likely to be found in more congested areas around the trailheads. One favorite among backpackers is the Painted Cave, a collection of impressive pictographs toward the lower end of Capulin Canyon. This is a strenuous 11-mile one-way effort and should be undertaken as an overnight trip. As always, while hiking in such a dry and remote area, bring sufficient water or locate reliable sources before heading out. Filter all water, as giardia contaminates the streams and ponds within the monument. No fires are permitted, and a backcountry permit is required for all overnight trips. Pets are not allowed on any trails.

THINGS TO SEE:
The dwellings themselves are among the most interesting and easily viewed historic sites within the monument. The cavities in the rock were originally created as air pockets within the volcanic ash from eruptions that occurred several thousand years ago. Many of these were then enlarged and connected for use as living areas by the Ancestral Puebloans. The cavities represent a creative and unique manner of using natural surroundings for shelter.

Frijoles Creek, beginning from the snow-covered slopes of 10,199-foot Cerro Grande Peak, is

USEFUL CONTACTS:

Bandelier National Monument
15 Entrance Road
Los Alamos, NM 87544
505-672-3861

nps.gov/band

visitlosalamos.org

espanolanmchamber.com

a year-round stream that was critical for the early inhabitants of this area. Today you can follow it downstream to views of the upper and lower falls. Along the way, as you travel through the riparian areas of the canyon, you can appreciate the rich biodiversity this small stream affords. The creek itself continues for a total of 14 miles, dropping 4,000 feet as it cuts through the Pajarito Plateau before spilling into the Rio Grande.

Wildlife can be seen throughout the monument, especially deer and Abert's squirrels. Elk are often spotted during the winter when they come down from higher elevations to enjoy the forage.

In early October, the annual Bandelier's Fall Festival features Pueblo art exhibits, a Pueblo dance group performance, and a chance to learn more about local culture.

A variety of lizards can be found in the American West, not all of them in desert environments.

GETTING THERE:
From Los Alamos, take West Jemez Road south to NM State Road 4. Turn east (left) and drive about 6.0 miles to the monument entrance.

FACILITIES:
There is no lodging within the monument, but nearby Española, White Rock, Los Alamos, and Santa Fe offer a full range of accommodations.

Juniper Campground, located just outside the main gate and open year-round (weather permitting), has sixty-four sites with several pull-throughs. There is an RV dump but no hookups or showers. While the campground can accommodate vehicles up to 40 feet, the road leading to the entrance of the monument is steep and winding with hairpin turns that may limit overall vehicle length. There are forty-eight drive-in sites and sixteen walk-in tent sites available on a first-come, first-served basis. Reservations are not accepted unless you are staying at one of the two group sites along Abert's Squirrel Loop. Bookings can be made through reservation.gov.

46. Kasha-Katuwe Tent Rocks
National Monument

NEAREST TOWN:	Cochiti, NM
SIZE:	4,645 acres
BEST SEASON(S):	Year-round
NOTABLE ACTIVITIES:	Hiking, birding, wildlife and plant viewing, photography, geology

THE MONUMENT:

This geologically unique parcel of 4,645 acres presents a fascinating landscape in the southeastern Jemez Mountains of north-central New Mexico. The tent-shaped rock formations are composed of volcanic rock and ash that was deposited six to seven million years ago. The main body of the rocks is made of soft pumice, with a more erosion-resistant caprock at the pointed tops. The process of eroding these 1,000-foot deposits, over many millions of years, has caused the softer pumice to trickle down while the caprock remains in a distinctly pointed, tent-like shape. These rocks can range in

Outstanding examples of the geological process await those who visit this monument.

A shelter, with the roof blackened from hundreds of fires, is little more than a natural opening in the rock.

height from a few feet to 90 feet. It's easy to see where the next generation of these rocks will come from, as similar layers are evident in the still covered hillsides next to the exposed towers.

Kasha-Katuwe Tent Rocks National Monument was designated on January 17, 2001, by President Bill Clinton in an effort to protect the sensitive geological landscape as well as the culturally significant sites of the Pueblo de Cochiti. People have lived in this region since 5,500 BCE, and during the 1400s several large pueblos were constructed. Kasha-Katuwe translates into "white cliffs" in the native Keresan language of nearby Pueblo de Cochiti. Despite being on Bureau of Land Management lands, dogs are not allowed in the monument due to the fragility of the landscape and the very small area that is accessible to the public. Parking is also limited, and on busy days you may have to wait at the entrance for a space to open up. One visitor observed that there was a 90-minute wait in March.

Located on the Pajarito Plateau, the monument sits between 5,700 and 6,400 feet in elevation. Hiking here may be an adjustment for those arriving from the flatlands. Weather can be a factor as well; it can be quite warm in summer, reaching 90 degrees on many days with nighttime lows in the 40s. Precipitation totals only about 12 inches annually. Winter is cold with lows in the 20s and highs reaching only the upper 30s. Snow averages 4 feet annually. The good news is that there are 281 days per year of sunshine.

Reaching the monument can be a challenge. A printed road map is recommended, as cell service is limited. The easiest way is to leave I-25 at Exit 259 and head toward the Cochito Lake Recreation Area and then toward Cochito Pueblo along NM State Road 22. Follow the signs onto Tribal Route 92, then FR 266. Travel another 5 miles or so along a well-signed gravel road that ends at the monument entrance.

Most of the plant life here is confined to the washes in order to have adequate water and nutritious soil.

The result of volcanic eruptions 6 to 7 million years ago, the soft pumice and tuff are protected by a harder caprock, forming the familiar tent-like shape.

THINGS TO DO:

There are two hiking trails within the monument. The 1.2-mile Cave Loop Trail is rated as easy and takes you to an above-ground cave. The Tent Rocks Canyon Trail is a 3-mile round-trip hike rated as difficult because it requires you to squeeze along a narrow slot canyon and then ascend a steep 630-foot section to the top of the mesa. Grand views of the Sangre de Cristo, Jemez, and Sandia Mountains, as well as the Rio Grande Valley, serve as a reward. The 1-mile Veterans Memorial Overlook is a loop trail that is wheelchair accessible.

THINGS TO SEE:

Hiking the trails to see the Tent Rocks is the most popular activity. It's worth the extra effort to view and photograph the rocks from different angles and heights, as they can be quite dramatic in the right lighting.

Wildlife here is typical of the high-desert habitat. You can spot a variety of lizards and snakes, including the western diamondback rattlesnake. Birds range from rock wrens, juniper titmouse, and the sage thrasher to turkey vultures soaring overhead. The bizarrely named redwhisker clammyweed is, despite its name, a plant worth seeking out when in bloom, as it's a remarkable combination of color and form.

GETTING THERE:

From I-25, take Exit 264 and follow NM State Road 16 north for 8.2 miles. Turn right onto NM State Road 22 for 2.7 miles, then turn left onto NM State Road 22/Route 85 for 1.7 miles to the monument entrance.

One can clearly see the different layers of rock and visualize how they'll eventually form into the familiar tent shape over time.

FACILITIES:

There are no facilities within the monument, but there is access to drinking water. The nearby Pueblo de Cochiti has a store and a gas station but little else, and does not allow photographs, drawings, or paintings of the area. There are private inholdings within the monument as well. There are no campgrounds in the immediate area because all of the land is part of Jemez Pueblo or Zia Pueblo, which are closed to the public. The nearby Santa Fe National Forest has dispersed camping. Juniper Campground at nearby Bandelier National Monument is probably the best bet for those wishing to camp. It has forty-eight drive-in sites and sixteen walk-in tent sites and can accommodate RVs up to 40 feet, although the approach road can be tricky for large vehicles. All these sites are first-come, first-served. While there is an RV dump, there are no hookups or showers. RV parks are plentiful in the Santa Fe and Albuquerque areas as is food, fuel, lodging, and entertainment. Los Alamos offers a quieter pace and more relaxed atmosphere than the two larger cities.

USEFUL CONTACTS:

Rio Puerco BLM Field Office
100 Sun Avenue NE
Suite 330
Albuquerque, NM 87109
505-761-8700

blm.gov/programs/national
-conservation-lands/new-mexico
/kashakatuwe-tent-rocks-national
-monument

visitlosalamos.org

visitalbuquerque.org

santafe.org

47. Petroglyph
National Monument

NEAREST TOWN:	Albuquerque, NM
SIZE:	7,236 acres
BEST SEASON(S):	Year-round
NOTABLE ACTIVITIES:	Hiking, birding, petroglyph viewing, wildlife and plant viewing, photography, geology

THE MONUMENT:

Petroglyph National Monument is on the edge of the Albuquerque metropolitan area. Its 7,236 acres offer a wide variety of activities for people who want to enjoy relatively fair weather year-round. Those who study ancient history will be intrigued by the 24,000 petroglyphs on the eastern side of the monument, while those seeking something more active can roam on the elevated West Mesa where there are many trails for hiking and viewing petroglyphs.

Administered by the National Park Service and the City of Albuquerque, Piedras Marcades Canyon was the first tract of land protected in the area through its listing on the National Register of Historic Places in 1986. The current monument, spurred on by urban development, was established

I particularly liked how the artist used the natural features of the rock to accent the figure they created.

Black Volcano on the West Mesa with the Sandia Mountains behind. Albuquerque lies between these, in the Rio Grande Valley below.

on June 27, 1990, by Congress. Ike Eastvold, founder of the Friends of the Albuquerque Petroglyphs, was instrumental in organizing local groups to rally for national monument status. There is continuing friction among the local population, as demand for additional housing grows in the area surrounding the monument. Much remains to be resolved, but the City of Albuquerque and its citizens have clearly placed open space and recreational opportunities high on their list of priorities.

The climate here is fairly mild year-round, although June through August can be hot with highs in the upper 80s, while overnight temperatures drop to a pleasant mid-60s. Winter temperatures reach into the low 50s, although there is typically plenty of warm sunshine to take the edge off. Nighttime lows can dip into the 20s. As in most places in the West, spring and fall often offer the most comfortable temperatures. Rainfall is less than 10 inches annually, falling primarily from July through October. Snowfall is less than 10 inches and doesn't linger long.

Other national monuments in this region include Bandelier National Monument to the north, El Morro National Monument and El Malpais National Monument to the west, and Salinas Pueblo Missions National Monument to the south. Organ Mountains-Desert Peaks National Monument is near Las Cruces.

A petroglyph depicting an anthropomorph with elaborate, possibly ceremonial, headgear.

Fruit pods of one of twenty-three species of cholla cactus give seasonal color to the landscape.

THINGS TO DO:

Begin at the visitor center off the northern end of Unser Boulevard at Western Trail to acquire useful information about trail conditions, closures, and the namesake petroglyphs. You can reach Unser Boulevard by taking Exit 154 off I-40. Make sure you're dressed properly for the weather, use sunscreen, and drink plenty of water. You can also obtain free brochures for each of the petroglyph trails, with driving and hiking directions, at the visitor center.

This area, and the volcanoes and petroglyphs within it, are considered sacred to Indigenous people. Respect for these cultural beliefs and appropriate behavior is expected of all visitors. Climbing on, touching, or otherwise effacing the petroglyphs can cause irreparable damage.

Some petroglyph designs represent recognizable figures significant to the artists and their culture, while others are more abstract. The designs include anthropomorphs (human-like figures), concentric circles and spirals, animal figures, and geometric designs and shapes.

On the West Mesa portion of the monument, the Volcanoes Day-Use Area has three distinct cinder cones: Vulcan, Black, and JA volcanoes, all of which were active 200,000 years ago. The Black Volcano Loop is an easy hike on mostly level ground for a total distance of 2.25 miles. This takes you close to both the JA and Black volcanoes on a well-marked trail. The Vulcan Loop, while more difficult due to elevation gain, is an additional 0.95 mile from the junction with the Black Volcano Loop Trail. Either choice is a nice outing for a morning or afternoon stroll and leads to impressive views of the Rio Grande Valley. Climbing to the top of the volcanoes is not permitted. While the gate is only open from 9 a.m. to 5 p.m., you can still access the area for early or late viewing and hiking. Because it's a high and open mesa, this site may close during severe weather. There is a vault toilet at the trailhead as well as shaded seating areas, but there are no petroglyphs or water.

THINGS TO SEE:

Off-trail hiking, while allowed, is highly discouraged given the heavy visitation the monument receives and the subsequent damage to sensitive desert plants. There are plenty of trails here for exploring much of the monument.

Rinconada Canyon, 1 mile south of the visitor center, contains the largest number of petroglyphs. It's easily accessed via a 2.2-mile unpaved loop trail. Approximately 1,200 petroglyphs have been identified in this area. There is a parking lot with toilets and picnic tables, but no water.

The 70-acre Boca Negra Canyon, with the most developed trailhead within the monument, is about 1.5 miles north of the visitor center, 0.5 mile past Montano Road. There are three paved, separate trails that access more than 100 petroglyphs. Restrooms, shade, and drinking water are available.

The Piedras Marcadas Canyon site is in the northernmost section of the monument. It's day-use only and has no amenities. There is a 1.5-mile out-and-back sandy trail that leads along the base of the escarpment, from which 400 petroglyphs can easily be seen.

GETTING THERE:

From I-25, take Exit 228, Montano Road, for about 6 miles to the visitor center.

From I-40, take Exit 154, Unser Boulevard, and drive about 5 miles to the visitor center on your left.

USEFUL CONTACTS:

Petroglyph
National Monument
Western Trail NW
Albuquerque, NM 87120
505-899-0205

nps.gov/petr

visitalbuquerque.org

FACILITIES:

There are no facilities within the monument and limited access to drinking water. Given that it lies within the city limits of Albuquerque, however, there are virtually endless options for food, lodging, fuel, and entertainment in the surrounding area.

48. El Morro
National Monument

NEAREST TOWN:	Grants, NM
SIZE:	221 acres
BEST SEASON(S):	Year-round
NOTABLE ACTIVITIES:	Hiking, birding, wildlife and plant viewing, photography, geology, cross-country skiing, history

THE MONUMENT:

El Morro National Monument was established on December 8, 1906, by President Theodore Roosevelt. It's a small monument that encompasses only 221 acres.

The cuesta, a long upward-rising rock formation that drops off abruptly, is a prominent feature of the surrounding landscape. This conspicuous formation has long served as a landmark for travelers along ancient trade routes and, more importantly, a reliable source of water. "El Morro" is Spanish for "the headland." The Zuni Tribe called it Atsinna, "place of writings on the rock." Both names describe the site well, though for different reasons.

The cuesta, Spanish for "a long upward-rising rock formation that drops off abruptly," is prominent in this photograph. The Headland Trail continues around the right side of the formation and leads to the 7,000-foot top.

The pueblo sitting atop the rock formation, Atsinna Pueblo, was once home to an estimated 1,500 people. It has been dated to about 1275 CE and covered 60,000 square feet with as many as 875 distinct rooms. The rooms served as housing and included ceremonial kivas. These original inhabitants grew corn and other grains in irrigated fields on the plains below, part of a socially complex and interdependent lifestyle.

Camels were used as an early mode of transportation until a railroad was installed 25 miles to the north during the Civil War. The etchings on Inscription Rock, "Beale" and "Breckinridge," name two of these early camel wranglers.

The weather here is typical for west-central New Mexico. Summers are hot and dry, and July and August often have afternoon thunderstorms. You don't want to be walking the Headland Trail when they roll through, as you'll be the tallest thing around. Winters are harsh with temperatures dropping below freezing, and snow is not uncommon.

Some of the ruins of the Atsinna Pueblo, dating to 1275 CE, at the top of the formation.

THINGS TO DO:

Stop at the visitor center to get oriented. You can watch a 15-minute video on El Morro and peruse the exhibits. The staff is knowledgeable and helpful and can assist you in making the most of your visit.

A must-do walk here is the Inscription Rock Trail Loop, a paved 0.5-mile stroll along the base of the formation. You can clearly see the inscribed writings of dozens of early travelers, some dating back to the time of the Spanish in the 1500s. The trail is self-guided; make sure to borrow a brochure from the rangers. This booklet corresponds with numbered stops along the trail and explains their significance.

Water, a critical resource for life in this region, could be dependably found here, attracting travelers of all backgrounds and purposes.

The Zuni Tribe called this site Atsina, "place of writings on the rock" for all of the various inscriptions on the lower rock.

To extend an outing on the Inscription Rock Trail, continue on the Headland Trail. This trail is a roughly 2-mile loop that reaches an altitude of over 7,000 feet and passes by the ruins of Atsinna. You can observe, but not touch, the relics of the once-thriving community.

Despite the appearance of numerous crack systems in the sandstone, climbing is not allowed within the monument. There are no trails or paths for bicycles other than from the campground to the visitor center.

THINGS TO SEE:

The writings along the Inscription Rock Trail are a visceral reminder of the historical figures who passed through the area. It's quite fascinating to see a hand-carved inscription dating back 400 years that is still legible. Everything within the monument is protected, including the rock itself, so no further marking of the stone is allowed.

USEFUL CONTACTS:

El Morro
National Monument
HC 61, Box 43
Ramah, NM 87321
505-783-4226
nps.gov/elmo

grants.org

go-newmexico.com/Gallup

visitalbuquerque.org

There are other interesting sites and attractions to visit in the region. The nearby El Malpais National Monument, about 25 miles to the east, offers a look at a rugged and hostile volcanic landscape. Bandera Volcano and Ice Caves, just east of the monument, is a private enterprise that contains Bandera Crater, formed about 10,000 years ago. The Ice Cave, a partially collapsed lava tube that holds ice year-round, is a unique sight. Also nearby are the Enchanted Mesa and Acoma Pueblo and Mission sites, both of which are managed by the Acoma Tribal Council and open to the public with permission.

Looking back from the top of the Headland Trail, which generally follows the light-colored rock to the ruins.

The nearby Wild Spirit Wolf Sanctuary offers tours of the animals in their care. They rescue captive-bred wolves and wolfdogs. It's located between El Morro and the small community of Ramah.

GETTING THERE:
Take NM State Road 53, from Grants, for 40 miles to the monument entrance.

FACILITIES:
Camping is available within the monument on a first-come, first-served basis and without reservations or fees. There are nine sites, and RVs up to 27 feet may be accommodated. There are no hookups, electricity, or showers, and water is only seasonally available. There is a picnic area near the visitor center.

There are a few campgrounds as well as dispersed camping within the Cibola National Forest, north of El Morro. An RV park can be found about 1 mile east of the monument entrance.

The nearest town that offers limited food and gas is Ramah, about 12 miles west of the monument. For lodging and a greater variety of restaurants you will need to travel NM State Road 53 east about 40 miles to Grants or west to Zuni Pueblo. You can also find abundant accommodations in the town of Gallup, taking NM State Road 53 west to NM State Road 602 north. The large metropolitan area of Albuquerque lies 125 miles to the east and has just about anything you might desire in the way of lodging and restaurants.

49. El Malpais
National Monument

NEAREST TOWN:	Grants, NM
SIZE:	114,000 acres
BEST SEASON(S):	Year-round
NOTABLE ACTIVITIES:	Hiking, birding, wildlife and plant viewing, photography, volcanic geology, mountain biking

THE MONUMENT:

El Malpais National Monument is named for the extremely rugged landscape of these volcanic fields. "Malpais" means badlands in Spanish. President Ronald Reagan designated El Malpais National Monument on December 31, 1987. The monument's 114,000 acres are managed by the National Park Service, while the surrounding 262,000 acres are overseen as a National Conservation Area, much of which is wilderness and run by the Bureau of Land Management. The topography is difficult to negotiate, with many lava flows. The flows run 40 miles north to south and can be as wide as 15 miles in places.

The area's first inhabitants were Paleoindians during the period from 10,000 to 5,500 BCE. From 5,500 BCE to about 400 CE, many of the area's residents became more reliant on agriculture. It was not until the arrival of the Ancestral Puebloans (400–1600 CE) that more permanent pueblos were

Indian paintbrush or "prairie fire." Interestingly, this plant is a hemiparasite, meaning that it can appropriate nutrients from other organisms, namely perennial grasses. Amazingly widespread, the genus contains some 200 species found from the Andes in South America to Alaska in the far north.

Looking past a sandstone abutment over the vast expanse of lava fields that comprise much of this monument.

established and the people became more stationary. Widespread drought is thought to have been the demise of these populations, causing their eventual migration to the valleys of the Rio San Jose in the north and the Rio Puerco and Rio Grande to the east. The arrival of European cultures began in the 1500s.

The climate here is high desert and can be brutally warm in the summer as you walk among the lava beds. Highs reach the upper 80s to lower 90s with evenings cooling off into the 50s. Winters are generally moderate with highs in the 50s, but nighttime temperatures drop into the teens. Precipitation is average for this area, about 10 inches per year, with some snowfall during the winter.

THINGS TO DO:

The excellent Northwest New Mexico Visitor Center right off of I-40 (Exit 85) near Grants can provide you with all the information you need to enjoy this spectacular area. There is also an outdoor picnic area and sufficient parking to accommodate large RVs. Here you can plan your visit to both El Malpais and El Morro National Monuments. A 27-minute video, *Remembered Earth*, provides insight into the geological history of this region. The visitor center is jointly run by both the BLM and National Park Service.

Given the difficulty of constructing a trail in the lava rock, most trails in the monument are marked by cairns. Always keep the cairns in sight, as it would be easy to become disoriented without them. Hiking on this kind of terrain is also more difficult than most other places; sturdy boots, adequate water, and extra food are essential.

There are several hiking trails to choose from. A popular hike that can be combined with a car shuttle is the Zuni-Acoma Trail. This 7.5-mile trek, most of which is also part of the Continental Divide National Scenic Trail, has two entry points. The first is about 16 miles south from I-40 on NM State Road 53; the other is roughly 15 miles south of I-40 on NM State Road 117. This is a long and strenuous hike over lava flows and shouldn't be underestimated. It typically takes most people six to seven hours to complete the out-and-back trip. Continental Divide Trail blazes and concrete markers indicate the passage of the 1776 Dominquez-Escalante Expedition. This trail has been in use for over a thousand years, providing a critical link between the pueblos of Zuni and Acoma for trade, ceremonial functions, and co-mingling of their populations.

The more than 400 lava tubes in the monument are popular with cavers. You will need a free caving permit, available from the visitor center, and must ensure that your gear and clothing have not been in a cave previously without being disinfected afterward. Additionally, you should not explore a cave alone or without at least three light sources with backup batteries. As the temperatures tend to remain a constant 42 degrees in the caves, it can be much colder inside than outside; dress appropriately. A helmet is useful protection against the sharp rocks of ceilings and walls. Leave things as you found them, unless you're picking up someone else's litter. Caves are extremely sensitive and isolated environments, and even the smallest act can have long-term negative consequences. The easiest cave to access is Junction Cave, a short drive south from I-40 Exit 81 to the El Calderon Area.

The Big Skylight Cave and Giant Ice Cave offer more

USEFUL CONTACTS:

El Malpais National Monument
1900 E. Santa Fe Avenue
Grants, NM 87020
505-876-2783
nps.gov/elma

grants.org

go-newmexico.com/Gallup

visitalbuquerque.org

nps.gov/elma/learn/historyculture
    /upload/ELMA_hist.pdf

La Ventana, "the window" in Spanish, at 80 feet high and 130 feet across, is the second-highest arch in New Mexico and easily accessed from NM State Road 117 by a short stroll.

adventurous and challenging outings. Both are accessed from the same trailhead—take NM State Road 53 to County Road 42 south. Follow CR 42 a little more than 1 mile west of Bandera Ice Caves to National Park Service Road 300. The 8-mile road to the Big Tubes area is unpaved and can be impassable when wet. Once you arrive at the trailhead, it's a difficult 0.5-mile hike to the entrance of Big Skylight Cave. The reward of seeing the vast opening of this cave is worth the effort, and after a short downclimb, you can begin exploring all of its varied treasures. The entrance to Giant Ice Cave is about 0.1 mile beyond the entrance to Big Skylight Cave. Accessing this cave entrance is no more difficult than Big Skylight, but traveling inside the cave is considerably more challenging and requires a high level of experience over unstable terrain. Once inside you'll find a perennial ice floor toward the rear of the cave and seasonal ice columns.

There are additional, more arduous caves to explore. Inquire at the visitor center for more information.

THINGS TO SEE:

An activity that requires little to no effort is a visit to the Sandstone Bluffs Overlook, just off NM State Road 117 about 10 miles south of I-40. A short gravel road brings you to the parking and picnic area. You can view 3,000-year-old lava flows while standing on sandstone cliffs that were created by ancient seas 200 million years ago. The small *tinajas*, water-filled potholes, teem with life when filled with rainwater. They're home to fairy shrimp, spadefoot toad tadpoles, and various water bugs. There are no formal trails at this overlook, but you can explore the base of the cliffs on your own. Watch your step on both the steep cliffs and the sensitive cryptobiotic

Tinajas, "small jars" in Spanish, are vital sources of water in an otherwise dry environment. These pools of seasonal water are critical for the survival of their residents who have extremely short life cycles, some only ten days.

soil. This slow-growing soil, composed of bacteria, lichens, moss, and fungi, is crucial to stabilizing the soil and takes hundreds of years to form.

Although it's located in the adjoining El Malpais National Conservation Area, La Ventana (The Window) Natural Arch is both easily accessed and worth the slight effort it takes to walk to its base. Roughly 17.4 miles south on NM State Road 117 from I-40 (Exit 89), the arch is viewable to the east side of the road. It's the second-highest arch in New Mexico, formed over time via the forces of wind, rain, and temperature. The back walls of the arch can be dramatically lit during fall, winter, and spring afternoons due to its southwest aspect. The walk to the base is about 150 yards and provides an interesting and up-close perspective of the immense sandstone walls that support the arch.

GETTING THERE:

From Grants, take I-40 to Exit 81 for NM State Road 53, and continue south for about 10 miles to the northern monument boundary.

From I-40 Exit 89, go south on NM State Road 117 for about 7 miles to the eastern border of the monument.

FACILITIES:

There is no developed camping within the monument, but dispersed camping is allowed with a free backcountry permit. Off-road travel is prohibited, so it is necessary to use existing roads and campsites. Nearby Grants offers a limited range of lodging and dining. Depending on your direction of travel, Albuquerque to the east or Gallup to the west will have a greater selection for sleeping and dining accommodations. There is also camping both within and outside of nearby El Morro National Monument.

50. Salinas Pueblo Missions
National Monument

NEAREST TOWN:	Mountainair, NM
SIZE:	1,100 acres (total for all three sections)
BEST SEASON(S):	Year-round
NOTABLE ACTIVITIES:	Hiking, birding, wildlife and plant viewing, photography, history

THE MONUMENT:

This complex of three separate Spanish missions (Gran Quivira, Quarai, and Abo) is in central New Mexico at 6,500 feet near the town of Mountainair, roughly 45 miles south of Albuquerque. It was initially designated as Gran Quivira National Monument on November 1, 1909, by President William H. Taft, and it was listed on the National Register of Historical Places on October 15, 1966. It was renamed in 1988 as Salinas Pueblo Missions National Monument to include all three sites.

What remains of the original Abo Spanish mission constructed in the early 1600s.

Ruins at the Quarai site, once home to some 600 southern Tiwa peoples. This image shows the exceptional architecture and construction of the time.

Massive wooden beams support an archway. It's not likely that such large trees would have been found locally.

Built by seventeenth-century Spanish Franciscan missionaries to convert the Indigenous inhabitants of this region to Christianity, the missions thrived for about fifty years before most of the population, both Spaniards and Native Americans, departed the area. It is thought that disease, drought, and famine led to the abandonment of this region. All three sites total about 1,100 acres. The main visitor center is in Mountainair, and visitor centers are also located at both the Gran Quivira and Quarai sites. Each has information about and driving directions to the other sites. At the Mountainair visitor center, there's a museum and a 14-minute video that explains the history of the region and its inhabitants. Abo Ruins has a contact station that can provide you with basic information on the monument. Gran Quivira is the largest ruin of a Christian temple in the United States.

Weather here is typical of a high-altitude dry desert environment. Generally mild in spring and fall with highs in the 70s and nighttime lows in the 30s, summer temperatures can reach the upper 80s with lows in the 50s. Winter can bring up to 20 inches of snow and daytime temperatures in the 40s to low 50s, with nighttime lows in the 20s. Annual precipitation amounts to about 15 inches of rainfall, most falling between June and October.

THINGS TO DO:

Once you've oriented yourself at a visitor center, it's an easy day trip to visit each of the three different sites. Beginning at Quarai, the smallest of the three units, you'll note the presence of a year-round water source, Zapato Creek, which supported a large Indigenous pueblo before the Spanish arrived. The next stop would be the Abo site, a short drive from Mountainair. Here you'll also find indications of a large Indigenous community prior to Spanish arrival in 1581. There are numerous unexcavated pueblo

Large ruins at the Quarai site.

This modest kiva, a place for social activities such as religious ceremonies, teaching children, and telling stories, was built at the same time as the Catholic mission.

mounds. A small convent was built here that contained a circular kiva. Gran Quivira, the largest of the three units at 611 acres, should be the last on your trip, as it will take the most time to explore. There were existing pueblos in this area prior to the arrival of the Spanish missionaries, indicating a large and thriving population of Indigenous peoples. This site has also gone by the name of Las Humanas.

On October 13, 2016, a Citizenship Ceremony was held at Quarai Mission to celebrate the new citizenship of fifteen Americans. This was a joint effort by the National Park Service and the US Citizenship and Immigration Service. Check the monument website or Facebook page for current information on this unique opportunity to be inducted into US citizenship.

THINGS TO SEE:

Nearby Manzano Mountains State Park has several miles of hiking and interpretive trails. It's also a great location for high-altitude birding year-round.

The ruins, and their accompanying history, are the biggest draw for most visitors. As mentioned above, all three sites can be seen in a single day for motivated explorers. It's best to have a place to stay nearby. The monument was designated an International Dark Sky Place in 2016 and holds several evening astronomy events in the summer months. These are supported by The Albuquerque

USEFUL CONTACTS:

Salinas Pueblo Missions
National Monument
P.O. Box 517
Mountainair, NM 87036
505-847-2585

nps.gov/sapu

discovermountainairnm.com

Initially, I was reluctant to explore the ruins in the midst of a winter storm. Then I realized that people had actually lived here under similar conditions and without the benefit of central heating. It was certainly a harsh life.

Sheltered corridors gave some relief from the elements when moving from place to place.

Astronomical Society and the Lake County Astronomical Society.

GETTING THERE:
Take I-25 (Exit 175) and drive 40 miles on NM State Road 60 to the visitor center in Mountainair.

FACILITIES:
There are no facilities available, aside from restrooms at each of the visitor centers. Nearby Manzano Mountains State Park, about 15 miles away and at 7,250 feet, has twenty-three sites with full hookups and another nine with electricity only. There are developed and dispersed campgrounds within the nearby Santa Fe National Forest. There is also an RV park in Mountainair.

51. Gila Cliff Dwellings
National Monument

NEAREST TOWN:	Silver City, NM
SIZE:	553 acres
BEST SEASON(S):	Year-round
NOTABLE ACTIVITIES:	Hiking, birding, wildlife and plant viewing, photography, hot springs, history

THE MONUMENT:

This monument is within the Gila National Forest in southwestern New Mexico and just 45 miles north of Silver City. The monument protects historic structures and artifacts of the Mogollon people, who inhabited this region from about 1275 to 1300 CE. The area was the northernmost reach of the Mogollon culture's influence. Why they left remains a mystery. Although originally under the oversight of the National Park Service, management of this monument was transferred to the US Forest Service in 1975.

Sites were often chosen for their south-facing aspects, the better to gain what little warmth there was from the low winter sun.

Looking up the Gila River Canyon, site of the Melanie Hot Springs, a relaxing day outing.

The rocky alcoves provided both a refuge from the elements as well as a defensible position.

The monument is just 553 acres in size, small by most monument standards, yet it contains a wealth of priceless artifacts and a rich cultural history. Proclaimed by President Theodore Wilson on November 16, 1907, this is also one of the first national monuments designated under the Antiquities Act of 1906.

Ranging from 5,700 to 7,300 feet in elevation, weather here is typical of a mountain environment. Highs range from the mid-80s to the low-90s in the summer with lows in the upper 40s. Spring and fall are generally mild with daytime highs in the upper 70s and nighttime lows in the 20s to mid-30s. Winter is cold and highs rarely exceed the 50s during the day, dipping into the teens at night. Snow accumulation can be as much as 10 feet in the higher elevations, closing many of the trails.

Although the road to Gila Cliff Dwellings National Monument from Silver City is only about 45 miles, allow a good 90 minutes to get there. This is a slow, winding mountain road that lends itself more to scenic views than expedient travel. It's also a popular cycling route, so be mindful of bicyclists on the roadway. Another approach that may be a little flatter is to take NM State Road 35 from San Lorenzo north until it joins NM State Road 15.

THINGS TO DO:

The visitor center is a great source of information and includes a 15-minute video about the Mogollon people, the landscape, and the monument. It has an interesting collection of Mogollon and Apache artifacts, including a unique bracelet made from bittersweet clamshells. Its presence show-

Wooden ladders provide access to the various alcoves as well as protection since they could easily be pulled up and inside the shelter.

A diversity of geology can be found here in both the Gila Cliff Dwellings Caldera and the adjacent Bursum Caldera.

cases the vast trade network that was present from the Gulf of California across Arizona and to the upper Gila River. There are also kennels available for your pet, as they are not allowed on the trails, with the exception of service animals.

Once you've stopped at the visitor center, it's time to head out and explore these unique dwellings. The Cliff Dwellings Trail is a 1-mile loop trail beginning at the visitor center that rises about 180 feet to the habitation sites. The upper part of this trail can be muddy, icy, steep, and rocky. You don't have to travel the entire trail to encounter the first of the dwellings.

There are over 400 miles of trails within the surrounding Gila Wilderness. For those seeking a more strenuous outing with several scenic viewpoints, the 12-mile West Fork Loop offers access to the ridge between the middle and west forks of the Gila River. Starting at the TJ Corral Trailhead, it ascends 1,300 feet before looping back to the parking area.

Several hot springs can be found in the area. The easiest to access are the Jordan Hot Springs, from the Middle Fork Trailhead, a short 0.75-mile hike that includes several water crossings. The temperature of the springs is 140 degrees, so mixing this water with the colder water of the river is necessary to avoid serious burns. Another short hike is on the west side of Gila National Forest off NM State Road 180 near Glenwood, which leads to the San Francisco Hot Springs. A side road on the west of US Highway 180, north of Sheridan Corral Road but south of Black Mountain, leads to the trailhead. It's an easy 2.5-mile round-trip to the springs.

More information on hikes and hot springs can be found at the visitor center or via the links in the "Useful Contacts" section.

Restored stairs give easier, and safer, access to the ruins for the visitor.

THINGS TO SEE:

There is an unexcavated ruin about 1.5 miles east of the monument, perched on a high bluff overlooking the middle and west forks of the Gila River below. This is a large site that's estimated to have had over 200 rooms, three Great Kivas, and a plaza for community gatherings. Access is near the visitor center, so first check with staff about visiting these ruins to get current information. Visit the link below for details about the intriguing research completed at these ruins.

Wildlife is abundant, with over 100 documented species of birds—some permanent residents, some migrants passing through. Black-chinned and broad-tailed hummingbirds are common, as are Bewick's wren, spotted towhee, the plumbeous vireo, and northern flicker. You may catch a glimpse of rare wild turkeys or a northern goshawk. Mammals include black bears, mountain lions, mule deer, and elk. The Blue Range Wolf Recovery Area, which includes the Gila National Forest, is home to an effort to reintroduce the endangered Mexican Gray Wolf to its native range. As with most wildlife sightings, habitat is critical to finding the species you seek. Updates on recent sightings may be found at the visitor center.

GETTING THERE:

From Silver City, head north on NM State Road 15 for 44 miles along a slow, winding mountain road. Allow up to two hours of driving time.

FACILITIES:

While the monument has no camping facilities, the surrounding Gila National Forest offers both developed and dispersed camping.

The primitive and free Forks Campground is about 5 miles south of the monument on the east side of NM State Road 15, just north of the Gila River

A male red-naped sapsucker, common in mixed forests, is differentiated from the yellow-bellied by the red throat.

It does get cold here in winter, often into the teens as evidenced by frost on the windshield after camping out.

Bridge. Grapevine Campground is another primitive and free campground along the Gila River about 5 miles south of the monument and south of the Gila River Bridge. Both have no water aside from the Gila River, which must be filtered, treated, or boiled before consuming. These campgrounds are first-come, first-served, and RVs are not recommended due to the sandy and steep access road. There are vault toilets and fuel, food, and showers. There is a phone at Doc Campbell's General Store about 4 miles farther south.

Closer to Gila Cliff Dwellings National Monument, the Upper and Lower Scorpion campgrounds are 0.5 mile to the south on NM State Road 15. Camping is free, and there is potable water at the RV station at visitor center parking area. The USFS discourages RV camping at either of these campgrounds, though there is paved parking. Vault toilets, grills, and tables are available and fuel, food, and showers.

The largest nearby town is Silver City. It has 10,000 residents and relies heavily on tourism, so it's home to many amenities.

USEFUL CONTACTS:

Gila Cliff Dwellings National Monument
26 Jim Bradford Trail
Mimbres, NM 88049
575-536-9461

nps.gov/gicl

visitsilvercity.org

52. **Prehistoric Trackways**
National Monument

NEAREST TOWN:	Las Cruces, NM
SIZE:	5,255 acres
BEST SEASON(S):	Year-round
NOTABLE ACTIVITIES:	Hiking, birding, wildlife and plant viewing, photography, geology, fossil tracks

THE MONUMENT:

This monument was established on March 30, 2009, by President Barack Obama, the first for his administration. It features a significant deposit of Paleozoic Era fossilized footprints, many in the form of a series of tracks. The tracks were made along the coastline of a large tropical sea, the Hueco Seaway, which once existed along the southern part of New Mexico.

Looking east at sunrise along the well-marked Trackways Trail. The city of Las Cruces, the Rio Grande, and the Organ Mountains can be seen in the distance.

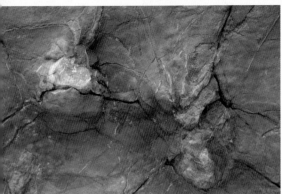

A fossilized imprint of a dinosaur track with
four, possibly five, toes. It's easy to walk right
past something like this, or step on it, at the
Discovery Site as none of the fossils are
marked.

White-winged dove enjoying the
flowers of an Ocotillo cactus.

These fossils date back 280 million years and are some of the finest preserved sets of dinosaur trackways in the world. Locals first discovered various tracks and other fossils in the 1930s. Jerry Paul MacDonald was the first to recognize their scientific significance in 1987 and has labored for decades to identify, preserve, and remove 2,500 slabs for safekeeping. Many of these trackways are now housed in the New Mexico Museum of Natural History and Science in Albuquerque, the Carnegie Museum of Natural History, and the Smithsonian Institute. There are two track sets at the nearby Las Cruces Nature and Science Museum.

The monument's 5,280 acres lie within the Robledo Mountains northwest of Las Cruces. The weather can be hot in the summer months with highs into the mid-90s while lows drop to the more comfortable upper 60s. Winters are cooler with daytime highs rarely above the upper 50s and nighttime lows dropping into the upper 20s. Early spring and late fall are more reasonable and likely the best times to visit. Highs during these times are in the 70s with lows in the 40s. Rainfall is scant at less than 10 inches annually, with most falling from July through October, so be aware of flash flooding. Snowfall amounts to about two inches a year.

The best and easiest access to the monument is from I-25 Exit 9, Dona Ana, north of Las Cruces. Here you'll head west on NM 320 to NM 185, turning north for about 0.5 mile to Shalem Colony Road. Go left here and follow this for about 1.5 miles, cross the Rio Grande, and turn right on CR Rocky Acres Trail. Go about 0.25 mile to Permian Track Road on the left and then about another 0.25 mile to the kiosk. As you cross the Rio Grande, you'll notice a couple of areas that are accessible to the river's edge, which make for a nice break after hiking the monument.

An osprey, also known as a fish hawk, finds a solitary perch to enjoy its catch of the day.

THINGS TO DO:

Hiking the Ridgeline Trail is a good way to access the general monument area from the parking lot. The Trackways Trail is a 2.3-mile out-and-back route that is rated moderate and is used by Bureau of Land Management guides to take visitors out to see the trackways at the Discovery site. A more moderate approach to the Discovery Site is to drive past the kiosk about 0.2 mile to the OHV staging area. Park here and follow the wash across the road through a fenced and gated track, staying to the right. You'll pass another cabled gate that you can walk around and then ascend the wash for about 1.0 mile to the site, which has a large sign. Tracks can be found in this area with a little searching.

If you're an off-road enthusiast, then this is an excellent area for riding trails from easy to extremely difficult and dangerous. There is a dedicated system of trails here that lie outside the restricted area of the monument.

Mountain biking is another popular activity here, especially during the milder winter months. This is the home of the SST Mountain Bike Trail, an extremely challenging and technical track that requires expert riding skills.

THINGS TO SEE:

The Discovery Site is the best place to see trackways in the monument. It's best to arrange a tour led by staff from the BLM Office in Las Cruces. When available, this can save you a lot of wandering around, especially if you're not sure what to look for, as many of these tracks are quite small. See the contact information below.

If you're not able to hike or the weather is uncooperative, visit the Las Cruces Museum of Nature and Science to see a trackway that was excavated from the Monument.

There are two other national monuments within a few hours of Las Cruces: Organ Mountains-Desert Peaks Monument in New Mexico and Chiricahua National Monument in Arizona.

If you're a birder traveling between November and February, a trip to the Bosque del Apache National Wildlife Refuge, about two hours north on I-25, is worthwhile. You'll have the opportunity to view thousands of sandhill cranes and snow geese that winter here.

GETTING THERE:

Take I-25 north of Las Cruces to Exit 9, Dona Ana. Head west on NM Highway 320 to NM Highway 185, turning north for about 0.5 mile to Shalem Colony Road. Go left here and follow this road for about 1.5 miles, crossing the Rio Grande. Turn right on NM County Road Rocky Acres Trail. Go about 0.25 mile to Permian Track Road on the left and then about another 0.25 mile to the kiosk.

FACILITIES:

This is an undeveloped monument and there are no facilities. Although this is a BLM-administered monument there are few drivable roads, so dispersed camping is not an option. The nearest public campgrounds are at Aguirre Springs in the Organ Mountains-Desert Peaks National Monument on the east side of San Augustin Pass going toward White Sands on NM 70. There are toilets here and a trash service but no water. Water can be had at the host campsite near the entrance. The Oliver Lee Memorial State Park south of Alamogordo is farther away with forty-four sites. Otherwise, Las Cruces has a number of food and lodging options.

USEFUL CONTACTS:

BLM Office Las Cruces
1800 Marquess Street
Las Cruces, NM 88005
575-525-4300
blm.gov/visit/ptnm

New Mexico Museum of
Natural History and Science
1801 Mountain Road NW
Albuquerque, NM 87104
505-841-2800

New Mexico Bureau of
Geology and Mineral Resources
801 Leroy Place
Socorro, NM 87801
575-835-5490

lascrucescvb.org

53. Organ Mountains–Desert Peaks
National Monument

NEAREST TOWN:	Las Cruces, NM
SIZE:	500,000
BEST SEASON(S):	Year-round
NOTABLE ACTIVITIES:	Hiking, birding, wildlife and plant viewing, photography, geology, astronomy, solitude, mountain biking, rock climbing, horseback riding

THE MONUMENT:

On May 21, 2014, President Barack Obama designated this nearly half a million acres as a national monument. This was a collaborative effort among local groups and communities, and nearly 75 percent of area residents supported the creation of the monument.

The monument is divided into four separate areas, each with its own distinctive characteristics and appeal. The Organ Mountains rise high above the surrounding Chihuahuan Desert to the top of Organ Needle, just under 9,000 feet. The Desert Peaks area lies northwest of Las Cruces and contains the Picacho Peak Recreation Area. The Potrillo Mountains are the most remote area of the monument with a distinctive landscape that includes cin-

Organ Mountains from the West with their distinctive jagged peaks reaching to an elevation of nearly 9,000 feet.

der cones, lava flows and tubes, and a volcanic crater, the Kilbourne Hole, which once served as training grounds for NASA's Apollo missions to the moon. The Doña Ana Mountains, while the smallest of the four areas, have a wide range of opportunities for hiking, biking, horseback riding, and rock climbing.

The weather can be harsh in the summer with highs reaching the mid-90s and lows into the 60s. Winters are more agreeable as daytime temperatures rarely exceed the low 60s and lows drop to the upper 20s. Precipitation is nine inches with an occasional dusting of snow during winter.

THINGS TO DO:

The Dripping Springs Visitor Center, on the west side of the monument should be your first stop. This facility, open year-round, is a great resource for information and daily bird sightings and other wildlife. The 3-mile round-trip hike to the old Dripping Springs Resort is on level ground and offers scenic views.

There are miles and miles of hiking trails within the monument's four units. Many are short and offer quick exposure to the area's biodiversity; longer hikes can involve multiple days. The 29-mile Sierra Vista National Recreation Trail is one of the most challenging and enjoyable. Horses, bicycles, and hikers are allowed on this route, which connects Las Cruces with Franklin Mountains State Park in Texas, traversing the west slope of the Organs.

Doña Ana Mountains, the northeastern unit of the monument, at sunset.

Loggerhead shrike, a common bird in brushy, treeless areas.

Spotted towhee, possibly Great Plains towhee due to the greater amount of white spotting on the scapulars.

Say's Phoebe, a fairly common flycatcher found in dry, open areas.

For rock climbers, the Organ Mountains offer a wealth of climbing on solid granite and rhyolite. Be advised: there are no easy approaches and route-finding may be the most difficult part of the climb. The east side of the mountains can be accessed from the Aguirre Springs Campground, while Baylor Canyon Road provides entry from the west side. Organ Needle, the northernmost and highest feature of the Organs, sits at 8,990 feet. Most of the technical climbs begin around 7,000 feet. Temperatures are high in the summer months with relentless winds. Nighttime temperatures can plummet, as is often the case at higher altitudes. Recommended routes within the main area of the Organs include the west ridge of The Wedge, which goes at 5.7, and the Left Eyebrow of Sugarloaf, 5.7 R. Both are long routes, especially when you include the approaches, so be prepared! Another great climbing location is in the Doña Ana Mountains, north of Las Cruces, which has eleven separate climbing areas. A favorite feature here is the Checkerboard Wall, which has a number of moderate lines. Check out mountainproject .com and the more recent (2006) *Rock Climbing New Mexico* by Dennis Jackson. The Jackson guide covers the entire state and offers climbing beta for the Organs.

THINGS TO SEE:
The Organ Mountains offer a wide-ranging diversity of rare plants, including some only found in this region. Many of the flowering plants are seasonal, so your visit should coincide with the most likely blooming season. The area can be a colorful mosaic of blooming zinnias, marigolds, daisies, barrel

▲ Moonrise at sunset in the Portillo Mountains Unit of the Organs.

◄ Sugarloaf Mountain, with several long moderate routes, attracts most of the climbers here in the Organs. Be advised that while these climbs are on moderately decent rock, expect runouts in the forty- to fifty-foot range as well as the potential for horrendous winds.

cacti, sunflowers, and summer poppy. Plants vary as the altitude changes, with juniper and mountain mahogany at the higher elevations and desert plants, such as creosote, ocotillo, and yucca at the lower elevations. The Rio Grande, alongside the monument, offers a rich assortment of plant and bird life that should not be missed.

Bird watchers can see such species as the bald and golden eagles, endangered peregrine falcons, and Montezuma quail. The rare aplomado falcon has been reintroduced in parts of the monument and a sighting should not only be treasured but also reported to monument management to help them track these gorgeous birds.

Representative mammals include mule deer, pronghorn, coyotes, mountain lions, and jackrabbits. Several reptile species, including snakes, are found here as well.

GETTING THERE:

To access the east side of the Organs, follow US Highway 70 over San Augustine Pass. Go about 1 mile to Aguirre Springs Road to the south and follow it approximately 6 miles, just below the base of the Organ Mountains.

For more detailed directions and information, go to the Bureau of Land Management District Office in Las Cruces.

The Rabbit Ears at sunrise from the Aguirre Spring Campground on the east side of the Organs.

FACILITIES:

There is a campground on the east side of the Organs, Aguirre Spring, just south of Highway 70 about 1.0 mile down the east side of San Augustin Pass. Look for Aguirre Springs Rd. to the south and follow it approximately 6 miles to just below the base of the Organ Mountains. There are fifty-seven sites available, but RV travel is restricted due to the twisting, narrow roadway. This campground is open year-round, but the gates are locked at night, depending on the season. It is a quiet and relaxing place. Water is available at the entrance.

Franklin Mountains State Park north of El Paso, TX, also offers camping. There are five RV sites and fourteen walk-in tent sites.

Additional camping is at Oliver Lee Memorial State Park south of Alamogordo on NM 54. There are forty-four sites here, sixteen of which are suitable for RVs. The Park is open year-round with showers, vault toilets, and hiking and interpretive trails.

Lodging and other amenities can be found in nearby Las Cruces, which also makes a convenient base for exploring the different units of the Monument.

USEFUL CONTACTS:

Organ Mountains–Desert Peaks National Monument
Las Cruces District Office BLM
Las Cruces, NM 88005
575-525-4300

lascrucescvb.org

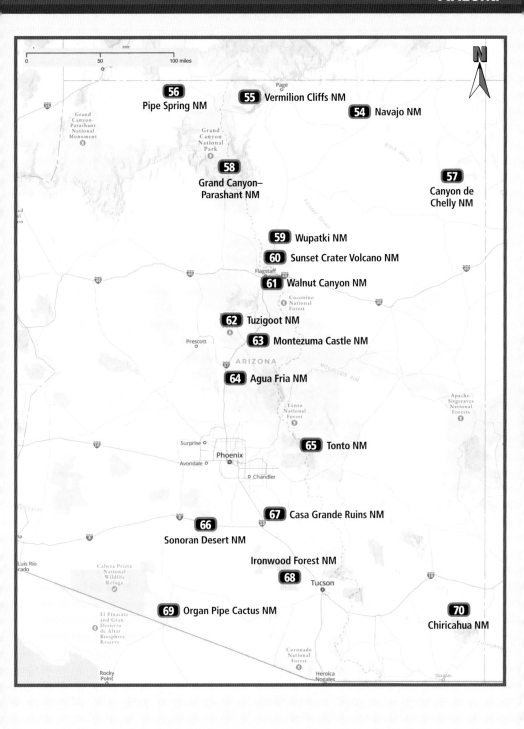

56 Pipe Spring NM

55 Vermilion Cliffs NM

54 Navajo NM

58 Grand Canyon–Parashant NM

57 Canyon de Chelly NM

59 Wupatki NM

60 Sunset Crater Volcano NM

61 Walnut Canyon NM

62 Tuzigoot NM

63 Montezuma Castle NM

64 Agua Fria NM

65 Tonto NM

67 Casa Grande Ruins NM

66 Sonoran Desert NM

Ironwood Forest NM

68

69 Organ Pipe Cactus NM

70 Chiricahua NM

54. Navajo National Monument

NEAREST TOWN:	Kayenta, AZ
SIZE:	470 acres (all units)
BEST SEASON(S):	Year-round
NOTABLE ACTIVITIES:	Hiking, birding, wildlife and plant viewing, photography, geology, astronomy, solitude, history

THE MONUMENT:

Navajo National Monument is in the northeastern corner of Arizona, just west of Kayenta. It's managed by the National Park Service and is an inholding of Navajo Nation lands. The monument comprises three non-contiguous parcels, with historic and modern villages scattered throughout the region, representing part of the past, present, and future of the various tribes that live on the Colorado Plateau.

Numerous rocky spires can be found in this region, particularly in the vicinity of Kayenta.

Part of the rationale behind establishing the monument was to prevent looting of historic sites in the late 1800s, which was a popular activity throughout the West. President William Taft declared monument status for these parcels on June 8, 1909.

Weather in this region is warm and dry, especially during the summer, with average highs in the mid-80s to 90s and lows reaching the upper 50s. The elevation is 7,300 feet, so the intensity of the sun is greater

The paved Sandal Trail offers excellent views of the Betatakin Ruins in the alcove. A pair of binoculars would be useful here.

than at sea level. Winters are cold, with daytime highs in the 40s and nighttime lows in the low 20s. Precipitation is just under 13 inches annually, while snowfall can be significant at nearly four feet.

THINGS TO DO:

Stop at the visitor center to view some of the artifacts and read about the history of Indigenous peoples in the area. You can also sign up for various ranger-led hikes to the two main ruin sites, Betatakin and Keet Seel. Betatakin is a combination of 160 acres of National Park Service land and 250 acres of land from the Navajo Nation. Keet Seel is about 160 acres. A third site, Inscription House, is located 40 miles away in Nitsin Canyon.

To get oriented, hike one of the three rim trails that begin from the visitor center. Tsegi Overlook involves hardly any walking at a mere 0.1 mile from the entrance road. You'll have solid views of Tsegi Canyon, but not the ruins. The 0.4-mile round-trip Canyon View Trail is also short and easy, ending at the Ranger Station. Here you'll have grand views of Tsegi Canyon and its many tributaries. The 0.6-mile round-trip Aspen Trail covers strenuous terrain, but it travels through beautiful forest within Betatakin Canyon. The easy and paved 1.3-mile round-trip Sandal Trail is the most popular hike, with sensational views of the Betatakin Ruins. The visitor center also has a video about Betatakin Ruins, if you're unable to visit on foot.

The omnivorous black bear is shy and reclusive, preferring solitary habitat and occupies a territory of up to fifty square miles.

THINGS TO SEE:

The easiest site to see is the Betatakin Ruins via the Sandal Trail. This trail puts you within site of the ruins to the north, but you'll still be about 500 feet above and 1,300 feet away from the actual ruins. Afternoon sun puts the ruins in shade from this location. A ranger-led 5.0-mile round-trip hike to Betatakin Ruins follows either the Tsegi Point Trail or the Aspen Trail, depending on the weather. The Aspen Trail drops 700 feet to the canyon floor as it makes its way to the ruins. Although led by a ranger, you can return at your own time and pace. The Tsegi Point Trail hike is limited to fifteen people per day. A longer and more strenuous trail to the ruins leaves the visitor center and follows the Sandal Trail to the Aspen Trail, covering 2.5 miles one-way. This hike has a twenty-five-person limit. Both hikes are offered daily during the summer hours; the Aspen Trail hike is offered only on weekends.

For those with the time, ability, and desire, a hike to the ruins of Keet Seel is an option. Reservations and a backcountry permit are required for this May through September hike. This is a long and difficult hike, about 8.5 miles one-

USEFUL CONTACTS:

Navajo National Monument
P.O. Box 7717
Shonto, AZ 86045
928-672-2700

nps.gov/nava

Information on camping and tours
discovernavajo.com

visitarizona.com/cities/northern
  /kayenta

A small hut made from local materials gives visitors an idea of how difficult living here would have been as well as the resourcefulness of the people.

way involving a 1,000-foot descent to the canyon floor followed by about 400 feet of elevation gain before reaching the ruins. To break up this trip, there is a primitive campground 0.25 mile from the ruins that you can camp in with prior arrangement. There is a mandatory orientation at 3:00 pm the day before the hike. The hike requires several crossings of Keet Seel Stream, so expect to get wet. Day hikers should plan on four to six hours of hiking this trail each way. The ruins here are among the best preserved in the entire Southwest.

GETTING THERE:

From Kayenta, AZ, take US Highway 160 for about 20 miles, then turn right onto AZ Highway 564 and drive about 9 miles to the visitor center.

FACILITIES:

There are no facilities within the monument aside from the campgrounds and no open fires are allowed. Limited supplies may be obtained at the Black Mesa Trading Post at the junction of Highways 564 and 160. The seasonal Canyon View Campground offers 14 free tent sites. Three are suitable for groups of up to fifteen tents. There are composting toilets and grills but no water, which can be found at Sunset View Campground. This free year-round campground is open to both RVs and tents. Length limit is 28 feet. There are thirty-one sites with tables, grills, parking, and a comfort station with running water. No hookups or RV dumps are available. Because the surrounding lands are Hopi and Navajo Reservations, no dispersed camping is allowed.

55. Vermilion Cliffs
National Monument

NEAREST TOWNS:	Fredonia, AZ, to the west, Page to the east
SIZE:	293,689 acres
BEST SEASON(S):	Year-round
NOTABLE ACTIVITIES:	Hiking, birding (California condor), wildlife and plant viewing, photography, geology, astronomy, solitude, mountain biking

THE MONUMENT:

Vermilion Cliffs, which sounds like a fairytale, is indeed an otherworldly experience. President Bill Clinton proclaimed it a national monument on November 9, 2000. The Paria Plateau is the dominant feature here, covering the majority of the monument's 293,689 acres. Within this timeless landscape are several gems of geological and photographic beauty, most notable the Coyote Buttes and Paria Canyon. Elevations range from 3,100 to 6,500 feet. The cliffs can rise as much as 2,000 feet above the surrounding lands. The cliffs are part of the "Arizona Strip," which is 7,878 square miles of stunning desert landscape across northern Arizona.

The warmth of the setting sun lights up the cliffs with a familiar reddish hue, giving the monument its name.

Weather here is typical of the high desert, hot and dry most of the year. Summer highs reach the upper 90s with nighttime lows in the 60s. Winter offers a slight respite from the searing summer heat, with temperatures ranging from the 40s to 50s during the day and dropping to the 20s at night. Precipitation is scant year-round, barely reaching six inches on average. June is the driest month with barely two-tenths of an inch of rainfall, although other months don't even receive one inch. This is a harsh and unforgiving landscape. A reliable standalone GPS/map app and current topo maps and compass are essential if you wish to venture off the main roadway.

The gorgeous lines of sandstone found in The Wave are well worth the nearly 6-mile round-trip hike and vying for a lottery pass.

THINGS TO DO:

Obtain information at Navajo Bridge on US 89A, east and south of the monument at the Bureau of Land Management offices in Kanab, UT, or at the seasonal Paria Contact Station on the northern side of the monument off US 89. The visitor center in St. George, UT, on the north side or the seasonal visitor center at Big Water, UT, are the best sources for year-round information.

Most people drive House Rock Valley Road (HRVR), BLM 700, on the west side of the monument and south of US 89. HRVR travels along the prominent west-facing cliffs and is suitable when dry for vehicles with good clearance and tires. A full-size spare tire is highly recommended, as is plenty of water and food. The road is rough dirt and rock with occasional washes and runs for approximately 30 miles, connecting US 89 to the north with US 89A to the south. HRVR is also the access road for Buckskin Gulch, Wire

Moonrise over Sandstone cliffs. The various layers of sediment suggest this was a much different environment in the past.

Parking at the Wirepass Trailhead for The Wave, rarely crowded due to the limited permit system required for access.

Pass, and Lone Tree Trailheads; as well as Stateline Campground; and all the 4WD roads leading east into the monument.

A multiday backpack down the Paria River Canyon, which is 38 miles one-way, is not for the faint-hearted or inexperienced. Allow at least four days for this adventure and be outfitted with topographical maps, a compass, and the willingness to carry two gallons of water between sources. The trail follows the drainage of the Paria River to its confluence with the Colorado River and the site of John Wesley Powell's campsite, when his party explored this region in 1869.

The Buckskin Gulch Trail is an intimate and challenging canyoneering experience. It passes through one of the longest slot canyons in the country. The trailhead is 4 miles down HRVR from US 89. Then it's another 3.5 miles on foot to the beginning of the slot canyon. The trail continues for 13 miles to join Paria Canyon, if you desire. Otherwise, at 4.5 miles the trail meets the Wire Pass Trail, which you can follow west back to HRVR and then another roughly 5 miles up HRVR to the Buckskin Gulch Trailhead, for a 10-mile loop. Wire Pass Trail has several sections of five- to six-foot drops that must be negotiated along this loop; these can change with each flood, so it's best to check on conditions before heading out.

THINGS TO SEE:

The Wave, located in Coyote Buttes North, is undoubtedly one of the most popular destinations. Consequently, access is managed through a lottery system that only allows twenty people per day. Apply for the lottery through

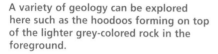

A variety of geology can be explored here such as the hoodoos forming on top of the lighter grey-colored rock in the foreground.

A kiosk with information on the endangered California condor. The cliffs are a common release site for these birds from captivity.

recreation.gov. This limit and the 5.7-mile round-trip hike that requires navigation skills maintains a true wilderness experience for each visitor.

You may also see the endangered California condor here, especially along the higher cliffs on the west side of the monument. As of spring 2021, there were only about 500 of these birds in the wild and/or captivity. While this may seem like an impressive number from their low point of 22 individuals in 1982, it still represents a fragile population. Condors lack a sternum, so there is no solid point of attachment for the large muscles of their wings. This means that while they flap their wings as many other birds do, condors rely primarily on soaring to move about once in the air. They can soar 160 miles in search of carrion and have been known to soar as high as 15,000 feet. There are regular condor releases at Vermilion Cliffs about 2.5 miles north of US 89A along HRVR, reached by passenger vehicles from the south. At present, about 71 condors inhabit this region.

In addition to condors, more than twenty different raptor species and dozens of bird species inhabit the monument. Plant life includes threatened Welsh's milkweed, known to exist here and in one other location in Utah. This plant is critical in the formation of sand dunes. Large mammals include the desert bighorn sheep, pronghorn, and mountain lions.

The Navajo Bridge on the southeast corner of the monument is an interesting stop and a good place for a picnic as you watch for a possible California condor sighting. You can still walk across the old bridge, which has views of the sandstone bluffs and Colorado River below. The monument's interpretive center has a bookstore and knowledgeable staff to assist with your trip.

Lake Powell and its dam are also in the area.

Life can be difficult here with very austere conditions and the size of a tree doesn't always indicate its age.

GETTING THERE:

From Bitter Springs, south of Page, take US Highway ALT 89 about 35 miles to the southern access for House Rock Valley Road.

Drive 14 miles north from Bitter Springs to get to Navajo Bridge. The visitor center there can provide additional driving information.

FACILITIES:

There are no facilities within the monument. Cell service is intermittent to nonexistent.

White House Campground is located on the northern side of the monument and has five sites for tents and self-contained campers as well as toilets but no water. Access via Monument Road #751 about 2 miles south of AZ 89 at the seasonal Paria Contact Station. This road may be impassable in times of high water.

Stateline Campground, located 8.5 miles south along HRVR, is on the border of Utah and Arizona. It has four shaded sites with vault toilets but no water. This is also the beginning of the 800-mile Arizona Trail that traverses the state north to south, ending at the Mexico border.

Dispersed camping is permitted throughout the monument but only in previously disturbed areas. No off-road driving is allowed. Additionally, most of the backcountry roads have deep sand and require a 4WD vehicle with good clearance and proper tires.

Coral Pink Sand Dunes State Park, west of Kanab, is handy if you're heading west or are in Kanab to get a walk-in permit for The Wave. The park is popular with OHV enthusiasts, so the dunes can be tracked up unless you're there right after a big windstorm. There are also dinosaur tracks here, embedded in the sandstone. Sites can accommodate RVs up to 40 feet but there are no hookups. Toilets and showers are available.

A crescent moon rises at dusk. The remoteness of the monument makes it an ideal place for stargazing or astrophotography.

There is lodging at Cliff Dwellers Lodge, Vermilion Cliffs Lodge, and Marble Canyon Lodge on the south side off US 89A. Lees Ferry has camping at the Lees Ferry Campground. There are fifty-four first-come, first-served sites with water, toilets, and a waste dump but no hookups. Overall length should be limited to 30 feet as the roads can be narrow. There is an adjacent boat ramp on the Colorado River. The Lees Ferry Lodge also has limited lodging and food. Nearby Marble Canyon has food, gas, and propane.

Seasonal (mid-May to mid-October) camping is available at Jacob Lake Campground in Jacob Lake, west of the monument on US 89A. There are fifty-three sites, thirty-seven of which are pull-through but no hookups. Toilets and water are on-site, but for RV fills you need to use the Chevron station across the highway.

Page, AZ, and Kanab, UT, offer food, fuel, and lodging as well as other attractions.

USEFUL CONTACTS:

**Vermilion Cliffs
National Monument**
345 E. Riverside Drive
St. George, UT 84790
435-688-3200
**blm.gov/national-conservation-lands
  /arizona/vermilion-cliffs**

**The Wave lottery and
Paria Canyon permits**
**blm.gov/programs/recreation
  /permits-and-passes/lotteries-and
  -permit-systems/arizona**

visitarizona.com/cities/northern/page

visitsouthernutah.com/Contact-Us

56. Pipe Spring
National Monument

NEAREST TOWN:	Fredonia, AZ, to the east
SIZE:	40 acres
BEST SEASON(S):	Year-round
NOTABLE ACTIVITIES:	Hiking, birding, wildlife and plant viewing, photography, history

THE MONUMENT:

The source of water at Pipe Spring, essential for early travelers, has drawn people to this area since as early as 300 BCE. Water present in this arid environment is largely due to sandstone aquifers that allow the water from snowmelt and rain to percolate to deeper, impervious layers where it then travels southward, surfacing in various locations as springs. Pipe Spring is located directly off AZ 389.

Winsor Castle and pond. This building housed people and dry goods in the mid-1800s and provided a water source for travelers.

▲ West Cabin, formerly used as a bunkhouse for the ranch hands here.

◀ A reconstruction of what living here was like in the early years of human inhabitation.

Pipe Spring was declared a national monument on May 31, 1923, by President Calvin Coolidge. Located along the Arizona Strip, it became a natural stop for tourists traveling between Zion National Park and the north rim of the Grand Canyon. It is administered by the National Park Service.

Temperatures here reach the low 90s during the summer but drop to the mid-50s at night. Winter highs are in the upper 40s to lower 50s, cooling off to the low 20s at night. Precipitation amounts to about 14 inches annually with about 20 inches of snowfall.

THINGS TO DO:

To access the grounds, you have to stop at the visitor center, where you can view artifacts such as pottery and a diorama depicting early life here. Longhorn cattle roam nearby as well.

The 0.5-mile loop trail above the grounds of the monument offers a spectacular view of the surrounding landscape, the Arizona Strip, and a self-guided tour of the plants along the way. The trail passes by the West Cabin, a bunkhouse used by workers for the Winsor Castle Stock Growing Company and others in the mid to late 1800s. The demise of cattle ranching was a result of overgrazing. Today, the landscape of tumbleweeds and sagebrush has displaced the native grasses due to overgrazing.

Everyone uses the water here, including this Western scrub-jay.

THINGS TO SEE:

The Kaibab Paiute Heritage Days are held every August. There are competitions in song, dance, and traditional games. The visitor center grounds have some original farming equipment and a kahn, which is a shelter of branches and brush, in which early Indigenous inhabitants lived. The Windsor Castle is a large two-story structure that housed people and supplies. You can visit it on a ranger-led tour. There is also a working orchard with peach, apple, plum, and crab apple trees. There is a pond fed by the spring that is the best place to find birds.

USEFUL CONTACTS:

Pipe Spring National Monument
HC65 Box 5
Fredonia, AZ 86022
928-643-7105
nps.gov/pisp

visitsouthernutah.com
  /Pipe-Spring-National-Monument

go-arizona.com/Fredonia

GETTING THERE:

From Fredonia, AZ, take AZ Highway 389 for approximately 15 miles west to the turnoff for the monument.

FACILITIES:

There are no services within the monument. Nearby Kaibab Paiute Tribal RV Park and Campground has fifty-eight RV sites with full hookups and a dump station. There are also sixteen tent sites and showers, laundry, a kitchen, and food storage. There is a gas and convenience store at the turnoff for the monument. The nearest towns with full services are Kanab, UT, and Fredonia, AZ. There are many public lands in the area so finding a dispersed campsite shouldn't be difficult.

57. Canyon de Chelly
National Monument

NEAREST TOWN:	Chinle, AZ
SIZE:	83,840 acres
BEST SEASON(S):	Year-round
NOTABLE ACTIVITIES:	Hiking, birding, wildlife and plant viewing, photography, geology, mountain biking, history

THE MONUMENT:

This monument was established on April 1, 1931, by President Herbert Hoover. It is located within the Navajo Nation and has a unique collection of ancient Indigenous structures and twisting high-walled canyons. This area is one of the longest continuously inhabited regions of North America; for the past 5,000 years it has been inhabited by Indigenous people including the Archaic, Ancestral Puebloans, Hopi, and Navajo. Each tribe used the landscape in different ways to construct habitats or shelters.

The view looking into the deep canyon. People still live and farm along the canyon floor as they have for hundreds of years.

Spider Rock, named for a figure in Navajo history, Spider Woman, is a 700-foot spire that resulted from differential erosion of the surrounding rock.

Canyon de Chelly National Monument consists of two primary canyons, Canyon del Muerto to the north and Canyon de Chelly to the south. Each is enclosed by sheer sandstone cliffs that reach over 1,000 feet high. The monument encompasses 83,840 acres, or about 131 square miles. It is managed as a joint venture by the National Park Service and the Navajo Nation.

With elevations over 6,800 feet, this is a high-altitude desert environment. In summer be prepared for daytime temperatures in the low 90s, at times exceeding 100 degrees. There can be a 30-degree drop in nighttime temperatures. Winter has daytime temperatures in the 40s and nights in the teens. Precipitation is minimal, only nine inches annually, primarily during the monsoon season, from June through August. About 12 inches of snow fall, mostly during December and January.

THINGS TO DO:

Stop at the visitor center to pick up a brochure that describes the monument and history of the area. You can also get a list of outfitters that operate tours within the canyons. There is an exhibit inside the center and a replica hogan outside. The center is staffed by Navajo.

The White House Trail is the only permitted access into the canyons without a park ranger or Navajo guide. The 2.5-mile round-trip includes a 600-foot descent through the canyon walls to the floor and then a short hike to the ruins. You can see the ruins from the pullout on the rim, but they are more impactful up close and you can better appreciate the white plaster that gives this structure its name.

Hiring a guide for a hike, horseback ride, or Jeep tour of the canyon floor is a great way to see the ruins and to appreciate the immensity of these chasms. This approach also tours near the farms the Navajo people cultivate and maintain. Corn, squash, and beans are still grown here, as they have

All of this land was initially at the same height as the cliff tops. Erosion and weathering caused the softer rock to deteriorate faster, creating the deep canyon.

been for centuries. In the spring, the lush vegetation fed by streams from the surrounding watershed contrasts brilliantly with the red hues of the canyon walls. In the fall, the intense yellow of the cottonwood leaves make for stunning photographic compositions. Winter is less crowded.

THINGS TO SEE:
Each of the ten pullouts along the rim drives have views of both canyons and the ruins below. This is a good option if you're pressed for time, although you should allow two to three hours for each drive if you wish to stop at the viewing points.

GETTING THERE:
From 6 miles west of Ganado, take AZ Highway 191 north for 50 miles to Chinle. From here drive 2 miles east on Navajo Route 7 to the visitor center.

FACILITIES:
There are no facilities or water within the monument. There is camping at the Cottonwood Campground, which is within walking distance of the visitor center and is among a large grove of cottonwoods which provide shade for nearly all of the ninety-two sites. There are flush toilets, but no hookups or water taps. RVs and trailers are

USEFUL CONTACTS:

Canyon de Chelly
National Monument
P.O. Box 588
Chinle, AZ 86503
928-674-5500
nps.gov/cach

A complex of ruins within the Chinle Wash are easily viewed from a pullout. Alternatively, one can hire an interpretive Navajo guide for a tour of the Wash.

It's always interesting to me to see something as hard as rock showing evidence of having once existed in a more liquid state.

limited to 40 feet. Availability is first-come, first-served, except for the two group sites, which require reservations.

Camping is also available at the privately owned Spider Rock Campground toward the end of the south rim drive. There are thirty RV and tent sites available, which include water fill-up, solar showers, and a dump station. Note: no credit cards are accepted but you can pay by check, travelers checks, or cash. The campground also offers Jeep tours of the monument.

Nearby Chinle has several lodging and restaurant options and gas and groceries. The Thunderbird Lodge, Navajo owned and operated, is located near the visitor center and offers lodging, tours, as well as a curated Navajo dining experience.

A spire in the making. Perhaps, in a few million years, erosion will create a spire from this nub of sandstone protruding from the top of the canyon wall.

58. Grand Canyon–Parashant
National Monument

NEAREST TOWNS:	Mesquite, NV, and St. George, UT
SIZE:	1,048,321 acres
BEST SEASON(S):	Year-round, although summers can be quite hot
NOTABLE ACTIVITIES:	Hiking, birding, wildlife and plant viewing, photography, geology, astronomy, solitude, mountain biking, 4WD trails, access to the north rim of the Grand Canyon

THE MONUMENT:

This monument was founded on January 11, 2000, by President Bill Clinton and is one of the largest in the system, encompassing 1,048,321 acres. Different areas are managed by the Bureau of Land Management and the National Park Service.

This is an extremely remote and isolated monument and is not for the casual traveler. Visiting here requires a high degree of self-sufficiency and a capable vehicle as there are no services available and cell phones do not work.

View from the rim of the western Grand Canyon with the Colorado River some 3,000 feet below.

The Colorado River winding its way westward at sunset, slowly carving through the rock of the surrounding Colorado Plateau.

All access roads are rough dirt roads with limited maintenance and become more difficult the farther into the monument you go. At least one full-size spare tire is recommended; the small temporary spare that most vehicles come with is inadequate. Tow service can run $1,000 to $2,000 and is likely not covered by insurance, given the remoteness of the roads.

Help could be hours or even days away. Be prepared to spend the night out by having adequate food, shelter, and water for your group. That said, if you're properly equipped and have the right mindset (i.e., know when to turn around), this is one of the most pristine and serene landscapes you'll find in the contiguous United States.

There are four federally designated wilderness areas within the monument: Grand Wash Cliffs, Paiute, Mount Trumbell, and Mount Logan. All have special restrictions and are limited to foot access only. A trip to any of these areas will give you a solitude rarely experienced these days.

This is a dry and hot region with summer highs easily over 100 degrees, cooling off to the upper 70s at night. Winter highs are in the 60s and 70s and nighttime lows in the 30s. Precipitation is nine inches with no recorded snowfall.

THINGS TO DO:

The Interagency Information Center in St. George, UT, should be your first stop for current road conditions and guidance about where to go and how

The road to Whitmore Overlook is several miles beyond where we're camped and becomes progressively worse for most vehicles.

to travel safely. You can also view the exhibits to learn more about the area and its history.

There are four primary access points into the monument. The Sunshine Route is CR 109, just 8.0 miles west of Fredonia off AZ 389, or 6.0 miles east of Pipe Spring National Monument. According to the Park Service, this is the most reliable route, but it is impassable when wet from either snow or rain. It's roughly 40 miles from CR 109 to the boundary. The road crosses tribal lands, which are off-limits.

The Clayhole Route follows CR 5 for 38 miles. It is rougher terrain than the Sunshine Route. To get here, take AZ 389 to about 3 miles east of Colorado City. Turn south onto Cane Beds Road.

The Main Street Route, originating in St. George to the west, follows BLM Road 1069 to CR 5 for 52 miles to the boundary near the Mt. Trumbell School House.

The last route follows I-15 west from St. George to Gold Butte Road at Riverside. It is roughly 24 miles along this road to the western boundary of the monument.

Several other roads lead into the monument, some better than others; talk with the staff at the information center in St. George for up-to-date information on their conditions.

THINGS TO SEE:

The petroglyphs at Nampaweap require a 48-mile drive on rough volcanic rock roads from the east but are worth the effort. Here you'll be able to see hundreds of ancient images chiseled into the basalt rock. Take either CR 109 or CR 5 to the boundary and then follow CR 5 as it turns west to the well-

The one-room Mount Trumbell Schoolhouse, which serves as a unique part of American history.

The interior of the one-room schoolhouse, which was first built in 1922 for the children of the region. Its doors closed in 1968 when there were too few students to justify a full-time teacher.

A nearly full moon setting at sunrise.

marked site. It is a 0.5-mile walk to the beginning of the petroglyph area. There are hundreds of individual petroglyphs here and the distance to the outcrops is less than 50 yards. Most of the rock art can easily be seen with binoculars. If you choose to hike along the base of the formation, be careful to not step on the many petroglyphs that are on flat-lying rock instead of the vertical faces above you.

Tuweep Overlook is a popular viewpoint in the southeastern portion of the monument. While the drive in on either CR 109 or CR 5 is decent, it deteriorates as you approach the Tuweep Ranger Station and farther south toward the overlook. The last 2.7 miles are strictly for proper 4WD vehicles with high clearance and appropriate tires. Overall vehicle length is restricted to 22 feet and trailers are highly discouraged due to extremely limited or nonexistent turnaround space. There is a parking area with signage on the west side of the road before you enter the more difficult portion. From here you can hike or backpack to Tuweep Overlook for either a day or overnight visit. The overlook provides stunning, and slightly unnerving, close-up views of the western portion of the Grand Canyon 3,000 feet below. Keep your pets on a leash and small children within reach. Sunsets here are spectacular, bathing the canyon walls in a warm alpenglow that highlights the river far below.

Two hiking trails originate at Tuweep, Tuckup and Saddle Horse

Loop. Tuckup is a 6-mile round-trip outing that leads to spectacular views of the Grand Canyon. There are two trailheads, one just before the Tuweep Campground off the roadway and the other at Site 10. Saddle Horse Loop Trail is a 45-minute loop that brings you to the edge of the canyon with views of the Colorado River. The trailhead is at Site 5 or about halfway between the campground and the overlook.

The Whitmore Canyon Overlook is another popular site to visit. From the Mt. Trumbell School House, take BLM 257 which turns into 1045 as it enters the monument. Follow it for about 23 miles past Bar 10 Ranch to the end of the road. Here you'll be treated to expansive views. If you wish to hike to the Overlook, the Whitmore Trail is a moderate 4-mile round-trip hike that leads to

Petroglyphs along the rock walls of the Nanpaweap Site. Binoculars can be useful here in order to avoid walking on the loose rocks.

a place 900 feet above the banks of the Colorado River. It has several hundred feet of elevation change, so what you hike down, you'll have to hike back up. There is also a trail that leads down to the Colorado River. There are petroglyphs on the surrounding rock as you travel the trail.

GETTING THERE:
Given the remote nature of the roads in this monument, stop at the Public Lands Information Center in St. George, UT, first. You can also download a more detailed road map of the monument from the NPS website for the monument.

FACILITIES:
There are no services or fuel within the monument and spotty cell service. The Tuweep Ranger Station cannot provide assistance beyond contacting a tow service, which may take hours or days to get there. It is possible to get a limited amount of gas at the Bar 10 Ranch with cash.

A Cooper's hawk perched on some sage searching for a potential lunch.

The hardy barrel cactus, also known as the "compass cactus" for its south-facing slant. This is due to phototropism, the process by which plant cells on the shaded side elongate, thus pushing the plant toward the sunlight.

There is a campground at Tuweep Overlook with ten sites. Site 10 is reserved for large groups. Permits are required for camping here, which can be obtained at Pipe Spring National Monument or the information center in St. George. There are two composting toilets here and another at the Overlook. No water is available. Horses and mules are prohibited, and pets must be leashed at all times. You must enter and exit this area after sunrise and before sunset unless you are camping at Tuweep Campground.

Dispersed camping is allowed on the BLM portion of the monument, using existing sites only. Driving off the primary roads is prohibited.

The very agile juniper titmouse, fairly common in juniper or pinyon-juniper woodlands, showing off for the camera.

USEFUL CONTACTS:

Grand Canyon–Parashant National Monument
345 East Riverside Drive
St. George, UT 84790
435-688-3200

nps.gov/para

59. Wupatki National Monument

NEAREST TOWN:	Flagstaff, AZ
SIZE:	35,422
BEST SEASON(S):	Year-round, although summer can be hot
NOTABLE ACTIVITIES:	Hiking, birding, wildlife and plant viewing, photography, geology, history

THE MONUMENT:

Despite its location in one of the warmest and driest locations on the Colorado Plateau, this was once a thriving and robust community of Ancestral Puebloan people. Several thousand others would eventually live within walking distance of this great center of culture and trade. Wupatki, the "Tall House" in the Hopi language, is a multistory structure that contained over 100 rooms. For at least 10,000 years, Indigenous people have lived and passed through this region, settling down in the 1100s. The nearby Wupatki Spring

The "Tall House," a 100-room structure that served as the centerpiece for a once-thriving culture of the Ancestral Puebloan people.

The architecture and construction here, as elsewhere in the region, was superb considering the resources available.

Wukoki Pueblo, standing alone and visible for miles, drew travelers and visitors for trade and possibly settlement here.

puts forth 500 gallons of precious water a day. For 150 years, this region prospered as a trading hub for the surrounding smaller communities, with goods from as far away south as Mexico and the Pacific Coast to the west.

The National Park Service manages this monument, which was established by President Calvin Coolidge on December 9, 1924, and listed on the National Register of Historic Places in 1966.

Weather data for Flagstaff is generally not applicable to this area as it's a few thousand feet lower and tends to be hotter and drier overall. Summer highs are in the upper 90s with nighttime lows in the 60s. Winter daytime temperatures are in the 50s and 60s with lows in the 20s. Precipitation, when it occurs, is six inches annually, with most falling in August and September. Snowfall is nonexistent, although you can look south to Humphreys Peak, Arizona's highest peak at 12,633 feet, and see white glimmers of snow atop its summit.

THINGS TO DO:

The Wupatki and Sunset Crater Loop Road, CR 395, leads to most of the hikes and walks to the ruins.

The Doney Mountain Trail is an easy 0.9-mile out-and-back hike along a maintained trail that offers excellent wildflower viewing in the spring. Walking to the higher peak gives views of the canyon lands and the distant San Francisco Peaks. There is an elevation gain of about 170 feet on this trail.

The Wupatki Ruins Trail starts at the visitor center and is a popular option. It's about 0.5-mile out-and-back; however, allow at least 90 minutes to explore the ruins. There are more hiking opportunities in the adjacent Sunset Crater National Monument.

The Citadel Pueblo ruins, located near a sinkhole that likely held water at the time, enjoys views of Humphreys Peak, 12,633 feet, the highest peak in Arizona.

Colorful flowers dot the volcanic landscape when conditions are suitable, breaking the monotony with their beauty.

There are also ranger-led backpacking trips to sites not normally open to the public, such as Crack-in-Rock Pueblo. This is a strenuous 20-mile, two-day effort limited to twelve participants. It's offered on weekends in April and October, and participants are selected based on a lottery system. There are also discovery hikes offered on Saturdays from October through April that explore the history and archaeology of the area. These include visits to the Kaibab House (ruins and petroglyphs), Antelope House (ruins, ranches, and geology), East Mesa (ruins and petroglyphs), and Coyote Water (petroglyphs). These also require online registration. Participants are selected based on a lottery system to minimize impact.

THINGS TO SEE:
There are five ruins here that are open and accessible to the public. They are Wupatki, Wukoki, Citadel, Nalakihu, and Lomaki Pueblos. All are within walking distance from their respective parking areas and are off CR 395, Wupatki and Sunset Crater Loop Road. The Wupatki Ruins are the most popular. Over 125 different species of birds may be seen at Wupatki; some are seasonal migrants, while others make their home in this difficult environment.

The Museum of Northern Arizona in Flagstaff offers a rich collection of artifacts, art collections,

USEFUL CONTACTS:

Wupatki National Monument
6400 Highway 89
Flagstaff, AZ 86004
928-679-2365

nps.gov/wupa

flagstaffarizona.org

flagstaff.com/camping

The circular pattern of this petroglyph is a fairly common design, in one form or another.

A Golden Prince's-plume, a tall, 5- to 6-foot, desert perennial showing bright yellow flowers when in bloom, typically April through September.

research facilities, and a variety of trips and workshops on a 200-acre campus.

GETTING THERE:

From Flagstaff, take US Highway 89 north for about 38 miles to the entrance for the monument.

FACILITIES:

There is a seasonal campground at the entrance to the nearby Sunset Crater National Monument. Bonito Campground has forty-four first-come, first-served sites suitable for vehicles up to 42 feet. Flush toilets, water, tables, grills, and fire rings are provided. The O'Leary Group Campground has three sites and can be reserved. To get here, drive 12 miles north from Flagstaff on US 89 and turn right onto FR 545 and continue for 2 miles. The Lockett Meadow Campground is another seasonal campground with seventeen sites, each with a table and fire ring. There is a vault toilet but no water. RVs and trailers are discouraged due to the steep and narrow access road. To get here, drive 12.5 miles north of Flagstaff on US 89 and turn left onto FR 552. Continue for 1 mile and turn right at the sign to Lockett Meadows.

The 53,000-acre Cinder Hills Recreation Area, 13 miles north of Flagstaff on US 89 at FR 776, is also available for dispersed camping. This is an OHV area and sees a lot of use due to its proximity to Flagstaff. There are no developed facilities here so you must be self-contained.

Flagstaff, just to the south, offers food, lodging, fuel, and entertainment as well as several RV parks and campgrounds.

Cameron, further north on US 89, offers a quieter and more relaxed atmosphere for those traveling north. Here you can find food, fuel, and lodging.

60. Sunset Crater Volcano
National Monument

NEAREST TOWN:	Flagstaff, AZ
SIZE:	3,040 acres
BEST SEASON(S):	Year-round, although summer can be hot
NOTABLE ACTIVITIES:	Hiking, birding, wildlife and plant viewing, photography, volcanic geology, astronomy

THE MONUMENT:

In 1928, a Hollywood film company wanted to use explosives on the flank of Sunset Crater as part of the special effects for a Zane Grey movie, *Avalanche*. There was significant public opposition that helped lead to the creation of this monument on May 26, 1930, by President Herbert Hoover. The 3,040-acre monument and its 1,120-foot cinder cone are managed by the National Park Service. It protects the cultural heritage of the Sinaguan people, who were thought to have lived here.

The eruption of Sunset Crater over a 100-year span between 1064 and 1180 CE created a landscape mostly devoid of life, but today there are signs of the slow process of recovery. Sunset Crater, the dominant feature in the

Unlike Capulin Volcano in nearby New Mexico, there is no road or trail to the 8,028-foot summit of Sunset Crater. In fact, it is off-limits to any type of travel.

Scattered ruins can be found throughout both Sunset Crater and adjacent Wupatki Monuments.

A colorful lizard, possibly a collared lizard, basking on the rocks of a ruin but positioned to catch a passing flying insect.

landscape, towers 1,100 feet above small pockets of pine and aspens, typical shrubs of the desert, and a variety of wildflowers. Wildlife includes bats, pronghorn, elk, and mule deer, and a large number of bird species. This area offers researchers a unique opportunity to monitor the return of an ecosystem. For example, researchers have found that lizards living on the black cinder fields are darker-colored, which appears to be an adaptation to avoid predatory birds.

Summer highs are in the upper 90s with nighttime lows in the 60s. Winter daytime temperatures are in the 50s and 60s with lows in the low 20s. Annual precipitation is six inches, with most falling in August and September, the "wet season."

THINGS TO DO:

Hiking to the top of the cinder cone has been prohibited since 1973 because of excessive erosion caused by foot traffic. There is a 1-mile loop trail at its base that allows hikers to get up close to the lava and cinder.

There is a paved 39-mile Scenic Loop through Sunset Crater and Wupatki National Monuments, which is the most common activity for visitors. This allows you to visit two monuments, enjoy the views at the Cinder Hills and Painted Desert pullouts, visit several impressive ruins, and have a picnic lunch along the way.

While it's not possible to ascend Sunset Crater, if you want to peer down the sides of a volcanic cone visit nearby Red Mountain Cinder Cone. Just 15 miles north of the Nordic Center on US 180 near mile marker 247, it offers a 3-mile round-trip hike and a ladder climb to the amphitheater. But beware, above the ladder there is little more than driftwood wedged into crevices for the barest of handholds to ascend farther.

Sunsets in the desert, seen here with virga, rain that evaporates before reaching the ground, can be particularly dramatic and colorful.

Despite the proximity to Flagstaff, this 20-second exposure clearly shows the Milky Way in the winter sky.

There are several hiking trails within the monument, all of which can be reached east of the seasonal campground at the monument entrance along Wupatki and Sunset Crater Loop Road. You can sign up at the visitor center to do these hikes with a ranger. The easy A'a Trail is a short 0.2-mile round-trip that goes along part of the Bonito Lava Flow, allowing you to see volcanic debris up close. The Bonito Vista Trail is accessible and easy, covering 0.3 mile out-and-back. It has grand views of the Bonito Lava Flow and some of the nearby volcanoes.

For a longer outing, try the Lava's Edge Trail, which travels through ponderosa pine forests alongside the edge of the Bonito Lava Flow. This is a shaded trail if you wish to avoid the sun on a hot day. The Lenox Crater Trail is longer, at 1.6 miles round-trip, and more strenuous as it gains 300 feet to the summit of Lenox Crater. This is an excellent hike to see a variety of birds.

THINGS TO SEE:
Both Sunset Crater and Wupatki National Monuments are part of the San Francisco Volcanic Fields, a 2,000-square-mile area with 600 distinct volcanoes. While Sunset Crater is the prevailing feature in this setting, the lava fields are intriguing when you examine how they originated and then flowed over the landscape.

Despite its proximity to Flagstaff, Sunset Crater is an International Dark Sky Park and has several night programs during summer. These take place at either the visitor center or the Lava Flow Trail parking area, 1.5 miles east of the visitor center. In August, at the height of the Perseids Meteor Shower, there is a viewing party at the Lava Flow Trail parking area where you can watch meteors fall at the rate of up to sixty sightings per hour. Since the best viewing for the event occurs after midnight into the early morning hours,

Dispersed camping on nearby USFS lands, under a cloudless night sky.

the monument typically remains open all night. The Astronomers of the Verde Valley help make these events possible.

GETTING THERE:
Take US Highway 89 north from Flagstaff for 16 miles to the monument entrance.

FACILITIES:
There is a seasonal campground at the entrance to Sunset Crater Volcano Monument. Bonito Campground has forty-four first-come, first-served sites suitable for vehicles up to 42 feet. Flush toilets, water, tables, grills, and fire rings are provided. The O'Leary Group Campground has three sites and can be reserved. To get here, drive 12 miles north from Flagstaff on US 89 and turn right onto FR 545 and continue for another 2 miles.

The Lockett Meadow Campground is another seasonal campground with seventeen sites, each with a table and fire ring. There is a vault toilet, but no water. RVs and trailers are discouraged due to the steep and narrow access road. To get here, drive 12.5 miles north of Flagstaff on US 89 and turn left onto FR 552. Continue for another 1 mile and turn right at the sign to Lockett Meadows.

The 53,000-acre Cinder Hills Recreation Area, 13 miles north of Flagstaff on US 89 at FR 776, is also available for dispersed camping. This is an OHV area and sees a lot of use due to its proximity to Flagstaff. There are no developed facilities here so you must be self-contained.

Flagstaff, just to the south, offers food, lodging, fuel, and entertainment as well as several RV parks and campgrounds.

Cameron, farther north on US 89, offers a quieter and more relaxed atmosphere for those traveling north. Here you can find food, fuel, and lodging.

USEFUL CONTACTS:

Sunset Crater Volcano
National Monument
6400 Highway 89
Flagstaff, AZ 86004
928-526-0502

nps.gov/sucr

flagstaffarizona.org

61. Walnut Canyon
National Monument

NEAREST TOWN:	Flagstaff, AZ
SIZE:	3,600 acres
BEST SEASON(S):	Year-round
NOTABLE ACTIVITIES:	Hiking, birding, wildlife and plant viewing, photography, geology, history

THE MONUMENT:

Located just 10.0 miles east of Flagstaff, Walnut Canyon National Monument was home to people of the Sinagua culture. The Sinagua people, a pre-Columbian culture, occupied the canyon rim for centuries, farming and hunting for subsistence. Between 1100 and 1250 CE they began to move into the canyon itself and built shelters within the natural limestone alcoves. As in many other locations, their reason for leaving the area is a matter of debate. More than eighty separate dwellings have been identified and many can be seen along the Island Loop Trail that circumnavigates the prow of

While not open to visitors, ruins across the canyon from the main site can be viewed with binoculars.

The creamy yellow flowers of a yucca plant, one of 40–50 species in North America. The petals can be eaten, the leaves used to hang meats for drying, and the roots of the Soaptree Yucca have been used as a shampoo.

Undeniably spartan quarters, these stone refuges served to keep the occupants sheltered from the elements.

rock 185 feet below. There are other ruins within the monument, but all of these are off limits to the public. Some are visible by looking across the canyon on either side and studying the cliffs there. Binoculars can be useful. The ruins at Tuzigoot and Montezuma Castle National Monuments are other sites where the Sinagua people formerly dwelled.

The threat from scavengers and looters in the early 1900s compelled President Woodrow Wilson to declare this a national monument on November 30, 1915. Initially, it was managed by the US Forest Service, but was later transferred to the National Park Service in 1933. The monument consists of 3,600 acres, within which 6 miles of Walnut Canyon are contained. The rock here was created from ancient sand dunes thousands of years ago when this area was an enormous desert. The rock reveals this history in the way it is laid down along the canyon sides. The name Walnut Canyon is derived from the species of walnut trees within the creek bottom on the canyon floor.

At nearly 7,000 feet there are four distinct seasons here. Summer highs barely get into the 80s with chilly nights in the 30s and 40s. Winter sees up to six feet of snowfall annually and daytime highs in the low 40s, while nighttime temperatures can drop to the teens or less. Spring and fall are mild and comfortable; these are the best times to visit. Thunderstorms are frequent from July through September, so take precautions. Only May and June drop below one inch of precipitation, with most months having one and a half to two inches of rainfall.

THINGS TO DO:

You must stop at the visitor center to access the ruins, so it's a good place to start your visit. The parking area is limited and vehicles over 40 feet will not be able to turn around here. This is a busy monument, so it's best to get here early in the morning or late in the afternoon before closing to avoid crowds. The visitor center has a bookstore, restrooms, and a picnic area. Arizona does not observe Daylight Savings Time and remains on Mountain Standard Time throughout the year. Christmas Day is the only day the monument is closed. Guided hikes along the canyon ledge and to a nearby ranger cabin are offered during the summer months; reservations are required for the strenuous Canyon Ledge Hike.

Looking down from the visitor center at people walking the one-mile loop of the Island Trail. What's out of view here are the 240 steps and 185 feet of elevation required to return.

The Rim Trail is easy and on level ground. The first part is paved. It's 0.7-mile round-trip and takes about 30 minutes to complete. The complete trail will bring you to two overlooks with expansive views into and across the canyon below.

THINGS TO SEE:

The Island Trail offers close-up views of the ruins along a paved walkway. It's just 1 mile round-trip, but the tough part is climbing up its 240 steps and 185 feet back to the visitor center. This can be a real workout if you're not accustomed to high altitude. Once you're on the level of the ruins, you can go in either direction, but most people go counterclockwise. There are twenty-five ruins to investigate as you walk along. You'll also have the opportunity to see much of the plant life here as well as some of its wildlife, especially birds.

The pale wolfberry, Mormon tea, nuts from the piñon pine, wax currant, various cacti, and the ever-present yucca plant all were integrated into the daily diet of the Sinaguan. These were supplemented with wild game as the opportunity arose. Wildlife in this region includes mule deer, elk, cottontail rabbits, jackrabbits, rock squirrels, wild turkeys, and a number of different lizard species. There are 121 species of birds within the monument, including raptors such as the peregrine falcon and Cooper's hawk, great horned and Mexican spotted owls, mourning doves, western tanagers, and the lesser goldfinch. A study looking at the effect of increased emissions and the subsequent effect on climate change shows several species have been extirpated from this area while others come in to potentially colonize the region.

USEFUL CONTACTS:

Walnut Canyon National Monument
6400 US 89
Flagstaff, AZ 86004
928-526-3367

nps.gov/waca

flagstaffarizona.org

GETTING THERE:

Take I-40 to Exit 204, which is 7 miles east of Flagstaff, and follow the spur road south for 3 miles to the visitor center.

FACILITIES:

There are restrooms and a picnic area at the visitor center but there are no camping facilities within the monument, nor is backcountry travel or camping allowed. Bonito Campground, at Sunset Crater Volcano National Monument, about 18 miles north on US 89, then right on FR 545, is open seasonally and has 44 sites. There are no hookups but tables, fire rings, grills, drinking water, and toilets are available. Vehicle length is restricted to 42 feet.

Ft. Tuthill County Park, a few miles south of Flagstaff off I-17 Exit 337, offers seasonal camping with 101 shaded sites, some with water and sewer but no electricity. There are portable toilets and drinking water available, except from November until May when these services are shut off, but the park is still open for camping. There are lots of outdoor activities available here as well.

Dispersed camping can be found in the Coconino National Forest about 15.0 miles north of Flagstaff and off Leupp Road.

Flagstaff is close, which means you should have no trouble finding RV parks, lodging, food, fuel, and entertainment.

62. Tuzigoot
National Monument

NEAREST TOWN:	Clarkdale, AZ
SIZE:	834 acres
BEST SEASON(S):	Year-round
NOTABLE ACTIVITIES:	Hiking, birding, wildlife and plant viewing, photography, history

THE MONUMENT:

Tu zighoot, an Apache word meaning "crooked water" in reference to the meandering path of the nearby Verde River, was first proposed as a name for the historic site by Ben Lewis, a Tonto Apache working on the site. The word was truncated to Tuzigoot. The Yavapai word for the area is Aha-gahlahkvah, which also means "crooked water." The monument is one of the smallest at only 834 acres, but the adjoining public lands offer considerably more to do and see.

Sitting on some of the highest ground near water and fertile croplands, the location of Tuzigoot was perfect for the 8,000 Sinagua people that lived here during its peak.

Even today this location is prized for the rich river bottom soil and nearly endless sunshine for growing. Being high on the hill likely helped to keep mosquitos at bay as well.

This region has long been a place of cultural and archaeological significance. The rich ecosystem of this valley has attracted people for hundreds of years and sustained a population of as many as 8,000 Indigenous people by the year 1300. Choosing to live on a hilltop offered a commanding view of the surrounding area, preservation of critical farmland, and avoidance of mosquitoes that likely infested the lowlands below.

One of the most valuable commodities of the area was blue salt, the only rock we consume, which was also used as a form of currency. For people who relied on a diet of mostly vegetables, it was critical to have a supplementary source of sodium chloride.

Initial excavation and preservation work had begun in 1932 with funding from the Federal Emergency Relief agency, followed by the Civil Works Administration and eventually the Works Progress Administration. Forty-eight men and women worked on the site to preserve the ruins for generations to come.

The weather here is typical of central Arizona. It is hot in the summer (up to 110 degrees) with heavy rains common from late June through early August. Nighttime temperatures drop to 70 degrees. Winters are more moderate, with daytime temperatures averaging around 55 degrees but dipping into the teens at night. Snowfall is a rare occurrence.

Locally gathered stones were used for the main structure.

Timbers, likely gathered from the Verde River banks, were used to support the roof.

THINGS TO DO:

Stop at the visitor center and museum for a history of the ruins and the adjoining valley. Here you can walk through the timeline of human occupation and learn what brought each culture to this area. Access to the Tuzigoot ruins is via a short paved walkway that rises to the top of the ridge. It is not too steep, but wheelchairs are not recommended. This loop circles the ruins and there is a short staircase leading into the interior of one of the rooms. You can also look down on the wetlands below and imagine working the fields of maze or squash to have enough to eat through the coming winter.

An organization called the Sacred Scarlets presents monthly lectures and demonstrations on the significance of the scarlet macaw to the Indigenous cultures of the Southwest. These striking birds, more often thought of as residents of locations much farther south, were traded and valued for their brightly colored feathers. You can participate in one of these demonstrations on the last Sunday of each month at 10 a.m. Or you can attend a demonstration of the close relationship between prehistoric cultures and their environment given by the Echoes from the Past School of

USEFUL CONTACTS:

Tuzigoot National Monument
P.O. Box 219
Camp Verde, AZ 86322
928-634-5564
nps.gov/tuzi

Dead Horse Ranch State Park
675 Dead Horse Ranch Road
Cottonwood, AZ 86326
928-634-5283

azstateparks.com/dead-horse

visitsedona.com

Engelmann's prickly pear cactus. The pads, once the spines are removed, are widely consumed in the Southwest and can be roasted, steamed, pickled, or fried.

Ancient Technology on the third Saturday of each month from 10 a.m. to noon.

A unique way to experience the monument area and the surrounding lands is a balloon ride. Contact Verde Valley Balloons at verdevalleyballoons. com. Or you can float different sections of the Verde River. A number of outfitters offer trips as short as a few hours up to multiday excursions down different sections of the river.

THINGS TO SEE:

The six-mile stretch of the Verde River known as the Verde River Greenway State Natural Area is unique for its ecological features. This bionetwork, one of fewer than 20 worldwide and an Audubon Important Bird Area, is well-known for its remarkable biodiversity. Sitting at about 3,300 feet, this range hosts up to 175 species of birds throughout the year. While many are permanent year-round residents, most are seasonal or migratory. Depending on the time of year, you may have the opportunity to see ring-necked pheasants, golden and bald eagles, lesser nighthawks, five different species of hummingbirds, flycatchers, and eleven species of wood warblers. A good number of sightings occur along the riparian zone of the Verde River or one of the three lagoons within the State Park.

GETTING THERE:

From Clarkdale, take S. Broadway for a few miles to its junction with Tuzigoot Road. Follow this to the visitor center.

Up to 175 species of birds can be found in this area, especially along the Verde River corridor. **A** Common yellowthroat warbler **B** Summer tanager **C** Black-crowned night-heron **D** Female red-winged blackbird with dragonfly.

FACILITIES:

There are no facilities. Fortunately, there are a range of choices in the surrounding area for food and lodging. The excellent Dead Horse Ranch State Park a few miles away has 100 sites that accommodate large RVs up to 40 feet and truck/trailer rigs up to 65 feet along with 30/50-amp service. There are also seventeen non-electric tent sites as well. There are showers, but no laundry. Additionally, there is a twenty-three-site group/equestrian camping area with one electric site. There are also eight cabins for rent, although you must bring your own linens. Visit AZStateParks.com to make recommended reservations. Nearby Cottonwood offers plenty of choices for food and lodging if you aren't camping. Sedona, 20 miles to the north, makes for a wonderful visit and the gorgeous drive through the canyon has pullouts and parks for hiking, photography, and relaxing. There is also a wide range of dining and lodging options available there.

63. Montezuma Castle National Monument

NEAREST TOWN:	Camp Verde, AZ
SIZE:	860 acres (both sites)
BEST SEASON(S):	Year-round
NOTABLE ACTIVITIES:	Hiking, birding, wildlife and plant viewing, photography, geology, history

THE MONUMENT:

President Theodore Roosevelt declared Montezuma Castle National Monument on December 8, 1906, to protect the unique and historically irreplaceable artifacts found in these 860 acres. In 1943, Congress incorporated the lands surrounding Montezuma Well into the Monument. Montezuma Castle is also on the National Register of Historical Places as of 1966.

Fed by a natural spring that puts forth 1.6 million gallons per day, this was a bountiful source of water in an otherwise arid landscape. Looking closely at the left side of the photograph, above the water but within the rock band one can see several dwellings.

Early inhabitants likely chose this site due to the availability of water, fertile ground, and a means of constructing safe shelter in the cliffs above Beaver Creek. The main ruin is estimated to have been as large as 4,000 square feet and rose to five stories high. This was an exceptional accomplishment given the methods available at the time, made from stone and mortar masonry; the stone is the surrounding limestone, and the mortar was made from mud or clay from along the creek bed. The site was abandoned in the mid-11th century due to the eruption of the nearby Sunset Crater Volcano. It was re-inhabited later and the last estimate of occupation dates to around 1425.

Montezuma Well, a sub-unit of the monument, is 7 miles northeast of Montezuma Castle at

Upwards of 200 people once called this area home and lived along Beaver Creek. The ruins are still standing after 700 years.

I-17 Exit 293. The well is a limestone sinkhole fed by underground springs that offers a year-round water source. It has been calculated that approximately 1.6 million gallons of water flow from two main vents deep in the well every day through 150 feet of limestone before exiting an outlet into an irrigation ditch built 1,000 years ago. The water is not recommended for consumption as it contains an extremely high concentration of carbon dioxide, eighty times higher than in most lakes, as well as other contaminants. Fish and amphibians are unable to survive in this environment, but the well is home to the world's only populations of a shrimp-like amphipod, a leech, a miniature snail, water scorpion, and diatoms, a microscopic one-celled plant species.

Summers are hot and dry with temperatures exceeding 100 degrees in July but often cooling to the 60s at night due, in part, to the altitude of 3,150 feet. Winters are cooler with daytime highs in the 60s and lows down to the

Dwellings above the well are evidence of human habitation here, close to a reliable source of water.

20s. Precipitation falls primarily in the form of rain during the late summer and through March.

THINGS TO DO:

Montezuma Castle is a popular accessible monument. About 400,000 people take Exit 289 off I-17 and drive the 3 miles to the visitor center parking area every year. Here you'll find a small museum highlighting the Southern Sinagua lifestyle and artifacts from the area, as well as a bookstore.

Walking the hard-surfaced 0.33-mile trail is the only option for getting about. The ruins have been off-limits to the public since 1951, but the walkway lies close to the ruins and there's a diorama that replicates the main ruins above. Numerous trailside markers explain the ruins and the local foliage. You can return to the visitor center the same way or follow the loop around as it parallels Beaver Creek.

A 0.5-mile trail leads up a steep incline to the edge of Montezuma Well. It has great views of the well and ruins and information displays. The trail continues down to the water's edge and nearby ruins.

USEFUL CONTACTS:

Montezuma Castle National Monument
P.O. Box 219
Camp Verde, AZ 86322
928-567-3322
nps.gov/moca

flagstaffarizona.org/things-to-do

THINGS TO SEE:

Winter visitors to Montezuma Well include migratory waterfowl such as American widgeons, cinnamon teal, and the occasional Canada goose. Spring and summer provide birders with possible views of Gambel's quail, Gila woodpecker, great blue herons, American kestrels, and a number of others suited for these conditions. Resident mammals include white-tail deer, foxes, porcupines, javelinas, and even beavers. There are snakes in the area, including rattlesnakes, so be mindful of where you step.

Before arriving at Montezuma Well, you can stop to view a typical Hohokam pit house on display under protected housing that dates to approximately 1100 CE.

Velvet mesquite has numerous uses: flour was made from the seeds and pods while the sap could be turned into candy, resin, and an adhesive.

GETTING THERE:

At North Verde on I-17 take Exit 289, then drive about 2 miles down a side road to the entrance of Montezuma's Castle.

For Montezuma's Well, take I-17 Exit 293, Highway 17, to E. Beaver Creek Road. Follow this for several miles through McGuireville and Rimrock to the entrance of the monument, using the posted signage.

FACILITIES:

There are none within the monument. The closest town is Camp Verde, about 4 miles to the south, which has campgrounds and RV parks in the area. Cottonwood, Flagstaff, Prescott, and Phoenix are nearby and offer a broad range of accommodations and dining. Dead Horse Ranch State Park near Cottonwood offers 100 sites for RVs up to 65 feet along with 30/50-amp service and a laundry.

A black-chinned hummingbird feeding on a prickly pear cactus flower.

64. Agua Fria
National Monument

NEAREST TOWN:	Cordes Lakes, AZ
SIZE:	71,000 acres
BEST SEASON(S):	Year-round
NOTABLE ACTIVITIES:	Hiking, birding, wildlife and plant viewing, photography, geology, astronomy, solitude, mountain biking, history

THE MONUMENT:

Proclaimed a national monument by President Bill Clinton on January 11, 2011, Agua Fria consists of 71,000 acres and includes over 450 archaeological sites and thousands of petroglyphs. Currently managed by the Bureau of Land Management, the site suffers from a lack of personnel and funding, so, as in other monuments, be sure to leave no trace here. Only a few of the archaeological sites are easily found; the rest are protected by their isolation.

Sitting at an elevation between 2,100 and 4,600 feet, this is a semi-desert grassland with a distinctly seasonal climate. Summer temperatures

Ponds are going to be the best places to spot wildlife, especially birds. Early morning and dusk will likely be the best times.

reach 110 degrees and are dry while winters are mild with more moisture. Mild spring temperatures make it even more enjoyable, although the winds are continuous and gusty. Seasonal flash floods, common to these areas, occur without warning and can result from rainstorms miles away. Be alert and monitor weather reports for the region. Fires of any type, as well as smoking outside a vehicle or structure, are prohibited. It doesn't take much imagination to see what a fire would do to this landscape or how difficult and hazardous it would be to try and fight it.

A colorful Western tanager enjoying the fruits of a thorny desert scrub.

Despite being a short 40-mile drive from Phoenix, Agua Fria is largely undeveloped and remote. Agua Fria has a rough dirt road that quickly becomes impassable when wet, the occasional pit toilet, miles of minimally maintained roadways, and an isolation not found in many other locations.

Along with solitude, there are endless vistas in all directions. If ever there was a place for quiet contemplation, this is it. The sun rising over the Mazatzal Mountains to the east is a sight to see and the night sky is filled with countless stars.

A western version of the yellow-rumped warbler, the Audubon's warbler is distinguished by the yellow throat patch in the males. They favor thickets, found throughout the monument, during winter and migration.

THINGS TO DO:

The Pueblo la Plata is a popular archaeological ruin to visit. Drive approximately 8.3 miles from the monument entrance to a northbound dirt track on the left and drive past two water tanks on the left. After this, the road gets rough and if wet, it's best to walk the remaining distance. The Pueblo la Plata is at the end of this mile-long track.

The ruins were once home to a thriving culture of about 3,000 Perry Mesa and Black Mesa Peoples that inhabited this area from about 1200–1450 CE. Comprised of eighty to ninety rooms during its peak, the site has since fallen victim to time and the elements. The construction technique was "massed room block," which means stacking rocks and then covering them with wood, mud, and straw. Numerous potsherds are visible.

If you're lucky enough to find an agave plant in bloom, which doesn't happen very often, you'll be treated with a variety of birds and insects who show up for the sweet nectar, much like this Bullock's oriole.

Your best bet for finding petroglyphs is likely along Badger Springs Wash. Look for them on the rocky hillsides as you make your way downstream toward the Agua Fria River.

During the warmer seasons be mindful of the presence of black-tailed rattlesnakes, which are often found in or near burrows within rock piles.

THINGS TO SEE:

Enjoy the views, which are endless in every direction, even though you may be only a few miles from I-17.

There is a variety of wildlife within the monument, but not usually present in great numbers due to sparse resources. Pronghorns, javelinas, mountain lions, Gambel's quails, desert tortoises, and Gila monsters represent unique adaptations to this environment. Birding is a popular activity with 170 species of birds documented within the monument; this takes some effort, given the open spaces and distances between the various habitats. Many of these species are seasonal migrants, not year-round residents.

Agave plants, unique to high desert ecosystems, are easily seen above the surrounding landscapes with their tall stalks, which are put up during their once-only flowering period. After that effort the plant dies off, leaving a family of newer plants emerging from nearby runners. This plant was likely key to Indigenous peoples' survival in this harsh environment as all of it is edible once properly roasted. The leaves could also be boiled, beaten into a fiber, and used to make clothing as well as ropes and carpet. The pads of the prickly pear cactus are also edible, once cleaned of their menacing spines.

Petroglyphs are found near the pueblos in the monument. The best location, for sheer number and ease of access, is the Badger Springs Wash, off the Badger Springs Trail. The trailhead is located about 1 mile down a gravel road at I-17 Exit 256. As you make your way down Badger Wash, look for the confluence of Badger Springs and the Agua Fria River. Be sure to look both upstream and downstream in your search for panels, wildflowers, and the scenery of the narrowing canyon. You can also clearly see the high-water mark on the opposite bank of Agua Fria, over six feet above the typical water level.

Petroglyphs are categorized into four distinct types: animals, human figures, abstract/geometric, or a panel combining these. Unfortunately, modern-day visitors have colored some using chalk, which detracts from and damages the delicate elements of the artwork.

Removing artifacts from where they are originally found destroys the context of their location, hindering accurate archaeological studies. Taking them from any protected lands is a federal offense.

GETTING THERE:

The monument is south of Cordes Lake, AZ, and is accessible from I-17 Exits 262, 256, and 244.

FACILITIES:

There are no facilities, so prepare adequately. Sufficient water, food, and a sturdy shelter are essential. Fill your gas tank before entering the monument, as it's easy to drive farther than you may have planned. Make sure your vehicle is in good shape and carry a full-size spare. Dispersed camping is allowed throughout the monument but be mindful of private property.

USEFUL CONTACTS:

Agua Fria National Monument
21605 N. 7th Avenue
Phoenix, AZ 85027
623-580-5500
blm.gov/visit/agua-fria

arizonaruins.com

aguafriafriends.org

visitphoenix.com

There are limited services in nearby Black Canyon City or Cordes Lakes. For full services, head to Camp Verde or Cottonwood to the north or the greater Phoenix metropolitan area to the south.

65. **Tonto**
National Monument

NEAREST TOWN:	Punkin Center, AZ, to the north, Globe to the south
SIZE:	1,120 acres
BEST SEASON(S):	Year-round, although summer can be hot
NOTABLE ACTIVITIES:	Hiking (limited), birding, wildlife and plant viewing, photography, history

THE MONUMENT:

Tonto National Monument, managed by the National Park Service, is tucked into a south-facing hillside. Its two cave sites are representative of hundreds of such dwellings that have been found throughout the Tonto Basin. Supported by the rich farmland of the valley below and abundant wildlife and other natural food sources, thousands of people once called this landscape

Lower Ruins are accessed by a short, but steep, 1-mile outing on a paved walkway.

Interior of ruins at the lower site.

Cholla and saguaro cactus along the walkway to the lower ruins with Roosevelt Lake in the background.

their home. This 1,120-acre monument was established on October 21, 1907, by President Theodore Roosevelt. The construction of the Roosevelt Dam in 1906, along with soldiers and settlers, brought unwanted attention to the area. Destruction and looting of the lands occurred before the historic sites could be adequately protected. Much of what is known or surmised about the people who lived here has been gathered from potsherds and other relics found at these sites.

The first people to settle here did so in Eagle Ridge between 100 and 600 CE. Although primarily hunter-gatherers, they also grew crops such as corn, beans, and cotton. By 750 CE, people from the lower Gila and Salt River Valleys migrated to this area and began to settle. Their irrigation canals were visible until the Roosevelt Dam immersed the lower valley in water. Trade with other peoples from as far away as the Gulf of California and Mexico is evidenced by the presence of seashells and macaw feathers, a species of bird not found in this region.

By the 1300s, the Salado cave dwellings were established and inhabited by the Indigenous people of the land.

Plant species here are typical of the Upper Sonoran range with an abundance of saguaro and cholla, prickly pear and barrel cactus. Yucca and agave are also present, as is the indomitable creosote bush. Whitetail and mule deer may be seen but the mountain lion, while present, is more elusive. There are three known rattlesnake species found here. One-hundred bird species either make this area their home year-round or are seasonal migrants such as bald eagles, roadrunners, verdin, and a variety of wrens.

The weather here is hot during summer when temperatures often reach the mid to upper 90s, with nighttime lows around the mid-60s. Winters are milder, with highs in the 60s and lows down to the 30s at times. Rainfall is

Sunrise views along Apache Lake Drive.   View along the Salt River, a more scenic
                                          and relaxed drive to Phoenix.

abundant for such an arid landscape, about 17 inches annually. It falls during winter and the summer monsoon season in July and August.

THINGS TO DO:

To access the monument, you must stop at the visitor center, where you can watch a short movie about the region and its early inhabitants and look over some of the artifacts found in the area. You'll exit the visitor center to gain the uphill trail to the Lower Cliff Dwellings, a steep 1-mile round-trip hike to the ruins. Interpretive signs along the way describe the variety of plants that inhabit the hillsides and there are stunning views of Lake Roosevelt in the distant valley. Originally a nineteen-room structure tucked into a large alcove, much of the original ruins are still intact and show a rough construction when compared to other ruins of the southwest. To visit the Upper Cliff Dwellings, a much larger ruin with forty rooms, you have to register with

The prominent blue of Roosevelt Lake contrasts with the soil
and the vegetation of both shorelines.

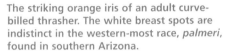

The striking orange iris of an adult curve-billed thrasher. The white breast spots are indistinct in the western-most race, *palmeri*, found in southern Arizona.

A vermilion flycatcher hunts for a flying insect, a staple of its diet.

the monument staff for one of their tours that occur from Fridays to Mondays in early November until the end of April. This is a 3-mile round-trip and gains 600 feet of elevation. Proper clothing and footwear are needed, as is sufficient water and sunscreen.

If you're heading to Phoenix, consider taking AZ 88/Apache Trail for 40 miles along the Salt River. Even if you don't wish to drive the entire distance, you can still see the Roosevelt Dam in the first mile or so from the monument. The route is a gravel surface suitable for most cars, although it does have some narrow sections and steep drop-offs along with the twisting, undulating roads typical of mountain travel. There are pullouts and dispersed campsites. Additionally, cross-country hiking and water activities are accessible from this route. Note that this is not a drive for an RV or a lengthy vehicle, especially if you're towing something.

While there are no hiking trails within the monument other than those leading to the cliff dwellings, the surrounding Tonto National Forest has several trails ranging from moderate to quite difficult.

THINGS TO SEE:

At the Lower Dwellings you'll be able to walk through some of the rooms under the watchful eye of a ranger and gain an inti-

USEFUL CONTACTS:

Tonto National Monument
26260 N. Arizona Highway 188, #2
Roosevelt, AZ 85545
928-467-2241
nps.gov/tont

visitarizona.com/cities/north-central
  /payson

visitphoenix.com

A chain-fruit cholla, reaching a height of 12 feet and whose fruit never ripens, provides nesting sites for cactus wrens and curve-billed thrashers.

mate sense of the space. You'll also have million-dollar views below to Roosevelt Lake.

GETTING THERE:
From Apache Junction on the east side of Phoenix, take Arizona Highway 88 for 36 miles to its junction with Arizona Highway 188. Turn right on Highway 188 and drive a mile to the monument entrance.

Alternatively, drive 30 miles north from Globe on Arizona Highway 188.

FACILITIES:
There are no services within the monument, and there is only one 0.8-mile paved road, which leads to the visitor center. The monument is open daily from 8 a.m. to 5 p.m.; however, the trail to the Lower Cliff Dwellings closes to uphill traffic at 4 p.m. No pedestrian traffic is allowed past the locked gate after hours. Vehicles over 40 feet are prohibited but there is parking for vehicles up to 30 feet below the visitor center.

The nearby Roosevelt Lake recreation area on AZ 188 has several hundred campsites for both tents and full-size RVs. There are no hookups, but water, flush toilets, heated showers, and dump stations are available. Many of the campsites offer views over the water and are peaceful, especially in the off-season.

AZ 188 toward Phoenix has side roads and dispersed camping sites along the way. There are also developed campgrounds.

The nearest town with services is Tonto Basin, about 20 miles to the north, with food, lodging, fuel, and propane. There are RV parks within the town limits. Globe, 35 miles to the south on AZ 188, also has food, lodging, and fuel. Phoenix is about an hour to the west.

66. Sonoran Desert
National Monument

NEAREST TOWNS:	Gila Bend and Casa Grande, AZ
SIZE:	500,000 acres
BEST SEASON(S):	Year-round
NOTABLE ACTIVITIES:	Hiking, birding, desert wildlife and plant viewing, photography, geology, astronomy, solitude, mountain biking, horseback riding

THE MONUMENT:

Located just a few miles southwest of Phoenix, this monument is a largely untouched tract of the Sonoran Desert ecosystem. It is recognized for its extensive forests of saguaro and is one of the most biologically diverse expanses of North American deserts. Established on January 17, 2001, by President Bill Clinton, the monument consists of nearly 500,000 acres of protected historic sites, Native American artifacts, and a wealth of desert plants and wildlife. The monument has a declaration that specifically addressed the negative impact of livestock grazing and directed that no further leasing for this purpose be allowed.

A saguaro cactus backlit by the setting sun.

A saguaro cactus in full bloom attracts
a wide variety of birds and insects.
Photo by Getty Images/iStock Photos

Roadrunners are common within the deserts of the southwest, typically running and
rarely flying more than short distances.

The monument is bisected by I-8, which offers easy access to the few
roads that exist within its boundaries. This is an undeveloped monument
with no facilities, and its roads are mostly rough tracks that are impassable
when wet. The Maricopa Road (AZ 238), between Maricopa and Gila Bend,
is a quick drive across the center of the monument. There are four wilderness
areas within the monument: Sierra Estrella in the northeast, North Maricopa Mountains in the north, Maricopa Mountains south of AZ 238, and
Table Top Wilderness in the southeast corner. Trailheads for these areas are
accessed via dirt roads that may require a 4WD vehicle. The climate here is
a desert: hot and dry for most of the year. It's not unusual to see triple digits
from June through September with nighttime lows in the lower 80s. November through March is a good time to visit, especially for hiking or camping.
During this period, daytime highs are in the 70s, with lows dropping to
mid-40s to mid-50s. Precipitation is eight inches spread out over thirty-six
days. Considering the weather, remoteness, and the inherent dangers of the
desert environment, this is not a place to take lightly or to visit unprepared.

THINGS TO DO:
Head to the Arizona Sonora Desert Museum. It's adjacent to the western
unit of Saguaro National Park and offers 98 acres of open-air desert with
1,200 types of plants and 230 animal species. There are also 21 acres set aside
for walking along 2 miles of paths that show various desert habitats and
plants. It's one of the most impressive museums in the West.

There are many hikes in the monument from easy to difficult. As always
in the desert, preparation is essential to an enjoyable outing as is knowing
when to turn back, even if you haven't reached your intended destination.

Saguaro cactus against the night sky with the Milky Way on display. Photo by Getty Images/iStock Photos

A common raven perched on the remnants of an old cactus.

Margies Cove Trail is a moderate and sandy 7.5-mile out-and-back hike with 450 feet of elevation gain. The trail is well marked with cairns and because it's out-and-back, you can decide your distance at any point along the way. Expect expansive views and solitude, but no shade.

The Butterfield Stage Route is an easy hike that you can stretch from 1 or 2 miles to as long as 25 miles. As the name suggests, it's part of what used to be the Butterfield Stage Route. It is level ground, with only 460 feet of elevation gain over its entire length. This would make a great multiday horseback trail ride or backpack in temperate weather. Access via S. 91st Avenue, about halfway between Gila Bend and Maricopa on AZ 238. Follow this north to the W. Butterfield Stage Access Road and the trailhead.

Quartz Peak, at 3,970 feet, is a hard 5-mile out-and-back trail to the top of the peak, gaining 2,400 feet of elevation along the way. The trail is within the Sierra Estrella Wilderness Area and is a remote outing, even for the experienced hiker. To get to the trailhead, take AZ 85 to Riggs Road and follow this to the power line road, heading south until its junction with Empire Boulevard. The track to the trailhead is about 0.75 mile farther south on the power line road. The hike heads east.

To visit the Sand Tank Mountains in the southern portion of the monument, you'll need a permit from either the BLM office or Range Control at Luke AFB.

THINGS TO SEE:
There are forty-nine species of birds and mammals here including the endangered and rarely seen Sonoran antelope. Nighthawks are common as are Gila woodpeckers and cactus wrens. A variety of desert lizards and

snakes, and the desert tortoise, can also be found here, most often at night when temperatures are cooler.

GETTING THERE:
The monument is located about 40 miles west of Casa Grande. It has no visitor center but see the contact information below for specific directions to the site you wish to visit.

FACILITIES:
None exist within the monument. Cell service is spotty, so use a paper map and compass. No water is available so you must bring all that you might need. Most roads are not well maintained. Flash floods can occur during the monsoon season (July through September); never attempt to drive across flooding streams or washes.

Picacho Peak State Park is about halfway between Tucson and Casa Grande on I-10 and offers eighty-five campsites with electricity and water but no sewer or water hookups, although there is a dump station. It has showers and Wi-Fi for a small fee. Generators are not permitted.

Dispersed camping is allowed throughout the monument, preferably in sites that have already been used. The region is typically dry year-round, so open fires are discouraged if not prohibited due to high fire danger.

The monument's proximity to both Phoenix and Tucson allows ready access to lodging and dining options.

67. Casa Grande Ruins
National Monument

NEAREST TOWN:	Casa Grande, AZ
SIZE:	472 acres
BEST SEASON(S):	Year-round
NOTABLE ACTIVITIES:	Hiking, birding, plant viewing, photography, history

THE MONUMENT:

This monument was first protected as Casa Grande Reservation in 1892, as the first prehistoric and cultural reserve in the United States. It was designated a national monument by President Woodrow Wilson on August 3, 1918, under the administration of the National Park Service.

Built by Ancestral Puebloans, Casa Grande is a 40-foot by 60-foot, four-story structure with walls up to four feet thick. It is thought to have been both a regional gathering place and an astronomical viewpoint, since its four walls are aligned with the four points of the compass and have windows that correspond with specific positions of the moon and sun. One such opening

The ruins with the protective cover in place to shield the materials from the elements and further erosion.

Despite the overhead covering and restoration efforts, one can easily see how vulnerable this ancient structure is to the elements.

in the upper west wall lines up with the setting sun on the summer solstice. The structure is composed of caliche, a hardened natural cement of calcium carbonate that can be found worldwide and is used today in construction applications, including Portland cement.

A complex system of irrigation canals and ditches was created throughout the region, drawing critical water to grow foods in the rich soil of the valley. The river was also used to float large fir logs used to build various structures within the complex, some from as far away as 60 miles.

The Civilian Conservation Corps built several of the administrative buildings that are still in use today. They used Ancestral Puebloan traditional methods of constructing the adobe buildings to complement the original structures.

This is a hot place, with summer highs exceeding 100 degrees from June through September. It cools off to the 60s and 70s at night. Thun-

USEFUL CONTACTS:

Casa Grande Ruins National Monument
1100 West Ruins Drive
Coolidge, AZ 85128
520-723-3172
nps.gov/cagr

visitarizona.com/cities/phoenix
-and-central/coolidge

visitcasagrande.org

derstorms are common during July and August. Winters and the shoulder seasons are milder with temperatures in the 60- to 80-degree range. Precipitation is approximately nine inches annually, with most falling during winter.

THINGS TO DO:

The only way into the monument is through the visitor center, where you can watch a short video on the monument and walk through the interpretive displays. Guided tours are offered from late November through early April, when the temperatures are more comfortable. These tours are led by either volunteers or National Park Service staff. You can also tour the grounds at your own pace using the interpretive signs.

Some of the restoration done on the building to help stabilize the fragile structure.

THINGS TO SEE:

In addition to the Casa Grande, you can also explore the surrounding walls, rooms, and courts that made up the Indigenous site.

GETTING THERE:

From Phoenix, take I-10 east for 36 miles to Exit 185. Turn onto Arizona Highway 187/387 going over the overpass. Turn right onto Arizona Highway 387 and go 7 miles east to Arizona Highway 87. Drive another 7 miles to Coolidge. At the junction of Arizona Highways 87 and 287, turn right onto Arizona Blvd. and drive less than 1 mile to the entrance.

From Tucson, take I-10 for 47 miles to Exit 211, Arizona Highway 87. Drive north for 19 miles to Coolidge and continue another 3 miles to the monument entrance.

FACILITIES:

There are no facilities within the monument, but several nearby towns have food, lodging, and fuel. Coolidge is a mile south of the entrance, Casa Grande is 22 miles away, Chandler is 30 miles away, and Marana is 45 miles away. Phoenix, about an hour to the north.

68. Ironwood Forest National Monument

NEAREST TOWNS:	Red Rock and Avra Valley, AZ
SIZE:	60,000 acres
BEST SEASON(S):	Year-round
NOTABLE ACTIVITIES:	Hiking, birding, wildlife and plant viewing, photography, geology, astronomy, solitude, mountain biking

THE MONUMENT:

Established on June 9, 2000, by President Bill Clinton, Ironwood Forest National Monument falls under the management of the BLM and consists of 188,619 acres. Nearly 60,000 of these acres are non-federal and include private land holdings and Arizona State School Trust lands. The monument is named for the long-lived desert ironwood tree that grows in the area. It includes 200 Native American archaeological sites that date as far back as 600 CE.

Several species of cacti thrive here in an environment well suited for their growth. Ironwood trees are one of the longest living species within the Sonoran Desert as well as a "nurse plant" for over 500 plant species here.

To get to the monument take Interstate 10 Exit 226 or Exit 236 to Silver Bell Road, just west of Tucson. This road travels through the monument in a long loop.

This is an undeveloped monument, aside from the roads established by early miners and Indigenous peoples. Silver Bell Road is suitable for 2WD vehicles when dry, while many of the mining roads are best left to high-clearance 4WD vehicles, dirt bikes, mountain bikes, or hikers. Signage is nonexistent so a good map is essential to experience all the monument has to offer and to avoid private or State lands.

Temperatures in mid-summer can approach 100 degrees while winter temperatures seldom reach freezing. Annual precipitation averages less than 12 inches with little to no snow.

THINGS TO DO:

Along with camping in the monument, activities include hiking, mountain biking, wildlife viewing, or visiting archaeological sites. If you choose to travel in the backcountry, it is advisable to have a good map and compass/GPS. Ample food and water are essential.

A visit to the ghost site of Southern Arizona Smelting Company is an interesting look at the area's mining history. The Silver Bell mine site and cemetery are a reminder of the intense copper mining that occurred here starting in the 1860s. While some mining continues, no new mining claims or motorized off-road travel, are permitted.

The Arizona-Sonora Desert Museum provides an excellent guide the natural history of this area and is worth a visit, ideally before you explore the monument.

THINGS TO SEE:

Nichols Turk's head cactus and the lesser long-nosed bat, both endangered species, may be found here, although the bats are thought to be migratory. The cactus ferruginous pygmy owl makes its home here, as does the last viable population of desert bighorn sheep in the Tucson basin. There are 560 documented species of plants

USEFUL CONTACTS:

Ironwood Forest
National Monument
3201 E. Universal Way
Tucson, AZ 85546
520-258-7200
blm.gov/visit/ironwood

desertmuseum.org/programs
 /ifnm_index.php

ironwoodforest.org

Wildflower blooms: desertusa.com

A say's phoebe, common in dry, open areas, perched high in the scrub looking for insects.

A cristate, likely the result of an injury early in the life of this saguaro, caused this deformity in its growth.

and fifty-seven species of birds within the monument. Saguaro cacti are abundant and you may be able to see a "cristat" saguaro, one that has been damaged while young and whose crown grows into a fan-like shape. Much of the wildlife benefit from the eighty or so man-made water sources scattered throughout the monument and the fourteen water sources maintained by the Arizona Game and Fish Department and Arizona Desert Bighorn Sheep Society.

Catching the spring bloom of wildflowers is often a hit-or-miss proposition, as many factors come into play. Sun, wind, water, temperature, and elevation all play a role in predicting when they might bloom. A winter with small amounts of rain and a spring with temperatures less than 85 degrees will usually produce a good showing. At elevations between 1,000 and 3,000 feet, February through April are good times for annuals, while March through May are best for altitudes of 3,000 to 5,000 feet.

GETTING THERE:

Exit I-10 at Rillito, Exit 242. Follow Avra Valley Road for about 10 miles to the monument border. Then follow Silver Bell Road, which leads back to the interstate at Marana. This route also allows access to other roads within the monument.

FACILITIES:

There are no established camping facilities within the monument, although dispersed primitive camping is allowed. Water is not available so bring enough for everyone in your party, as well as extra for your vehicle. Nearby Picacho Peak State Park offers full camping amenities including showers. Tucson has plenty of lodging and dining.

69. Organ Pipe Cactus National Monument

NEAREST TOWNS:	Why, AZ, to the north and Lukeville on the southern boundary with Mexico
SIZE:	330,688 acres
BEST SEASON(S):	Year-round
NOTABLE ACTIVITIES:	Hiking, birding, desert wildlife and plant viewing, photography, geology, astronomy, solitude, mountain biking, history

THE MONUMENT:

Both a national monument and a UNESCO Biosphere Reserve, Organ Pipe has much to offer the visitor willing to accept the harsh desert landscape. Established as a monument on April 13, 1937, by President Franklin D. Roosevelt, it was later designated a Biosphere Reserve in 1976. The area has been inhabited for 16,000 years by various cultures, changing hands often over time. The Old Salt Trail, near Quitobaquito, has been used for centuries as a

The rugged landscape of the monument, a UNESCO International Biosphere Reserve, with an organ pipe cactus in the foreground.

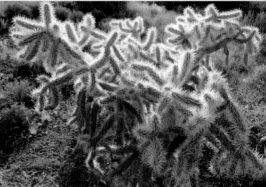

An archway, looking a bit like the Kissing Camels in the Garden of the Gods in Colorado Springs, Colorado, but without the crowds of tourists.

A side-lit cholla cactus, sometimes called a teddy-bear cactus because it mistakenly looks soft and cuddly from a distance.

major trade route connecting the salt beds of Sonora, Mexico, with cultures around the region. This is also the only home to the endangered pupfish of the same name, as well as the sonoyta mud turtle and the desert caper. This region is the only place where the organ pipe cactus grows wild. Some of these cacti are more than 150 years old. May is a good time to see the saguaro cactus blooms.

Bounded on the west by the massive Barry M. Goldwater Air Force Range, to the east by the Tohono O'Odham Nation, and on the south by the US-Mexico border, this is a remote place.

Organ Pipe National Monument is subject to some of the hottest and driest climates in the United States. June through August can see high temperatures in the triple digits, while during May and September they reach the upper 90s. Lows during this time reach the upper 50s to upper 70s. Winter is the best time to visit with more reasonable temperatures in the 60s and 70s during the day and the 40s to 50s at night. Precipitation, nearly negligible by most standards, amounts to less than seven inches annually.

THINGS TO DO:

There are numerous opportunities for hiking within the monument. There is a free hiker shuttle during the busier winter months that will get you to either the Senita Basin or Red Tanks Tinaja Trailheads, allowing you to walk back to the Twin Peaks Campground at your leisure and without fussing with your vehicle. This is an easy 4.6- or 6.7-mile hike, respectively, back to the campground. Call the visitor center to reserve a seat on the shuttle.

Around the visitor center there are three easy hikes. The first is the 0.1-mile round-trip Visitor Center Nature Trail on a brick pathway where you

A forest of saguaro cacti spreads evenly across the desert floor against a back-drop of rugged mountains reaching to 10,378 feet.

A male verdin in breeding colors can be found throughout the southwestern deserts, particularly in mesquite and other dense, thorny shrubs.

can see exhibits of desert life. Another slightly longer trail is the Campground Perimeter Trail, a loop of 1 mile that has wide views as well as excellent birding. The last trail is the Desert View Trail, another easy loop of 1.2 miles that offers expansive views, especially at sunrise or sunset.

There are more difficult trails along the Alto Mountain Drive. The Estes Canyon Trail is a moderate 3-mile round-trip trail with great birding. The difficult Bull Pasture Trail is a 3-mile out-and-back effort with outstanding views of Mexico and the monument. This can be combined with the Estes Canyon Trail for a loop trip that totals roughly 3 miles.

There is a series of trails that may be combined as you wish in the Puerto Blanca Mountains. The trailheads can be accessed from Twin Peaks Campground, North Puerto Blanco Drive, or the Senita Basin parking area. A visitor center map shows the options, and the staff can provide more information on levels of difficulty and what to expect.

An easy walk that favors birding is the Alamo Canyon Trail. It's a mild hike to a historic mining site with plenty of birding en route. Take care around any of the mines here as they may have open shafts and unstable shoring.

Bike riding is allowed on all roads open to vehicle use but not on any trails. There are over 100 miles of riding available.

THINGS TO SEE:
Bird life here is abundant despite the harsh environment. Over 270 species have been documented, 36 as year-round residents and the remainder as seasonal migrants. Seasonal timing impacts which species you may be able to see. Many visitors come here for the excellent birding and a chance

Ocotillo, "little torch" in Spanish, flowers bloom in the desert from March through June. Hummingbirds are their primary pollinators.

to add a few rare species to their life-list. The visitor center has several birders who can provide tips on where to go, when to be there, and what you might see, as well as a list of recent sightings.

The area around the visitor center has a variety of birds that include cactus wrens, phainopepla, roadrunner, varied buntings, and Gambel's quail. Golden eagles are present in the Monument and crested caracaras can often be seen, sometimes intermingled with groups of turkey vultures. Alamo Canyon is the best birding site within the Monument.

Other wildlife includes mountain lions, desert bighorn sheep, javelina, mule deer, desert tortoise, and a variety of rattlesnakes. The uncommon Sonoran pronghorn, smaller than its cousin of the Plains, is threatened by loss of habitat and climate change. Within the monument, their primary habitat, there were only twenty-five individuals in 2002. A captive breeding program was initiated in 2004 with pronghorn from Mexico to extend their genetic makeup. The first release of male yearlings occurred in 2006 and was followed by additional releases over the next several years. As of 2015, there were eighty individuals on monument lands, giving hope that this effort will create a viable, genetically diverse population that is self-sustaining.

USEFUL CONTACTS:

Organ Pipe Cactus National Monument
10 Organ Pipe Drive
Ajo, AZ 85321
520-387-6849
nps.gov/orpi

visitgilabend.org
  /museum-visitor-center

ajochamber.com

Kitt Peak Observatory
noao.edu/kpno

GETTING THERE:
From Gila Bend on I-10, drive south on Arizona Highway 85 approximately 80 miles through Ajo and Why to the monument visitor center.

FACILITIES:
Cell reception is limited at best. Off-road traffic along the border created over 200 miles of illegal track in the monument until a 30-mile barrier was put up in 2004 to protect the natural and cultural resources as well as to provide for visitor safety and

national security. The successful Wilderness Restoration Project was begun in 2015 to restore this land to its natural state.

Twin Peaks Campground, 1.5 miles from the visitor center, is the main location for camping with 208 first-come, first-served sites. Four of these sites can handle RVs up to 45 feet while 34 are tent-only. There is running water,

A well-maintained road, lined by saguaro cactus, leads back into one of the canyons of the monument.

showers, flush toilets, and RV dumps, but no hookups. Alamo Canyon Campground offers primitive tent camping only; no generators are allowed nor are RVs or trailers. There are four permit-only sites and campers must self-register at the campground. It's located at mile marker 65.5 on the east side of AZ 85, north of the concrete bridge, and involves a 3-mile drive/ride on a gravel road. Pit toilets, tables, charcoal grills (no other fires allowed), and trash cans are provided. Backcountry camping is allowed with permits from the visitor center, where you can also store your valuables. Fires are prohibited in the backcountry, as are pets. There are nine zones for backcountry camping to minimize impact.

The nearest town with food, fuel, and lodging is Ajo, just 11 miles north of the AZ 85/86 junction. Otherwise, Gila Bend, 55 miles north of the monument on I-8, is the best option for those not camping. It has a visitor center that can provide additional information on area attractions, food, and lodging, and a 1,200-square-foot museum with over 2,000 artifacts.

If you wish to travel south to the border on Highway 85, Lukeville has an RV park, fuel, and a general store.

Nearby Kitt Peak National Observatory is free and open to the public. In operation for over forty-five years, it is currently tasked with creating the largest 3D map of the cosmos. Located within the Tohono O'Odham Nation, there are Indigenous practices that must be respected. Kitt Peak, at 7,000 feet, is considered sacred by many and should be respected. Ask permission to take photos if you're uncertain whether they are allowed. There are several evening programs available to the public; see the "Useful Contacts" section.

70. Chiricahua National Monument

NEAREST TOWN:	Willcox, AZ
SIZE:	12,000
BEST SEASON(S):	Year-round
NOTABLE ACTIVITIES:	Hiking, birding, wildlife and plant viewing, photography, unique geology, astronomy, solitude, history

THE MONUMENT:

This monument was established on April 18, 1924, by President Calvin Coolidge to preserve and protect these "standing up rocks," as they are known to the Chiricahua Apache. The monument consists of roughly 12,000 acres in southeastern Arizona. Eighty-four percent of the monument was designated as wilderness in 1976 and is accessible only by foot or horseback. The rock formations are the result of an enormous volcanic eruption 27 million years ago. The Turkey Creek Volcano was a thousand times more powerful than the 1980 eruption of Mount St. Helens. As much as 2,000 feet

"Standing Up Rocks" as they are known by the Chiricahua Apache, are bathed in the warm glow of a setting sun.

The fire watch building on top of Sugarloaf Mountain, 7,310 feet, built in the 1930s by the CCC, is still used today to monitor fire activity.

Faraway Ranch House, a guest ranch run by Neil and Emma Erickson, was built in 1915 and is open to tours on Saturday and Sunday.

of ash was deposited in the area, much of which has since eroded away, leaving the rhyolite tuff rock formations seen today. The enormous valleys to the east and west were once at the same elevation as the Chiricahua Mountains. Lillian and Ed Riggs, daughter and son-in-law of the original Faraway Ranch settlers, were both strong advocates for protection of this area, a place they called "A Wonderland of Rocks." Their intimate knowledge of the rock formations allowed them to oversee much of the trail building that the Civilian Conservation Corps undertook. The Civilian Conservation Corps also built the original Interpretive Center, campground, trails, and housing and maintenance facilities. Much of the trail construction was supervised by Ed Riggs. Many of the buildings remain today, built to blend in with the environment.

The climate here is mountainous and high desert, warm in the summer with little precipitation and record temperatures up to 109 degrees. Typical highs are in the upper 80s, with nighttime lows in the upper 50s. Winter daytime temperatures can be in the 60s, with nights in the 30s. Snow is occasionally reported, especially at higher altitudes. As with similar environments, the best times to visit are spring or fall when you can enjoy

USEFUL CONTACTS:

Chiricahua
National Monument
12856 East Rhyolite Creek Road
Willcox, AZ 85643
520-824-3560

nps.gov/chir

southernarizonaguide.com
 /things-to-do-in-willcox

tombstoneweb.com

douglasaz.gov

The white-nosed coatimundi, a wily member of the raccoon family, uses its flexible snout to search out food in tree hollows, or the cooler you forgot to secure last night.

The beautifully delicate canyon wren, whose appearance is matched only by its melodious descending song. Often found in canyons near a water source.

moderate temperatures. Springtime offers the best chance to see local plants flowering, given that there's been enough rainfall. Most precipitation falls in July and August with minimal snowfall occurring between November and March. Thunderstorms are common from July through September, so plan your time outdoors accordingly. Elevation ranges from 5,124 feet at the visitor center to 7,310 feet at the summit of Sugarloaf Mountain.

THINGS TO DO:

Driving the winding 8-mile Bonita Canyon Drive to the top of Massai Point (at 6,870 feet) is the most popular activity within the Monument. Pullouts along the way have views of the San Simeon Valley to the east and, from the top, Sulphur Springs Valley to the west. The parking area accesses several trails of varying length and difficulty that allow you to explore the rock formations up close. Massai Point is a great place to view hundreds of rhyolite pinnacles in the canyons and hillsides below. The massive 12-mile Turkey Creek Caldera, just south of the monument in the Coronado National Forest, is the site of an enormous eruption that occurred 27 million years ago, blanketing the region with volcanic ash that eventually formed the rhyolite pillars that are exposed today.

Hiking all or part of the 17-mile trail system is sure to give you an up-close appreciation of the geology and wildlife to be found here. There are trails for all levels of ability. The 0.8-mile round-trip to the Echo Canyon Grottoes is a great outing for beginners while more experienced hikers can tackle any combination of the trails from Massai Point. One option that requires a car shuttle, or the Park Service shuttle when running, is to go to Massai Point and then hike 4.5 miles using a combination of trails downhill back along Rhyolite Canyon to the visitor center. Along the way you'll pass some of the most notable formations in the monument and gain a better understanding of the ecosystems here.

The Heart of Rocks Loop, a moderately strenuous hike, provides examples of the geology of the area while the short hike to the Echo Canyon Grotto puts you up close with rock formations, including the Grotto. Here you can see balanced rocks and clear evidence of the layering of rock as it was laid down millions of years ago.

Hiking to the top of Sugarloaf Mountain at 7,310 feet can be strenuous, although it's just 1 mile one-way. The reward is 360-degree views of the monument, its wilderness areas, and the vast valleys to the east and west. You can even spot Dos Cabezas, a double-summited peak far to the northwest. If you're comfortable hiking back to the parking area in low light, this is an outstanding place to watch the sunset or sunrise. The original fire watch structure built by the Civilian Conservation Corps in the 1930s still stands and is used today to monitor potential fires.

There are several trails open to horseback within the monument. They are restricted to the trail and not allowed on paved roadways except designated crosswalks. Camping with stock is not allowed in Bonita Canyon Campground but is permitted in nearby Coronado National Forest.

Stop at Faraway Ranch for a look into life on the frontier in the late 1800s. It's a 0.5-mile round-trip walk along level ground, from 30 minutes to an hour, depending on your interest. The original residents, Neil and Emma Erickson, settled here in 1887, eventually building the present-day structure in 1915. For a time, it was run as a guest ranch, offering visitors the chance to visit the wilds of Arizona yet enjoy the comforts of 1920s modern living. In 1903, Neil was appointed as the first ranger for the Chiricahua Forest Reserve and served here until he was transferred to Flagstaff in 1917.

THINGS TO SEE:

Birding is popular here with over 200 identified species of migrants and residents. Seeing, or hearing, the Mexican jay or an acorn woodpecker is easy in the wooded areas, especially around the campground. You might get lucky and see a covey of Montezuma quail near Massai Point or, even more rewarding, a sighting of the greater trogon, an occasional summer resident. There are also 13 species of hummingbirds in the Chiricahua Mountains, of which five have been seen within the monument. The diversity in bird species is due to the range of habitat available at the monument's location on a major north-south migration route. The area has been identified as an

Looking west across the Sulphur Springs Valley at Dos Cabezas
from the summit of Sugarloaf Mountain, 7,310 feet.

Important Bird Area by the American Bird Conservancy, so even if you're a novice at birding you'll likely spot birds that aren't found in other areas.

The white-nosed coatimundi (nasua narica), a member of the raccoon family, can be found within the monument at the northernmost edge of its range. While they are omnivorous, they like the berries of the manzanita shrub, which are plentiful within the monument. Much like their raccoon cousins, they are prolific eaters and quite intelligent, so be sure to secure your food in a hard-sided vehicle or the bear storage boxes at each campsite. Other mammals include the black bear, coues (Arizona whitetail deer), and the Chiricahua fox squirrel, only found here among the unique Sky Islands of these mountains. Historically, both the endangered ocelot and jaguar have inhabited this region and been documented north of the Mexico border, not far from the monument.

There are tours of the historic Faraway Ranch near the entrance to the monument. It was so named by Lillian Erickson, daughter of Neil and Emma Erickson, because it was so "awful faraway from everything."

The 10th Cavalry Buffalo Soldiers from the encampment at Bonita Canyon built a stone monument to President Garfield and many inscribed their names or initials on the rocks used. Ed Riggs later acquired some of these stones to preserve them to build a fireplace at the ranch. Remarkably, these signatures can still be seen today on the outside of the fireplace as you walk around the property.

A visit to the nearby Ft. Bowie National Historic Site is an enjoyable and educational outing for a day. Drive the unpaved Apache Pass Road south from the town of Bowie, or north from AZ 186, along the edge of the San Simeon Valley to the parking area and trailhead. This road may be impassable from either direction after heavy rains; otherwise, it's suitable for passenger cars. There is a vault toilet here and the trailhead for a 1.5-mile hike to the ruins. For those unable to walk, prior permission can be granted for access using the National Park Service road. The fort was in operation during the Apache Wars from 1868–1894, after which it was abandoned and left to the elements. There is a staffed visitor center and a permanent ranger residence, and you'll pass an old cemetery and stagecoach station along the way. There has been no reconstruction of the fort, so you'll be able to see the original adobe structures.

GETTING THERE:

From Willcox, drive 31 miles on Arizona Highway 186 to the junction with the monument entrance road. Take the entrance road for 3 miles to the visitor center.

FACILITIES:

There are no services within the monument. While there is no developed camping here, you can camp outside the site boundary in previously used locations, but never on private land. No open fires are allowed due to the dry and windy nature of this region.

There is a twenty-six-site campground at Bonita Canyon near the visitor center for vehicles up to 29 feet. Vehicles beyond this length are not allowed past the campground. Water and flush toilets are provided but no showers, hookups, or waste dumps. It's located within a large grove of trees, so shade can be found during warmer weather. There are food storage lockers at each site, and you are expected to use them unless you have a hard-sided vehicle. This campground fills during the busier months, so reservations are recommended through the link in the "Useful Contacts" section.

Dispersed camping is in the Coronado National Forest south of the Monument along Pinery Canyon Rd. on the right just before the monument entrance. This road is often closed and not maintained regularly during the winter months so it may be rough. If you're up for the adventure, it can take you all the way to New Mexico.

The nearest town is Willcox, 34 miles north, where you can find lodging, food, fuel, and several RV parks. Propane can be found at the Chevron Station on the west side of town. Tombstone is about 73 miles away and offers food, lodging, and fuel. Tombstone also offers a bit of the Wild West, with its famous Boothill Cemetery and OK Corral. Douglas, AZ, is located about 100 miles to the south along the Mexico border. It has full amenities.

ACKNOWLEDGMENTS

I would first like to thank Garry Harshbarger and Dustin Kemp for the use of their images. Both help to make this a better guidebook for a wide variety of readers.

I extend my thanks to Tyler Stuart for his invaluable assistance with the identification of many of the birds in this guide.

I wish to acknowledge the constant support and encouragement from my wife, Gana. It's been a long endeavor; her confidence in this project has been unwavering even when my own was less so.

I would also like to dedicate this book to all of the veterans who have served honorably in our nation's military, who stepped up and met the challenge of the uncertain.

About the Author

Originally from Fairbanks, Alaska, Mike Endres has had the unique pleasure of traveling a good part of the world in search of adventure and exceptional photography. His lengthy career in the US Army facilitated his opportunities for unique experiences in the outdoor world. With camera in hand, he has journeyed throughout the Western Hemisphere and Asia, visiting many ancient cultural sites and striking scenery along the way.

Mike has personally explored all the monuments in this guide at least once—with the exception of Devils Postpile National Monument in California (due to avalanche hazard on not one, but two attempts)—striving to understand the significance of each and to attain the best photographic representations of these protected areas.

When not on the road, Mike lives in Colorado Springs, Colorado, with his wife, Gana, and his ever-faithful and adventurous canine companion, Jake.

Recreate with
RIMS

Give back to the land you love with the CMC RIMS (Recreation Impact Monitoring System) mobile app: If you spot a downed tree, trail erosion, trash, or poor signage while you're exploring the places in this book, open the app and submit a quick report so that land managers can address the issue. Learn more and get started at www.cmc.org/RIMS.

Illustration by Jesse Crock

Join Today.
Adventure Tomorrow.

The Colorado Mountain Club is the Rocky Mountain community for mountain education, adventure, and conservation. We bring people together to share our love of the mountains. We value our community and go out of our way to welcome and include all Coloradoans—from the uninitiated to the expert, there is a place for everyone here.

www.cmc.org